Anderson Guide to
ENJOYING GREENWICH

Connecticut
An insider's favorite places

*I've lived in Greenwich all my life and
I'm finding new places to go and
restaurants to try in* The Anderson Guide.
It's really a great resource.
- Dr. Robert L. Ailleo, DMD

A real insider's guide. I keep it next to my phone.
- Darius Toraby, Architect

The Anderson Guide *is user-friendly and loaded with
information. It answers questions about Greenwich
we didn't know we had. Since buying our first copy
in 1998, we have relied on* The Anderson Guide *for
everything from researching pre-schools to finding
the best fried chicken in town.*
- Heather Picchione, Homemaker

This is the best directory for town resources.
- Caroline Frano, RTM, District 8

This indispensable guide is invaluable for new residents
- Hillary Watson, Past President of
The Old Greenwich-Riverside Newcomers Club

Anderson Guide to
ENJOYING GREENWICH

Connecticut
An insider's favorite places

Fifth Edition

Anderson Associates
Greenwich Real Estate Specialists

with illustrations and maps
by Vanessa Y. Chow

IG
Avocet Press

Anderson Guide to
Enjoying Greenwich, Connecticut
An insider's favorite places

Written by:
Carolyn Anderson &
Anderson Associates, Ltd.
www.anderson-real-estate.com
164 Mason Street, Greenwich, CT 06830
203.629.4519

Illustrations and maps by: Vanessa Y. Chow

Published by:
Ickus Guides, Avocet Press Inc
19 Paul Court, Pearl River, NY 10965
www.avocetpress.com

ISBN 0-9677346-1-4

On the cover: Photographs by Carolyn Anderson ©2002

Printed in the United States of America

WHAT KIND OF GUIDE IS THIS ?

This is a guide to our favorites . . . simply that. It is *not* a book of advertisements. No place mentioned in this Guide had any idea that it would be included. Establishments are here only because we like them. Although this Guide is about enjoying Greenwich, you will note that some of our selections are outside of Greenwich's town limits. These easy-to-reach places complement our many in-town resources.

Finding favorite spots takes a while. We have lived in Greenwich for many years. If you are just beginning life in America's number one town, we hope that some of the resources in this guide will give you a headstart in feeling right at home.

Initially, we prepared this Guide for our private real estate clients. Then the calls came in... their friends needed a copy. The Anderson Guide, the book we dedicated to our new friends who had selected Greenwich as their home, was published! We hope you will find it useful, too. Please let us know what you think of this guide. We love your comments!

Sincerely,

Carolyn Anderson
Amy Zeeve   *Jennifer O'Brien*
Jerry Anderson   *Maurice Hunt*
Marilyn Secord   *Robert Skorvanek*
Rebecca Kuperberg *Monica Vallejo*

...and all of us at Anderson Associates.

Disclaimer:
The purpose of this guide is to educate and entertain. Every effort has been made to make this guide accurate; however, it should not be relied upon as the ultimate source of information about Greenwich or about any resource mentioned in the Guide.

There may be mistakes both typographical and in content. We have done our best to lead you to spots we hope you will like. This is by no means a complete guide to every resource in Greenwich. Unfortunately, even the best are not always perfect. If you have tried one of our favorites and are disappointed, if we have missed your favorite, if we have made a mistake in a description—please let us know: fill out the feedback form in the back of the book and send it to us.

A note about "Hours":
The hours and days of operation are intended as a guide, but they should not be considered definitive. Establishments change their hours as business dictates. In addition, many change their hours for winter and summer and during holidays. Finally, just about every establishment takes a vacation.

CONTENTS

CONTENTS

CONTENTS

CONTENTS

CONTENTS

CONTENTS

CONTENTS

GREENWICH

AT A GLANCE

www.state.ct.us/munic/Greenwich

- Average age: 39.9
- Median family income: $82,900
- Median home sale price: $995,000
- Assessed value of all residences: $16.2 billion
- Average annual increase in the value of homes: 9.1%
- 50 square miles
- Population: 58,440
- 1,500 acres of public parks
- 32 miles of shoreline
- 150 miles of riding trails
- 37 houses of worship (34 churches, 3 synagogues)
- 9 yacht clubs, 8 country clubs and 1 tennis club
- 98 special interest organizations
- 15 garden clubs
- 40 languages spoken
- School system rated #1 in Connecticut
- Rated safest community in Connecticut
- Town of Greenwich budget: $269,000,000

GREENWICH

RATED BEST TOWN IN CONNECTICUT

Time and again, Greenwich is rated as Connecticut's number one place to live. Greenwich is the premier town along what is called the Connecticut Gold Coast. The town's unique beauty has been preserved by very careful town planning and zoning. Like Beverly Hills, Greenwich has the rare distinction of being one of those recognizable names. But unlike Beverly Hills, which is a 5.7 square mile enclave, Greenwich extends over fifty square miles with rolling hills, woodlands, meadows and 32 miles of gorgeous shoreline bordering the Long Island Sound. Greenwich is not isolated—it is a real community and a wonderful place to raise a family.

Although Greenwich conjures up thoughts of stately country homes and waterfront estates reserved for the select few, Greenwich is much, much more. As you will discover, Greenwich offers a wealth of diversity, not only in real estate and architecture, but also in residents. Greenwich is home not only to a cosmopolitan group of executives, but to a great variety of professionals, artists, writers, diplomats, actors and sports figures.

In addition to being rated number one in safety and education by *Connecticut Magazine*, Greenwich is rated the number one city in Connecticut for quality of life. Greenwich has a vast wealth of attractions. Whether you look at the picturesque shopping areas, the personal service provided by its mix of elegant shops, its fantastic library (the most used in Connecticut), its ultra-modern hospital or its fifty fabulous restaurants, Greenwich has it all. Recently *Connecticut's Best Dining Guide*, which covers the entire state, gave 19 of Greenwich's restaurants top honors. Of the 20 best restaurants in the state, 4 were located in Greenwich. *The New York Times* recently declared that Greenwich has more Very Good and Excellent restaurants per capita than any other community in Connecticut. One of the many unique things about Greenwich can be found on Greenwich Avenue every day between the hours of 8 am and 6:30 pm: the police officers at the street corners directing traffic. These officers help to preserve the feeling of a small town and, of course, also help keep the town's crime rate low.

GREENWICH

TOWN FACILITIES

Greenwich is still 25% green. It has 32 miles of coastline, with its main beaches at Greenwich Point (147 acres), Byram Beach and the 2 city-owned islands (Captain's Island & Island Beach). Greenwich has 8,000 acres of protected land, over 1000 acres of town parks, 35 town tennis courts (not including the YMCA and YWCA Courts), an indoor ice rink (open only to residents), 14 public marinas and a 158-acre, 18-hole golf course (open only to residents). Music lovers enjoy the Greenwich Philharmonic, while the Bruce Museum appeals to everyone and is rated one of the best museums in Connecticut.

EDUCATION

Greenwich public schools (eleven elementary, three middle and one high school) are rated number one in Connecticut - 40% of the graduates go to the "Most Competitive Colleges." The school budget is approximately seventy million dollars. The average class size is twenty and 90% of the teachers have masters degrees. In addition, Greenwich has thirty independent preschools and nine excellent private and parochial day schools. For details, see section SCHOOLS.

TIP: MAKING YOUR VOICE HEARD IN GREENWICH
If you feel strongly about an issue in town which you feel is not being addressed, gather 20 signatures of Greenwich registered voters and deliver it with your petition to the Town Clerk's office in Town Hall. Your petition will be put on the RTM's next call. Be sure to carefully define in your petition what action you want and to bring a few articulate, concise speakers to support your cause. When you deliver the petition, it would be best to tell the Town Clerk who wants to speak.

GREENWICH

LIBRARY - GREENWICH

www.greenwichlibrary.org

The Greenwich Library is a special treasure used by young and old alike. In a typical year the Library loans 675,000 customers an average of 4.5 books per minute. It is no wonder the library has been rated the best in the country. The library recently received a $25,000,000 bequest from Clementine Peterson. Based on this bequest and funds raised by the Friends of Greenwich Library, Architect Cesar Pelli designed the 31,000 square-foot addition as well as renovations to the original building. The Byram Shubert branch has also been enhanced and we have a wonderful new Cos Cob Library. These branches provide convenient neighborhood locations and serve as community centers. The library provides a large number of programs which are noted in other sections of this guide.

Use the website to check book's availability or phone 622.7910 to reserve items, and ask to have your reserved materials sent to one of the branches. There is no limit to the number of books you can check out.

Greenwich Library (Main Library)
101 West Putnam Avenue, 622.7900
Hours: weekdays, 9 am - 9 pm (June - August, 5 pm);
Saturday, 9 am - 5 pm; Sunday, 1 pm - 5 pm (September - June).

Byram Shubert Library (Branch)
21 Mead Avenue, 531.0426
Hours: Monday - Wednesday & Friday, 9 am - 5 pm;
Thursday, 1 pm - 8 pm; Closed Saturday & Sunday.

Cos Cob Library (Branch)
5 Sinawoy Road, Cos Cob, 622.6883
Cos Cob has a new library, perfect for family enjoyment. While the youngest ones enjoy playing or reading in the children's corner, older ones can read favorite books or search the Internet. The dynamic staff organizes events for both children and adults. In just a short while it has become an important part of Cos Cob community life.
Hours: Tuesday - Saturday, 9 am - 5 pm, Thursday until 6 pm; Closed Sunday & Monday. Children's story time: 10:45 am, Thursday.

GREENWICH

LIBRARY - OLD GREENWICH

Perrot Library of Old Greenwich
(Independent Library)
90 Sound Beach Avenue, 637.1066;
Children's Library, 637.8802
The Perrot Memorial Library is a non-profit institution independent of the Greenwich Library. It is open to all residents of Greenwich, although it principally serves the residents of Old Greenwich, Riverside and North Mianus. Perrot has recently completed a beautiful $3.3 million, 7,000 square-foot Children's Library.
Hours: Monday, Wednesday, Friday, 9 am - 6 pm;
Thursday, 9 am - 8 pm; Saturday, 9 am - 5 pm; Sunday, 1 pm - 5 pm.

HOSPITAL

Greenwich Hospital
5 Perryridge Road, 863-3000
www.greenhosp.chime.org
The 160-bed Greenwich hospital is an affiliate of Yale University School of Medicine. It is a world-class hospital, providing the town with excellent health care. Patients from all over Fairfield and Westchester seek treatment at Greenwich Hospital. Greenwich Hospital is carefully gearing up for the twenty-first century. The hospital has just built a state-of-the-art cancer center (Bendheim) as well as a $129,000,000 expansion to make it a high-tech diagnostic and healing center without the austere look, normal delays and "red-tape" often associated with hospitals. Plans are underway for another $98,000,000 expansion to be called "The Watson Pavillion." For more information on the Hospital and other medical services, see HEALTH, MEDICAL CARE.

GREENWICH

LOCATION

Greenwich is in the southwest corner of Connecticut, providing residents with the convenience of being close to a big city, while living in the comfort and security of the country. Greenwich has an excellent transportation system and is just minutes from Westchester Airport, which makes trips to nearby cities such as Boston or Washington convenient. Greenwich is only 29 miles from Times Square (43 minutes by one of the 78 trains that operate daily between New York City and Greenwich). There are 4 train stations conveniently located throughout the town. U.S. Route 1, the historic Post Road, is the main commercial artery. Locally, it is named Putnam Avenue. In addition, Interstate 95 and the Merritt Parkway traverse Greenwich, giving it excellent regional accessibility. It takes about 10 minutes to drive to Stamford, about 60 minutes to Danbury and approximately 15 minutes to White Plains. Limousines provide easy and quick access to New York City's international airports; La Guardia Airport is about a 45-minute drive. The Merritt Parkway, built in 1935 for cars only, was placed on the National Register of Historic Places in 1993. For more information, see TRAVEL.

TIP: LOCAL GOVERNMENT IN ACTION
The best way to understand how our town can be run so efficiently by the largest legislature in Connecticut - The RTM or Representative Town Meeting - is to attend some of their meetings. Meetings are open to the public and are held in the beginning of most months at the Central Middle School auditorium. Ask the Town Clerk (622.7700) for a schedule of their meetings and for an agenda, "The Call". Guests always sit in the last rows.

GREENWICH

POPULATION & HOUSING

The population of Greenwich grew until about 1970. Since 1970, the resident population has been stable or declining slightly. This has been accompanied by the construction or conversion of more dwellings to house the same number of people. In 1950, the population of 40,835 lived in 10,524 households, with an average of 3.9 persons in each. In 1990, the population of 58,441 persons lived in 23,515 households, with an average of 2.6 persons. Two-thirds of Greenwich homes are for single families, mostly detached, one to a lot. The town's residential zones provide a wide variety of housing types, from small condominiums to single-family homes of more than 10,000 square feet on 4 acres or more. Greenwich is divided into several strictly enforced zoning areas. In or near town, the density is high as a result of condominiums and apartments. Further from the center of town, the zoning changes to 1 acre per family, then to 2 acres per family and north of the Merritt Parkway it is a minimum of 4 acres per family. The population of the town continues to be diverse. One-sixth of all public school students, with 38 different first languages, are learning English as a second language.

JOBS & INCOME

Greenwich is a job center where 33,093 people are employed. More people now come to work in Greenwich than go to work elsewhere. As a result of the many offices moving to the suburbs, Greenwich has become a net provider of jobs during the past twenty-five years. At the same time the median household income in Greenwich has been growing steadily. In 1979 it was $30,278. Ten years later, in 1989, it was $65,072. Today it is over $80,000.

GREENWICH

TAXES

The Town of Greenwich operates on a "pay as you go" basis and does not carry debt. This allows Greenwich to keep property taxes low while maintaining a budget of over $268,000,000. Real estate taxes are based on assessments limited by statute to 70% of market value (presently 10.26 cents + sewer .85 cents per thousand of assessed value (mill rate)). There are no separate school taxes. There is a personal property tax on cars equal to the mill rate. There is no town income tax. The state has an income tax of 0.044 (4.4%). By 2017, the state inheritance tax will be phased out.

CRIME

Greenwich is rated the safest community in Connecticut and one of the safest in the country—and it's no wonder: with fourteen police cars on the road at all times, traffic downtown directed by police officers, and with a force of 158 police officers, the average response time to a call is less than four minutes.

TRENDS

Greenwich is in the largest metropolitan area of the United States, and is fortunate in its location, natural features, and historic development. Within the New York metropolitan area, Greenwich is the most desirable place to live. The migration of business and jobs from New York City to White Plains, Greenwich and Stamford has increased the demand for housing here. Greenwich intends to keep its place as the premier town to live in. To maintain control of its future, Greenwich has developed a Plan of Conservation and Development. This plan, filled with maps and information on the town, is very influential in preserving the town's goals. It can be purchased from the Planning & Zoning Commission at Town Hall, 622.7700. Greenwich is also bringing its information systems to meet the needs of the twenty-first century. The town is working on a Geographic Information System (GIS) which will allow the town and residents to access information such as property boundaries, assessments and building lines.

GREENWICH

GOVERNMENT

www.state.ct.us/munic/Greenwich

Unlike many towns and cities, there is a great feeling of community here. Greenwich is run primarily by volunteers, not politicians. The town is governed by a Board of Selectmen (one full time and two part-time) who are elected every two years. Although town departments are staffed by paid professionals, except for the Selectmen, all town boards (such as the Board of Estimate and Taxation, which serves as the town's comptroller) and the Representative Town Meeting, are made up of unpaid citizen volunteers. In addition to the volunteers in government offices, Greenwich depends on many residents who serve in unofficial capacities. The volunteer network supports and supplements the work of town departments and gives the town its unique cultural and social values.

REPRESENTATIVE TOWN MEETING

Greenwich still retains the traditional New England Representative Town Meeting (RTM). The RTM consists of 230 members selected by the voters in the town's 12 districts. It is larger than the State's House and Senate combined. Candidates run on a non-partisan basis and serve without compensation. As a result, the composition of the RTM is very egalitarian. The RTM serves as the town's legislative body and most issues of importance, including appointments, labor contracts, town expenditures over $5,000, town ordinances and the town budget, must be approved by the RTM. Any town issue may be brought before the RTM by a petition of twenty registered voters. Because many of the RTM members are quite successful in business and other careers, the town is run efficiently, honestly, conservatively and in the interest of its citizens. RTM meetings are held at night about once every month. RTM meetings are open to everyone and are a good source of information about the town. Call the League of Women Voters (352.4700) for a schedule. The League is very active and is a great way to get involved. They publish an informative guide on Greenwich Government, *People Make it Happen*.

GREENWICH

VOTER REGISTRATION

622.7889, 7890
You must be registered at least fourteen days before a regular election and by noon of the last business day before a party primary. You must be registered by the day before a special election or referendum.

HISTORY

Greenwich is the tenth oldest town in Connecticut. Named after Greenwich, England, the town began as a temporary trading post founded by Captain Adrian Block in 1614. Greenwich was settled in 1640 when it was purchased from the Indians as part of the New Haven Colony, with allegiance to England. The settlers grew restless under the Puritan influence and, in 1642, the settlers withdrew their allegiance to England and transferred it to the more liberal Dutch. At this time, the Cos Cob section of Greenwich was occupied by the Siwanoy Indians and a toll gate was set up between them and the central part of Greenwich, called Horseneck. In about ten years the town was forced back under the domination of the New Haven Colony. Greenwich supported the British during the French and Indian War, but during the Revolution the town was sacked several times by the King's troops. The advent of the New Haven Railroad in 1848 began the transformation of Greenwich into a residential community. This period saw many wealthy New Yorkers, including Boss Tweed, building summer homes. In the twenties, the town began to grow rapidly and land values began to soar. By 1928, Greenwich led the nation in per capita wealth. In 1933 the town had grown so large that it had to abandon open town meetings and adopted the Representative Town Meeting (RTM). Although the population growth has abated (because of the scarcity of buildable land) the property values have continued to climb.

The Greenwich Library and The Greenwich Historical Society have developed an Oral History of Greenwich. This program records the memories of residents who were influential in the town's development or who observed important events in the town's history. The Library has more than 130 volumes of recorded conversations. These interviews are a unique and wonderful way to learn about the town.

GREENWICH LAYOUT

MAIN STREETS

The central street connecting the main part of Greenwich with the Riverside, Cos Cob, and Old Greenwich sections is Putnam Avenue (a.k.a. Post Road, US 1). It runs essentially east to west through the town (of course out-of-town maps show US 1 running North/South from Stamford to Port Chester). Greenwich Avenue, the main shopping street, is the dividing line between East and West Putnam Avenue. Sound Beach Avenue on the eastern end of Putnam Avenue, is the main shopping street for Old Greenwich and runs to the Greenwich Beach.

AREAS & VILLAGES

Greenwich is made up of a number of small villages and neighborhoods, each with it own character and charm. The largest of these are: Byram, Banksville, Back Country, Central, Cos Cob, Mianus, Old Greenwich, Glenville, Riverside. All parts of Greenwich share the same government, school system, property tax rate and access to public facilities.

HIGHWAY MAP

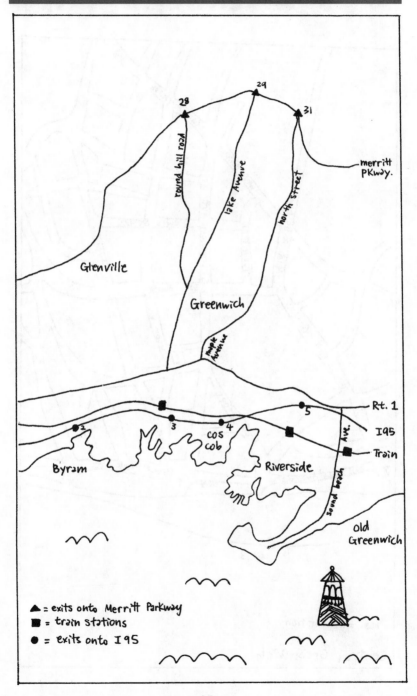

Glenville

Greenwich

round hill road

lake avenue

north street

maple avenue

merritt
Pkwy.

28

29

31

Rt. 1

I95

Train

5

3

4

2

cos
cob

Byram

Riverside

sound beach ave.

Old
Greenwich

▲ = exits onto Merritt Parkway
■ = train stations
● = exits onto I95

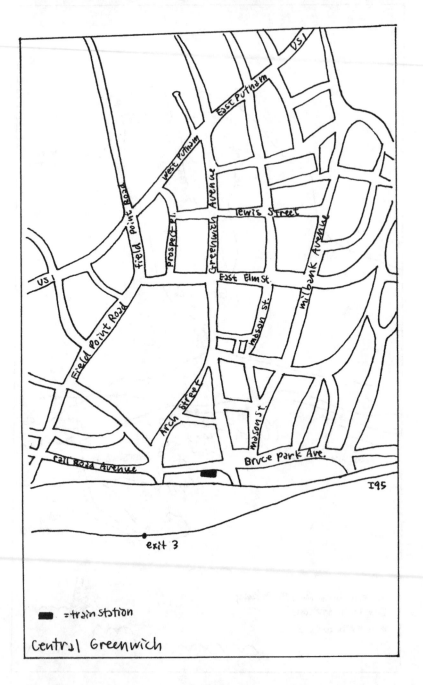

Central Greenwich

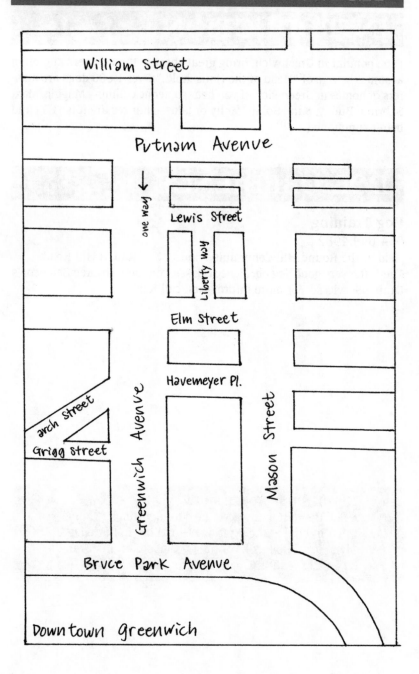

ANIMALS

INTRODUCTION

Pets, popular in Greenwich, bring great cheer to their owners and often assume the role of "Head of the Household." Over 1,600 dogs are masters of homes in Greenwich. If you hear someone calling—Maggie, Max, Sabrina, Buddy, Sam, Solan, Molly or Jake—chances are it isn't a child being summoned.

DOG OBEDIENCE

Dog Training
914.699.4982
Held at the Round Hill Community House, 397 Round Hill Road.
They offer very good dog obedience classes, conducted by Ken Berenson's Canine Services. For more information call Ken.

TIP: OX RIDGE HORSE SHOW
Enjoy the nationally acclaimed hunter-jumper competition in June at the Ox Ridge Hunt Club in Darien, CT. Olympic as well as local riders compete in this Grand Prix event. Call 203.656.1743 for details.

PETS

Adopt-A-Dog

629.9494

www.adopt-a-dog.org

Since 1981, this unique, local, not-for-profit animal agency has helped over 7,000 homeless dogs find loving families. If you have a soft spot in your heart for animals, consider adopting or becoming a foster "parent." You are always welcome to call or visit their kennels. They hold the annual show, "Puttin' on the Dog."

Best Friends Pet Resort & Salon

528 Main Avenue, Norwalk, CT, 888.367.7387

Doggy day camp with 4-legged playmates (assuming your pet can pass the interview process). Longer stays are available.

Hours: weekdays, 8 am - 6 pm; Saturday, 8 am - 5 pm; Sunday, 3 pm - 6 pm.

Directions: I-95 N to exit 15, follow Route 7 expressway N to the end, R on Main (next to the DMV).

Bow Wow Barber Mobile Dog Groomers

149 Cedar Heights Rd, Stamford, CT, 968-6214

Calls will be returned in the evening. They are on the road during the day.

Canine Athletic Club

40 Decatur Street, First Floor, Cos Cob, 561.9541

Perhaps your dog would like to belong to the Lunch Bunch. According to one of our pet friends, he is picked up every day, lunches with several of his dog buddies, and then returns home, ready for his afternoon nap. Kristin Leggio and Keith Fernim provide dog walking, exercise, and socialization service as well as in-home pet care services. If you are too busy to take your dog to the vet, they will do that too.

Connecticut Canine Law

Dogs over six months of age must have a license issued by the Town Clerk's office (622.7897) in Town Hall (8 am - 4 pm), and the dog must be immunized against rabies.

ANIMALS

PETS

Connecticut Humane Society
455 Post Road East, Westport, CT 203.227.4137
Although the Greenwich Animal Shelter sometimes has pets to adopt, the Humane Society is the major area resource. They have many hopeful dogs, cats and even rabbits and fish waiting to meet you. They maintain a lost-and-found file and will come to your home to remove injured or sick wild animals or birds.
Hours: Monday - Saturday 10:30am - 5:30pm, Sunday 10am - 4pm.

Dogs Dayz
Stamford, CT, 203.322.1262
Aileen Smith does daily dog walking, house and plant care while you are away. Excellent references.

Dog Parks
Generally Greenwich does not allow dogs with, or without a leash, on town property. However, at the present time the Town has agreed to let dogs with 10-foot or smaller leashes on the 75-acre Pomerance land which the town recently purchased for $17.6 million. For more information contact the Department of Parks and Recreation at 622.7830.

The Fish Doctor
a.k.a Winston Carmichael, Bridgeport, CT, 203.365.0269
He cleans, maintains and installs aquariums in Fairfield and Westchester County.

The Good Dog Foundation
718.788.2988
www.TheGoodDogFoundation.org
This foundation, part of a nationwide group, operates training sessions in Greenwich for people willing to bring their animals to visit local patients. The dogs ease depression in the elderly and calm hyperactivity in children.

ANIMALS

PETS

Greenwich Kennel Club

Cos Cob Community Center, 54 Bible Street, Cos Cob,
203.426.6586 or 203.426.2881

The GKC is a non-profit organization whose membership is comprised of area dog enthusiasts with interests in conformation, obedience and performance events. The GKC holds an annual all-breed dog show every June. If you are not sure whether you want to bring a beagle or vizsla into your home, attend this show. It is a wonderful way to meet them all, as well as to find a suitable breeder.

North Wind Kennels

Route 22, Bedford NY, 914.234.3771

If you would like to leave your dog or cat where Glen Close and Chevy Chase are said to leave theirs, go no further. Jake Feinberg's well known kennel has four "doggie suites" and can house 225 dogs and 45 cats. Our experience was less than satisfactory.

Hours: Monday - Saturday, 9:30 am - 5:30 pm. On Sunday or off-hours, their machine takes no messages.

Directions: North Street to the end, L on Route 22, kennel is on the right in about a mile.

Pet Finders Club of America

661 High Street Thurman NY 12810, 800.666.5678
www.petclub.org

The oldest nonprofit lost and found service in the US.

Pet sitters

When in need, try www.petsitters.org or www.petsit.com. These are national organizations that usually have reliable sitters. However, it is wise to ask for references and to make sure they are insured and bonded.

Puttin' On The Dog - Annual Dog Show

Roger Sherman Baldwin Park, Late September

Run by Adopt-a-Dog, 849 Lake Avenue, 629.9494, this show is a great place to show your dog, learn about dogs, or adopt a new friend. Always a hit with children of all ages.

ANIMALS

PETS

Sherlock Bones
800.942.6637
www.sherlockbones.com
Since 1975 this California pet detective has helped recover missing pets around the USA.

Stray Cats
Project Save-A-Cat, 661.6855
PAWS (Pet Animal Welfare Society) Norwalk, 203.854.1798
SCAT (Southern Connecticut Animal Trust) Stamford, 968.9385
If you know of a stray cat that needs to be captured or you would like to adopt a cat, call these volunteer organizations.

TIP: LYME DISEASE
Ticks, unfortunately, also live in Greenwich—even some carrying Lyme Disease. If you remove a tick you might want to take it "Dead or Alive" to the Department of Health in Town Hall. They will test it for the Lyme Disease bacteria. For information on Lyme disease, call the Greenwich Lyme Disease Task Force at 203.531.5090.
www.cdc.gov/ncidod/dvbid/lyme/

ANIMALS

VETERINARIANS

Animal Eye Clinic
at the Veterinarian Referral & Emergency Center
123 West Cedar Street, Norwalk, CT 203.855.1533
www.AnimalEyeClinic.net
People from all over the area bring their pets here for eye problems.
Hours: Monday & Tuesday, 8 am - 5 pm;
Wednesday & Thursday, 1 pm - 7 pm; Friday, 8 am - Noon.

Blue Cross Animal Hospital
530 East Putnam Avenue, 869.7755
The ladies behind the desk are very kind and caring. Dr Wolff provides holistic pet care, including acupuncture and homeopathy as well as conventional care.
Hours: weekdays, 8 am - 6 pm, Saturday 9am - 3 pm. Closed Sunday.

Greenwich Veterinary Hospital
358 West Putnam Avenue, 661.1437
Many of our knowledgeable friends take their pets to Dr Sean Bell.
Hours: weekdays, 7am - 5 pm, Saturday, 9 am - 2 pm. Closed Sunday.

Just Cats Hospital
1110 East Main Street, Stamford, CT 327.7220
Located off of I-95 at exit 9. They provide excellent medical services, boarding, grooming and TLC, just for cats.
Hours: weekdays, 7:30 am - 8 pm (Friday until 6 pm);
Saturday, 8 am - 5 pm.
Directions: I-95N to Exit 9; L at light; L on East Main.

Parkside Hospital for Animals
336 West Putnam Avenue, 661.6493
For over twenty years, Dr. Vitka has cared for many of Greenwich pets with skill and loving care.
Hours: Available around the clock. All visits are by appointment.

VETERINARIANS

Veterinarian Referral & Emergency Center

123 West Cedar Street, Norwalk CT, 203.854.9960

If your vet is not available, this is a wonderful emergency room for your pet. During normal hours, appointments must be made for specialists.

Hours: 24-hours a day, 7 days a week.

Directions: I-95 N to Exit 13; R on US 1; L on W Taylor; L on W Cedar.

TIP: DOG VOLUNTEERS NEEDED

Adopt-a-Dog shelters and places abandoned dogs and cats in loving homes. They need volunteers to help with functions such as: fundraising, dog walking, public relations and animal care. If you have a warm place in your heart for these sweet creatures, call 629-9494 for information.

ANIMALS

WILDLIFE & ANIMAL RESCUE

Animal Control
Dog Pound, Museum Drive, 622.8299, 622.8081
A Town of Greenwich Police Department service that handles dead or sick animals as well as stray dogs. We have a kind animal control officer, Allyson Halm. If your pet is missing, call her first. A few dogs are available here for adoption.
Hours: Every day, 8 am - 3:30 pm.

Bats and Wildlife
323.0468
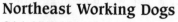
They carefully remove wildlife from your home and relocate it so you won't have unwanted pets. They can also help prevent furry intrusions.

Northeast Working Dogs
914.937.4421
If you have too many Canada Geese on your lawn this is the place to go for effective and humane control. A husband and wife team, Rob and Betsy Drummond, use border collies to herd the geese off your property. Treatment often takes six weeks or more.

Wild Life Trust
Contact: Jean 869.5415
She takes in orphaned and injured mammals and birds. This incredible Greenwich woman also breeds endangered species.
Hours: weekdays, 9 am - 5 pm.

Wild Wings, Inc.
637.9822 or 967.2121 Wildlife Hotline: 203.389.4411
Alison Taintor and Meredith Sampson are state and federally licensed wildlife rehabilitators who operate a wildlife rescue and rehabilitation center in Old Greenwich and Stamford. They respond to oil spill emergencies that affect wildlife.
Hours: They are on call 24 hours a day, 7 days a week for emergencies. For general information, call weekdays, 9 am - 5 pm.

ANTIQUES -PUBLICATIONS

Antique and consignment shops thrive in and around Greenwich (see SHOPPING). Although many antique shops take consignments, stores that are primarily consignment are often less expensive. They sometimes have outstanding selections. We have included the places we like best, but if you really want to get into the antique scene in a big way you might want to get one or both of the following:

Antiques and the Arts Weekly
Bee Publishing, Newtown, CT, 203.426.8036,
www.thebee.com, info@thebee.com.
A thick newspaper with a treasure trove of articles, advertisements and information on shows, auctions and events in the world of paintings and antiques. Good coverage not only of Connecticut, but of the tri-state area.

Sloan's Green Guide to Antiquing in New England, published by Antique Source, Inc, Belmont, Vermont, 888.875.5999, www.antiquesource.com.
A large book covering over 2,000 antique shops throughout New England & Eastern NY State. It includes a map which highlights the antique shops in Greenwich.

AUTOMOBILES

Travel Information

See also TRAVEL

Local commuters can untangle their morning commutes by consulting the following commuter transportation web sites:

MetroPool: www.metropool.com
The site offers news and information on commuting in and around Fairfield and Westchester counties.

TravTips www.smarttraveller.com
The latest traffic information for Connecticut and New York.

Pretrip travel information: www.hsa.org

Greenwich traffic cams: www.connecticut.com

Car Wash Center of Greenwich (SPLASH)

625 West Putnam Avenue, 531.4497
Hours: weekdays, 8 am - 6 pm (Friday until 6:30 pm);
Saturday, 8 am - 6 pm; Sunday, 9 am - 4 pm.

Classic Shine Auto Fitness Center

67 Church Street, 629.8077
This car detailing firm does not often advertise, but has been in business for many, many years. They operate on the strength of recommendations alone.

Concours of Elegance

To exibit a concours-quality car, call Bruce and
Genia Wennerstrom, 661.1669 (Co-chairs)
The Concours takes place in the Roger Sherman Baldwin Park the weekend after Memorial Day is observed. This exciting event for all ages features an exhibit of outstanding motorcars from the last decade of the nineteenth century through the late 1970's. It is one of the most prestigious Concours events in the country, attracting over 10,000 spectators.
Hours: 10 am - 5 pm.

Cos Cob Car Wash

73 Post Road, Cos Cob, 625.0809
A good place to have your car cleaned, inside and out.
Hours: Monday - Saturday, 8 am - 4:45 pm.

AUTOMOBILES

Department of Motor Vehicles Bureau

540 Main Avenue (Route 7), Norwalk, CT, 800.842.8222

860.263.5700

www.dmv.ct.org

New residents must obtain a Connecticut driver's license within sixty days, even if they hold a valid license from another state. Vehicles must also be registered within sixty days after the owner has established residency. The car must pass an inspection before being registered.

Hours: Tuesday - Saturday, 8 am - 4:30 pm (Thursday, until 7:30 pm, Saturday, until 12:30 pm); Closed Sunday, Monday and holidays.

Directions: I-95 N to exit 15, Rte 7 N; follow Rte 7 expressway to end, R and straight into the DMV.

Driver's License Renewals

Licenses can be renewed at the DMV in Norwalk or at the Connecticut License Bus, which stops in front of Town Hall the first Tuesday of every month from to 10 am - 6 pm.

Parking Meters

Parking meters in Greenwich are not expensive, but parking tickets are. Parking meters are a must weekdays, 9 am - 5 pm and Saturday, 9 am - noon. On Sundays and holidays, parking is free. Old Greenwich is still free of parking meters.

Parking Permits

622.7730

Call for details about train station parking permits and the location of municipal lots.

Police Directing Traffic

We still have the privilege of having police direct traffic on Greenwich Avenue. They are always helpful and friendly. When you can't find something, they are a great source of information. However, be warned— pedestrians and drivers alike are expected to pay attention. Follow their crossing instructions or face humiliation!

Vehicle Inspection

Automobiles must pass an emissions test annually. The nearest inspection station is located on I-95 between exits 9 and 10 in Darien. Call 800.842.8222 for directions and times. This station is scheduled to be closed.

AUTOMOBILES

VEHICLE RENTALS

Enterprise Rent-a-Car
15 Edgewood Ave (Just off West Putnam Avenue, next to McDonalds)
622.1611
www.Enterprise.com
They often have the lowest rates, but charge for mileage.
Hours: weekdays, 7:30 am - 6 pm; Saturday, 9 am - noon.

Hertz Rent-a-Car
111 West Putnam Avenue, 800.654.3131   www.Hertz.com
At the Exxon Station next to the Library, 622.4044
Hours: weekdays, 6:30 am - 6:30 pm; Saturday, 9 am - noon.

Ryder Truck Rentals
142 Railroad Avenue, 661.5548; 622.9353
www.yellowtruck.com
At the Mobil gas station. Hassle-free.
Hours: Every day, 7 am - 7 pm.

U-Haul
Jefferson Street, Stamford, CT 324-3869
www.uhaul.com
U-Haul rents every thing from a van to a large truck. They also have a
large stock of boxes and other moving supplies. Their vans are well
kept and are great for local moves. Their best trucks are saved for long
distance runs, so for local runs you might be better using a truck from
Ryder. Don't expect customer service to be a high priority.
Directions: I-95 N to Exit 8, R on Canal (second light), L on Jefferson.
Turn down the small side street next to the first building on the Right.
Hours: Monday - Thursday, 7 am - 7 pm, Friday, 7 am - 8 pm,
Saturday, 7 am - 7 pm, Sunday, 7 am - 5 pm.

BOOKS

Book Clubs
The Libraries often sponsor book clubs, such as the Brown Bag Book Club which meets on the second Wednesday of each month at the Cos Cob Library. All are welcome. Bring your own lunch and have a good time. For information on the Brown Bag Book Club, call 622.6883.

Book Exchange
At the Greenwich Recycling Center, Holly Hill Lane, 622.0550
This is fun you cannot miss. Residents drop off unwanted books. A volunteer "librarian" organizes the books by topic and author. Free books are available on all subjects. Just follow the rules: keep the shelves neat, ten books per family, enjoy your reading!
Donation hours: Monday, Friday & Saturday, 7 am - noon.
Exchange open: weekdays, 7:30 am - 3 pm.

Darien Book Aid Plan
1926 Post Road, 203.655.2777
This worthy group has been sorting and shipping donated books to countries around the world, since 1949. They are particularly interested in children's story books, books in braille, grammar texts, teenage literature and books on medicine, agriculture and gardening.

Smith College Book Sale
Waveny House, South Avenue, New Canaan, CT, 203.966.0502
This annual event benefits the Smith College Scholarship Fund and has more than 80,000 well-priced, quality used books including cookbooks, art histories and bound sets to decorate your home. Just a visit to Waveny House is worth the trip. Dealers descend early on the first morning, grabbing books which they later resell at a substantial profit. It's fun to arrive early with them, but be prepared for pushy, over-zealous types. The first day there is an admission charge. On the last day books are free. Don't forget to bring a big book bag.
Look for it at the beginning of April.
Directions: Merritt Parkway N to exit 37, L on South.

CHILDREN

INTRODUCTION

Children are our most treasured citizens. Greenwich has the top-rated school system in Connecticut and is ranked among the best in the country. Children nurtured in Greenwich have unique opportunities to develop their skills and to grow into happy, healthy, mature individuals. Young people in Greenwich have lots of fun.

AFTER-SCHOOL PROGRAMS

The following elementary schools have on-site after-school child care programs for students enrolled in that school.

Cos Cob School, 869.4670
Glenville School, 531.9287
Hamilton Avenue School, 869.1685 (2nd grade scholars)
International School of Dundee 637.3800
Julian Curtiss School, 869.1896
New Lebanon School, 531.9139
North Mianus School, 637.9730
North Street School, 869.6756
Old Greenwich School, 637.0150
Parkway School, 869.7466
Riverside School, 637.1440

BANC
Byram Archibald Neighborhood Center
After School Program
289 Delavan Avenue, 622.7788
Ages: 5 - 13 yrs. Four days per week.
Follows public school calendar.

Children's Center of Cos Cob Inc.
300 East Putnam Avenue, 625.5569

CHILDREN

AFTER-SCHOOL PROGRAMS

Girls Inc.

Western Civic Center, 531.5699

Girls, grades 1 - 5, Hours: 2:45 - 4:45 pm.

An excellent four day-a-week, math and science-based enrichment program for girls. Girls are picked up from Julian Curtiss, Hamilton Avenue & New Lebanon Elementary Schools, taken to Western Civic Center and returned to the school by 4:45. They have an excellent summer camp.

Greenwich Boys and Girls Club

Horseneck Lane, 869.3224

Co-ed, Ages: 6 and up, Hours: 3 - 9 pm. On school holidays, the program starts at 8 am. Summer hours are 8 am - 6 pm.

Kaleidoscope - YWCA

259 East Putnam Avenue, 869.6501, x 225

Co-ed, Ages: K - grade 5, Hours: 2:30 - 6 pm. Follows the public school schedule, including early release days. Social, educational and recreational enrichment. Transportation is provided from all Greenwich schools. Kaleidoscope also provides childcare services during school closings for holidays and vacations.

Rainbow Express - YMCA

869.3381

They run after-school childcare programs at Hamilton Avenue, New Lebanon, Julian Curtiss and North Mianus Schools.

42

BABYSITTING

Au Pair & Nannies Club
YWCA, 259 East Putnam Avenue, 869.6501 x 248
Area nannies meet to share care-giving ideas and to make new friends.

Babysitting Training
If your son or daughter wants to be a babysitter, the Red Cross sponsors a comprehensive all-day babysitting course which is open to 11 - 15 year-olds and offered two to three times a month: 231 East Putnam Avenue, 869.8444
Greenwich Hospital "Tender Beginnings" runs a baby sitting course for students 11- 13. Call 863.3561.

Child Care and Parenting Services
A wonderful pamphlet compiled by Community Answers and Greenwich Early Childhood Council. Available at the Community Answers desk at the Greenwich Library.

Child Care Infoline
800.505.1000
They provide information on licensed daycare, summer camps and nursery school programs throughout Connecticut.

Helping Hands
921.1530
www.helpinghands.com
An au-pair/nanny service that has been in business for ten years and focuses on the local area. Their Child Temp Service offers weekend, evening and occasional babysitting.

CHILDREN

BABYSITTING

Kid's Night Out
YMCA, 50 East Putnam Avenue, 869.1630
On the second and last Friday of every month, parents of children in grades K - 6 can enjoy an evening out, while their children enjoy an inexpensive, fun, safe night of activities, including gym games, swimming, movies, popcorn and board games.

(The) Sitting Service
Suzanne Pappas, President.
679 Post Road, Darien, 203.655.9783 or 4123
www.TheSittingService.com
English babysitting, pet sitting and house sitting referral service has been in Fairfield County for over 20 years. Yearly membership is $225 per family plus an hourly rate.

Student Employment Service
Greenwich High School, 625.8008, 8000
The office has limited hours, keep trying. During the summer, the service is run through Community Answers, 622.7979.
Children, ages 3 - 4. Full-day, year-round child care; tuition based on need.

> **TIP: CHILDCARE RESOURCES**
> Community Answers gathers information about programs and places of interest to children and parents in the CHILDREN'S NOTEBOOK. Community Answers also publishes an excellent leaflet on CHILD CARE AND PARENTING SERVICES. Our list of childcare resources is not complete, so be sure to ask for these informative pamphlets at their desk in the Greenwich Library.

CHILDREN

CHILDCARE

Children's Day School
139 East Putnam Avenue, 869.5395
8 Riverside Avenue
Children, ages 6 weeks - 5 years; Hours: 7:30 am - 6 pm.
Director: Maryane O'Rourke

Family Center
Joan Warburg Early Childhood Center
22 Bridge Street, 629.2822
Children, ages 6 weeks - 2 years; Hours: 7:30 - 6 pm.

Gateway School
2 Chapel Street, 531.8430
Children, ages 3 - 4. Full-day, year-round childcare; tuition based on need.
Hours: 7:30 am - 6 pm.

Little Angels Play Group
Greenwich Catholic School
471 North Street, 869.4000
Children, ages 3 - 4; hours: 1 pm - 3 pm.
Pre-K program, ages 4 - 5; 8:30 am - noon.

Tutor Time
25 Valley Drive, 861.6549
Children, ages 6 weeks - 5 years; hours: 6:30 am - 6:30 pm.
Early drop off, 6:30 am; late pick-up, 6:30 pm.
Also 2, 3 and 5-day programs, either half or full-day.

YMCA Magic Rainbow
2 Saint Roch Avenue, 869.3381
Children, ages: 6 weeks to 5 years.
All-day, year-round childcare. Hours: 7:30 am - 5:30 pm.

YWCA Playroom and Playroom Plus
259 East Putnam Avenue, 869.6501 x 221
Children, ages 15 months - 3 years. Professional on-site childcare services, either for parents attending Y classes or pursuing off-site activities. Morning or afternoon sessions available.

CHILD ENRICHMENT

ART

Art Workshop for Juniors
Greenwich Art Society, 299 Greenwich Avenue, 629.1533
Elaine Huyer teaches a lively, creative course in all media: clay, paint and collage for children ages 7 to 10.
Hours: Classes are conducted year-round. In the winter, classes are held after school on Tuesdays and Wednesdays, 3:45 am - 5:30 pm.

Easel in the Gallery
Bruce Museum, 1 Museum Drive, 869.0376, x 325
www.brucemuseum.org
Experts teach children from kindergarten through 5th grade. Children explore the current Bruce Museum exhibits, sketching in the galleries and creating art projects inspired by what they have seen.

Parent & Child Art Work Shop
YWCA, 259 East Putnam Avenue, 869.6501
Multi-media art projects from paints to clay for children age 2½ to 4.

COMPUTERS

Children's Computer Corner
At YWCA, 259 East Putnam Avenue, 869.6501
For children ages 9 - 12, introduction to computers and programming.

Computer Tots
At YWCA, 259 East Putnam Avenue, 869.6501
Hands-on classes for ages 3 - 5.

DANCE & ETIQUETTE

Allegra Dance Studio

37 West Putnam Avenue, 629.9162

Claudia Fletcher has been teaching dance to children in Greenwich for over twenty-five years. Ages 3 - adult; classes in jazz, ballet, tap, hip-hop and modern.

Barclay Ballroom Dancing for Young Children

Lois Thomson, Director, 908.232.8370

Friday evening classes, starting in September, are held at the Round Hill Community Center. The one-hour classes teach ballroom dancing and social etiquette to children in grades 4, 5, & 6. Children's attire is dressy. Girls should apply early.

Dance Adventure

230 Mason Street, 625.0930

www.danceadventure.com

Programs for parent and child, 4 months to 2½ years; pre-ballet for ages 3 - 5; ballet, tap & jazz for 1st graders to teens.

Mayfair Ballroom Dancing for Young Children

Donna Byrnes 661.5963 or call the Brunswick School (625.5800)

Mayfair is sponsored by the Brunswick Parents Association, but is open to all children in Greenwich. Like Barclay, they teach ballroom dancing and etiquette to children in grades 4, 5 and 6. Friday evening classes start in September and are usually taught at Brunswick. If you have a boy who wants to attend, there is usually no problem. For girls, there may be a waiting list.

Greenwich Ballet Workshop

Directed by Felicity Foote, 869.9373

Felicity coaches dedicated children (up to age 18) who want to look their very best on stage. See her Ambassador in Leotard Program under Young Adults.

CHILD ENRICHMENT

GYMNASTICS

US Academy of Gymnastics
6 Riverside Avenue, Riverside, 637.3303
Tumble Bugs and Snuggle Bugs for children 18 months to 5 years.
Serious gymnastics training for children from 1st grade through high school.

YWCA Programs
259 East Putnam Avenue, 869.6501
Jelly Beans - ages 16 - 36 months.
Tumble Tots - ages 2½ - 3 years.
Pre-Gymnastics - ages 3 - 5 years.
Gymnastics - ages 6 - 8; 9 and over.
Advanced Gymnastics.

YMCA Programs
50 East Putnam Avenue, 869.1630
Baby Power - 12 to 24 months.
Toddler Gym - 24 to 36 months.
Rockers - 3 to 4 years.
Rollers - 4 and 5 years.
Beginner - 6 to 10 years.
Intermediate - 6 to 10 years.

Western Greenwich Civic Center
449 Pemberwick Road, Glenville, 622.7821
www.jackrabbitsgym.com
Jumping Jackrabbits (1-5 years). A great way to wear your children out.

CHILD ENRICHMENT

LANGUAGES

Alliance Française
299 Greenwich Avenue, 629.1240
www.afusa.org/af/greenwich
Classes for beginners, intermediate and advanced are given in the French Center for children ages 3 - 13 years old. "Mommy and Me" lets 2-year-olds learn with their mothers. On Tuesdays French classes are offered for native French-speaking children who are enrolled in English-speaking schools.

German School
135 School Road, Weston, CT, 203.222.1228, 792.2795
50 Partridge Road, White Plains, NY, 914.948.6513
www.dsny.org
Monday and Saturday morning German language and cultural instruction for novice to native speakers. Available for children preschool through high school. They also have an adult program. Closed during the summer. Classes begin in September.

Language Workshop for Children
800.609.5484
Headquartered in New York City at 888 Lexington Ave, 212.396.1369, they have a branch in Greenwich. Morning and afternoon programs for children 6 months - 3 years, accompanied by a caregiver: French for Tots, Spanish for Tots and Le Petite French. Preschool for children 3 - 5 years. Programs for children 3 - 12: French for Children, Spanish for Children. New York City only programs for children 3 - 10 during the summer. Winter & spring breaks: Le Club des Enfants (French-American Day Camp), El Club de los Niños (Spanish-American Day Camp). Classes are conducted in Greenwich at the First United Methodist Church across from the YMCA.

CHILD ENRICHMENT

MUSIC

Drama Kids International
Classes held in various locations, call 637.8990
Developmental program helps young people 5-12 act confidently and speak clearly.

Kinder Musik
Old Greenwich Music Studio
23 Clark Street, Old Greenwich, 637.0461
Pre-instrumental programs for infants to 8 years. A delightful way to begin a child's love of music.
Hours: Monday - Saturday, morning and afternoon sessions.

Music Academy
YWCA, 259 East Putnam Avenue, 869.6501
Contact: 914.761.3715
High-quality, individual instrumental instruction for children in violin, Suzuki violin, piano, guitar and woodwinds, provided by the Music Conservatory of Westchester. Music theory lessons also available.

Music Together of Fairfield County
76 Walbin Court, Fairfield, CT 203.2546.1656
Fun, informal family music making classes for babies to 4-year olds.

Riverside School of Music
1139 East Putnam Avenue, 637.7413 or 7415
Private lessons for violin, viola, cello, piano, guitar, voice & flute for children 2 ½ and up. They are great with kids.
Open 7 days a week.

Studio of Victoria Baker
call: 531-7499
Victoria Baker, an opera singer, writes a column in the Greenwich Post., She gives private voice and piano lessons.

Young Artists Philharmonic
PO Box 3301, Ridgeway Station, Stamford, CT 532.1278
A regional youth symphony organization for talented youngsters. They've been playing for over forty years.

CHILD ENRICHMENT

READING

Preschool Stories
Stories are read to preschoolers in the mornings most weekdays. During the summer, stories may be read in a nearby park.
Byram Shubert Library, 21 Mead Avenue, Byram, 531.0426
Cos Cob Library, 5 Sinoway Road, Cos Cob, 622.6883
Greenwich Library, 110 West Putnam Avenue, 622.7900
       Weewalkers at Greenwich Library 12 - 24 months,
       Thursday mornings 11 am
Perrot Library, 90 Sound Beach Avenue, Old Greenwich, 637.1066

Tales at Twilight
Greenwich Library, 110 West Putnam Avenue, 622.7900
The Children's Desk, 622.7942
Thursday evenings in the summer at 7 pm are a special time for parents and children. Children, dressed in pajamas, bring their favorite teddy bear and listen to stories.

Young Critics Club
Perrot Library, 90 Sound Beach Avenue, Old Greenwich, 637.1066
Children in grades 6 - 8, who love to read and talk about books, gather on Friday afternoons with Kate McClelland and Mary Clark for a guided discussion.

CHILDREN

FAIRS & CARNIVALS

These annual fairs—complete with midway rides, food tents and games—provide excellent, safe entertainment for young children and raise funds for good causes at the same time. Church fairs tend to run for five days (Wednesday - Sunday), from 6 pm - 10 pm on weekdays, and noon - 10 pm on weekends, although some of the spring carnivals may only last for two to four days. Be sure to call for the exact dates and times.

Cos Cob School Fair
300 East Putnam Avenue (early May), 869.4670

Glenville School Carnival
33 Riversville Road (late April), 531.9287

Mianus School Pow Wow
309 Palmer Hill Road (early May), 637.1623

St. Catherine's Carnival
4 Riverside Avenue (middle August), 637.3661

St. Paul's Episcopal Church
200 Riverside Avenue, (late May), 637.2447

St. Roch's Bazaar
10 Saint Roch Avenue, Byram (early August), 869.4176

United Way September Fest
Roger Sherman Baldwin Park at Arch Street
(middle September), 869.2221

CHILDREN

FAMILY OUTINGS

Many family museums are included here; however for a complete list of Museums see, CULTURE, MUSEUMS.

Audubon Center

613 Riversville Road, 869.5272
www.audubon.org/local/sanctuary/greenwich
686-acre sanctuary, including 15 miles of trails and exhibits. Gift shop.
Hours: Open year-round except for major holidays, Monday - Sunday, 9 am - 5 pm.

Bridgeport Barrage

500 Main Street (Harbor Yard), Bridgeport CT, 203-345-4800
www.BridgeportBarrage.com
Major League Lacrosse. Their Season is June, July and August.
Directions: I-95 N to Exit 27, Lafayette Boulevard/Downtown. At the bottom of ramp straight on South Frontage Road, go past Warren Street R on Lafayette Blvd. First L on Allen Street. Parking Lot D on R (gravel lot with chain link fence). Ballpark diagonally across the street.

Bridgeport Bluefish

Harbor Yard, 500 Main Street, Bridgeport, CT, 203.334.8499
www.bridgeportbluefish.com
Professional Minor League Baseball in the new Atlantic League.
Hours: May to September, Monday - Saturday, 7 pm; Sunday 1 pm.
Verify hours and ticket availability before you go.
Directions: I-95 N to exit 27.

Bridgeport Sound Tigers

Arena at Harbor Yard, Bridgeport, CT 203.334.4635
www.SoundTigers.com
Ice Hockey, New York Islanders "farm" team. They will begin playing their 40-home game season at the new Arena in October.
Directions: I-95 N to Exit 27 (Lafayette Blvd.). At the bottom of the ramp continue straight along South Frontage Road past Lafayette Blvd. The next street is Broad Street. Go through the light and the Arena is directly in front of you.

CHILDREN
FAMILY OUTINGS

Bronx Zoo

Fordham Road at Bronx River Parkway, Bronx, NY, 718.367.1010
www.bronxzoo.com
World-class zoo with terrific rides and exhibits. Easy to find. Wednesdays are free.
Hours: Open year-round, weekdays, 10 am - 5 pm; Weekends and holidays, 10 am - 5:30 pm; November - March, 10 am - 4:30 pm.
Directions: (30-minutes) I-95 S to Pelham Pkw W; or Merritt Pkw S to Cross County Pkw W, then Bronx River Pkw S.

Bruce Museum

1 Museum Drive, 869.0376
www.brucemuseum.org
Recently expanded, they have impressive rotating exhibits and many programs for adults and children. They have a terrific gift shop with a large selection of books. The Museum has been accredited by the American Association of Museums as being in the top 10 percent of US museums. The Museum sponsors 2 fairs in Bruce Park every year; the mid-May Craft Fair and the Columbus Day Arts Festival have juried artists from around the country and draw visitors from all over the area.
Hours: Tuesday - Saturday, 10 am - 5 pm; Sunday, 1 pm - 5 pm.

Bush-Holley House Museum

39 Strickland Road, Cos Cob, 869.6899
www.hstg.org
Home of the Historical Society, this is the place to learn about Greenwich history. They also have a good library and a shop with books on Greenwich history, as well as reproductions of 19th century children's toys and books. While you are there, pick up a list of their always informative programs.
Hours: March - December, Wednesday - Sunday, noon - 4 pm; January - February, weekends, noon-4 pm.

CHILDREN

FAMILY OUTINGS

Discovery Museum

4450 Park Avenue, Bridgeport, CT, 203.372.3521
www.discoverymuseum.org
Hands-on art and science exhibits for children of all age levels, including their parents. A special section is devoted to preschoolers with dozens of attractions based on principles of early childhood development. Families who have discovered the Discovery Museum go there on a regular basis.
Hours: Tuesday - Saturday, 10 am - 5 pm; Sunday, noon - 5 pm. Open Monday in summer.
Directions: Merritt Parkway N to exit 47, L on Park Avenue
(1 mile S on L).

Essex Steam Train & Riverboat

Essex, CT, 860.767.0103, 800.377.3987
www.essexsteamtrain.com
Take a trip back in history through the scenic Connecticut River valley. Passengers board the 1920 steam train at the Essex station for a one-hour ride. At Deep River Landing the train meets the river boat for a one-hour cruise. The North Cove Express offers brunch, lunch and dinner during a two-hour excursion. Call 860.621.9311 for reservations on the Dinner Train.
Hours: Call for seasonal hours.
Directions: I-95 N to exit 69, Rte. 9 N to exit 3, Left (W) 1/4 mile. Across from Sunoco station.

FAMILY OUTINGS

Flanders Nature Center - Maple Sugaring

Church Hill and Flanders Roads, Woodbury, CT 203.263.3711

www.FlandersNatureCenter.org

www.WoodburyCt.org

It is a lot of fun to spend an afternoon at a Sugarhouse and to learn how to make maple syrup. It is even more fun to taste the pure syrup. During a good season there is sugaring in Connecticut for six or seven weeks. In an off year, the season could be only a couple of weekends. So be sure to call before you go. The Flanders Nature Center is 1 ½ to 2 hours from Greenwich. Woodbury is a well preserved colonial town with a number of antique shops and some top restaurants. The syrup operation is open to the public. Demonstrations are given on weekends from 3 pm to 5 pm from late February through March.

Directions: I-95 N to exit 27A, Rte 8 N to exit 37, Rte 262 /Frost Bridge Rd/Echo Lake Rd towards Watertown, R on Rte 63/Main St, L on Town Hall Rd, L on US-6/Deforest Rd/Woodbury Rd/Main St N, R on Rte 61/ Bethlehem Rd, L on Church Hill Rd.

IMAX Theater

At the Maritime Aquarium, 10 North Water Street, Norwalk, CT, 203.852.0700, www.MaritimeAquarium.org

With a screen that is six stories high and eight stories wide and with a 24,000-watt sound system, the experience is awesome.

Hours: Open daily; September - June, 10 am - 5 pm; July - Labor Day, 10 am - 6 pm.

Directions: I-95 N to exit 14, R at light on West Ave, l at 3rd light on North Main, L at light on Ann.

CHILDREN

FAMILY OUTINGS

Kykuit (The Rockefeller Estate)

Shuttle bus from Philipsburg Manor Visitors Center
Sleepy Hollow, NY.
www.HudsonValley.org
Home to four generations of Rockefellers, this is the Hudson Valley's most exceptional house and gardens. Tours include Nelson A. Rockefeller's extraordinary collection of 20th-century sculpture as well as the Coach Barn with its antique carriages and autos. A garden and sculpture tour is offered most weekdays.
Hours: 10 a.m. to 3 p.m. daily except Tuesday from April 28 - November 4, 2001.
Directions: I-95 or the Merritt Parkway (Rt 15)S to the Cross Westchester Expressway (I-287) West. Exit 1, Tarrytown. At the end of the exit ramp L to Route 119 to the end. R at the light onto Route 9 N. Philipsburg Manor is on the L.

Lake Compounce Theme Park

Bristol, CT
www.lakecompounce.com
About 1 ½ hours north of Greenwich, their roller coaster built on the side of a mountain was voted the best wooden coaster in the world by the National Amusement Park Historical Association. It is simply "awesome". All rides in the Circus World Children's Area and some rides in Splash Harbor are designed for young children. Children must be under 54" tall to ride, however adults may accompany children on some rides.
In October the "Haunted Graveyard" can be lots of fun. Check it out at www.hauntedGraveyard.com
Directions: I-95 North to Rt. 8 North (EXIT 27A) to I-84 East to Exit 31 (about 61 miles)

CHILDREN

FAMILY OUTINGS

Lyndhurst

635 South Broadway, Tarrytown, NY 914.631.4481
www.lyndhurst.org or www.HudsonValley.org
America's finest Gothic Revival mansion. A visit to the house and its 67-acre park is a must for all who are interested in 19th century architecture, decorative arts, and landscape design.
Hours: Mid-April through October :Tuesday - Sunday and Holiday Mondays, 10:00 a.m. - 5:00 p.m. Entrance gate closes at 4:15
November - Mid-April: Weekends only and holiday Mondays , 10:00 a.m. - 4:00 p.m.
Directions: I-95 or the Merritt Parkway (Rt 15)S to the Cross Westchester Expressway (I-287) West. Exit 1, Tarrytown. At the end of the exit ramp L to Route 119. Then L onto Broadway (Route 9) Lyndhurst is 1/4 mile on R.

Maritime Aquarium

10 North Water Street, Norwalk, CT, 203.852.0700
www.MaritimeAquarium.org
Interactive exhibits often including a Shark Touch Pool. Cited as one of the 10 Great Aquariums to visit.
Hours: Open daily; September - June, 10 am - 5 pm;
July - Labor Day, 10 am - 6 pm.
Directions: I-95 N to exit 14. See directions for IMAX Theater above.

Mystic Seaport and Museum

Mystic, CT, 860.572.0711
www.mysticseaport.org
Mystic is a two-hour drive. The Mystic Seaport Museum has a world-renowned waterfront collection of ships and crafts that tells the story of America and the sea. Mystic also has a good aquarium, with exciting special exhibits.
While in the Mystic area, stop by Stonington, which is about five miles east on US 1. Stonington is a nineteenth century fishing village which has kept its charm and has become a center for antique shops.
Don't forget Mystic Pizza - which inspired the movie. There is one in Mystic, 860.536.3700 and one in North Stonington, 860.599.5126.
Hours: Open every day except December 25th; Ships & exhibits, 9 am - 5 pm; Museum grounds, 9 am - 6 pm.
Directions: I-95 N to exit 90. Rte 27 S.

CHILDREN

FAMILY OUTINGS

NY Botanical Gardens

Bronx, NY, 718.817.8700

www.nybg.org

They have recently undergone a $25 million renovation and are considered the best in the country.

Hours: Open year-round, Tuesday - Sunday, 10 am - 6 pm. Wednesdays are free. November - March, open until 4 pm.

Directions: (30 minutes) Merritt/Hutchinson Pkw S to exit 15; Cross County Pkw W to exit 6; Bronx River Pkw S to exit 8W (Mosholu Pkw), at second light, L into Garden.

Philipsburg Manor

Sleepy Hollow, NY, 914.631.8200, 914.631.3992

www.HudsonValley.org

An eighteenth century working farm, with water-powered grist mill and livestock. Tours are conducted by interpreters in eighteenth century costumes.

Hours: April - December, open every day except Tuesday, 10 am - 5 pm. Open on weekends in March; closed January & February.

Directions: I 287/87 W to exit 9; follow signs for Rte. 9.

Pick Your Own Fruits & Vegetables

Picking your own fruit and vegetables has become a popular pastime in Connecticut. There are nine farms in Fairfield County offering urbanites the opportunity to pick their own products.

For more detailed information go to www.state.ct.us/doag

Some you might consider are:

Jones Family Farm

266 Israel Hill Road & Route 110, Shelton, CT, 203.929.8425

www.jonesfamilyfarms.com

This pick-your-own farm is in its thirtieth year. They have strawberries in June, followed by blueberries in July and August, and pumpkins in the autumn. In December, come and cut your own Christmas tree. They even have hayrides in October.

Hours: Best to call, hours change seasonally. Closed Sunday & Monday.

CHILDREN

FAMILY OUTINGS

Silverman's Farm
Easton, CT, 203.261.3306
www.silvermansfarm.com
Peaches in July, apples in August. Three-acre animal farm for youngsters.
Hours: weekdays, 9 am - 5 pm. Closed on major holidays. Call for hours in January or in case of bad weather.

White Silo Farm
Sherman, CT, 860.355.0271
Strawberries, asparagus, raspberries, blackberries and rhubarb.

Playland Park
Playland Parkway, Rye, NY, 914.813.7010
www.ryeplayland.org
Recently renovated amusement park, just 15 minutes away. A wide variety of rides for older kids from Go-Karts to Zombie Castle and Old Mill. Kiddyland has 20 of Playland's 45 rides. Playland also has a beach, swimming pool, lake cruises, ice casino, miniature golf and sightseeing cruises on Long Island Sound.
Hours: Open May to mid-September. The ice rink is open from October to April. Call for hours.
Directions: I-95 S exit 19.

Putnam Cottage
243 East Putnam Avenue, 869.9697
Originally a tavern serving travelers along the Post Road, it is now a museum owned by the Daughters of the American Revolution. Each year on the last Sunday in February (1 pm -3 pm), the Putnam Hill Revolutionary War battle is recreated. A definite must-see for adults and children alike.
Hours: Wednesday, Friday, Sunday, 1 pm - 4 pm.

CHILDREN

FAMILY OUTINGS

Renaissance Faire

Route 17A, Sterling Forest, Tuxedo, NY, 845.351.5171, 5174
www.renfair.com
Over 300 actors, in costume, mingle with the visitors (who can also don costumes) in a mock sixteenth century village. A wonderful way to enjoy a day of improvisation and learning.
Hours: August to mid September weekends only; 10 am - 7 pm.
Directions: I287/I87 West to exit 15A. Route 17N to 17A, Left to Faire.

Six Flags Great Adventure

Route 537, Jackson, NJ, 732-928-1821
www.sixflags.com/parks/greatadventure/home.asp
The park is a 3-hour drive from Greenwich. But if you like roller coasters, it is worth a trip. Their large amusement park has rides for every age, although the Nitro and Medusa roller coasters (two of their eight) are well-known by coaster aficionados. Six Flags Wild Safari is the world's largest drive-thru Safari outside Africa. Hurricane Harbor has water rides. Be sure to call for hours of operation before you go.
Directions: Take the George Washington Bridge to NJ Turnpike south to exit 7A. Proceed on I-195 east to exit 16A, then one mile west on Rte. 537 to Six Flags.

Stamford Museum & Nature Center

39 Scofieldtown Road (corner of High Ridge Rd), Stamford, CT, 322.1646
www.StamfordMuseum.org
118-acres, with a 10-acre working farm, pond life exhibit, boardwalks, natural history exhibits, planetarium and observatory. If your child hasn't grown up on a farm, this is the perfect place to learn about farming and farm animals.
Hours: Open year-round except for major holidays, Monday - Saturday, 9 am - 5 pm; Sunday, 11 am - 5 pm; planetarium shows Sunday at 3 pm; Observatory, Friday, 8:30 pm - 10:30 pm.
Directions: Merritt Parkway N, exit 35 (Rte 15)

CHILDREN

FAMILY OUTINGS

Stepping Stones Museum for Children

303 West Avenue (Mathews Park), Norwalk, CT 203.899.0606
www.SteppingStonesMuseum.org
Excellent interaction museum for kids under 10.
Hours: Tuesday - Saturday, 10 am to 5 pm, Sunday Noon to 5 pm,
Open Mondays in the summer.
Directions: I-95 north to exit 14N.

Sterling Hill Mine & Museum
Franklin Mineral Museum

30 Plant Street, Ogdensburg, NJ, 973.209.7212
www.SterlingHill.org
A world famous collection of fluorescent rocks, many from the Sterling
Mine. For the tour of the mine wear sturdy boots and bring a jacket
(it's cool even in the summer). Not appropriate for children under six.
Museum Hours: everyday, April through November
Tour Hours: 11 am - 1 pm; everyday, July and August, weekends April
- June and September - November.
Directions: Cross the George Washington Bridge and take Route 80
West to exit for Route 23 North. Proceed 26 miles, L on Route 517
South, 2.5 miles through Ogdensburg, R on Brooks Flat Road, R on
Plant Street.
About 2.5 hours from Greenwich.

United States Military Academy

West Point, NY, 845.938.2638
www.usma.edu
Visitors need a military ID to enter the grounds of the academy, except
for the visitor's center and military museum. One-hour guided tours
are available but photo IDs are required.
Hours: Guided tours: Monday - Saturday, 9:45 am - 3:30 pm;
Sunday, 11 am - 3:30 pm
Directions: I-95 to I-287/I-87 (NYS Thruway). Over bridge, take exit
13N onto the Palisades Interstate Parkway heading north. Take the PIP
north to its end (Bear Mountain traffic circle). Follow signs for Route
9W north (3rd exit off traffic circle). Exit 9W via West Point exit, Stony
Lonesome exit, or Route 293 exit.

CHILDREN

PARENTING SERVICES

ARC Greenwich
50 Glenville Street, 531.1880
www.arcgreenwich.org
Family support services and after-school programs for families of children with special needs.

Child Guidance Center of Southern Connecticut
132 East Putnam Avenue, 869.7187
Professionally-staffed mental health center for children and adolescents. Individual, group and family therapy, parent guidance, 24-hour crisis services, and community education programs.

Community Answers
622.7979
www.greenwich.lib.ct.us (click on the Community Answers link)
Information on parent education programs, support groups, crisis programs, counseling services, nannies, au-pair and babysitting services.

Family Health
Greenwich Department of Health, 622.6495
Prenatal and postpartum home visits, well-child clinics (birth to age 5), immunization and hypertension screening clinic (5 years to adult); school health services; early childhood/daycare licenses.

Healthy Living Connection
Greenwich Health at Greenwich Hospital, 863.3780
http://www.greenhosp.org/programs_hlc.asp
Parents Exchange, parenting classes, infant car-seat loan program, preschool vision screening, Friend and Family Infant and Child CPR, First Aid, anti-smoking education.

Kids in Crisis
622.6556
www.kidsincrisis.org
Crisis intervention counseling and short-term shelter.
Ages: Newborn - 17 years.

CHILDREN

PARENTING SERVICES

Le Leche League
869.5344, 637.7621
Support groups and information on breastfeeding.

Parent's Exchange
Greenwich Health at Greenwich Hospital, 863.3780
Weekly discussion groups led by child development specialists. A good environment to stimulate and provide parents with opportunities to exchange ideas. Parents are grouped by their children's age from infants to adolescents. Babysitting is available.

Parents Together
P.O. Box 4843, Greenwich, CT, 06831-0417, 869.7379
An independent, non-profit organization working in cooperation with the PTA Council and public and independent schools in Greenwich. They publish two newsletters: birth to fifth grade and grades 6 - 12. Consider their newsletter a must! For an annual subscription, send a check for $10 and indicate the newsletter you want to receive.

Parent to Parent Network
50 Glenville Street, 531.1880, ext. 2300
Information network for families with children who have special needs.

Tender Beginnings
At Greenwich Hospital, 863.3655
Expectant parent classes, Lamaze classes, baby care and breastfeeding classes, nutrition, prenatal exercise, newborn parenting groups, grand parenting, baby food preparation, babysitting, sibling classes.

CHILDREN

PARTIES AT HOME

Many fabulous, fun parties are documented in Greenwich picture albums. Making children feel special on their birthday is not unique to Greenwich, but Greenwich parents find unique ways to do so. Many of the best parties are hosted by imaginative parents at home or in a town park. However if you want to consider assistance, the following may be of help.

Awesome Science Parties
203.227.8112, 800.311.9993
Hands-on, interactive parties—each child is involved with every experiment. Children have lots of science fun making edible gummy drops, or volcanos and launching rockets. Parties are age appropriate. They also do after school programs in our elementary schools.   Ages: 5 - 11.

Little Cooks
888.695.2665 or call Mary 203.331.8138
They have a variety of upscale parties for different age groups and themes, including holidays and international cuisine (youngsters cook recipes from—and learn about—a country). Parties include invitations, party favors, chef hats, aprons and all ingredients.   Ages: 5 - 18.

Mad Science of Fairfield County
888.381.9754
www.madscience.org/connecticut
Interactive experiments for children, combining science with entertainment. Party programs are tailored to the age group and can include: chemical magic, vortex generators, indoor fireworks, or model rocket launchings.   Ages: 5 - 12.

Pied Piper Pony Rides
203.431.8322
www.piedpiperponyrides.com
You may want to invite one of their gentle ponies and friendly staff members to your party. The children will have a good time and the pony droppings will be removed. Closes for the winter.

CHILDREN

PARTIES AWAY FROM HOME

Adventure Kids

16 Old Track Road, 861.2227, 629.5641

www.AdventureKids.com

A fun, indoor place for young children to play. Combines play with learning. Cafeteria where parents can relax while their children run amuck safely. Ages: 6 months - 12 years.

Hours: Daily 10 am - 6 pm; closed last two weeks of August and December 25th.

Dynamic Martial Arts

202 Field Point Road, 629.4666

A party where children can learn karate. Ages: 4 and above.

Hours: Saturday parties, noon - 1:30 pm.

Elmsford Raceway

17 Raceway Lane (formerly North Payne Street), Elmsford, NY, 914.592.5375

For 33 years the del Rosario family has entertained children and their parents with 6½" slot car racing. Ages: 4 to 99.

Hours: weekdays, noon to 9:30 pm; Saturday, 11 am - 9:30 pm; Sunday, noon - 7 pm.

Directions: I-95 South to I-287 West, exit 2, R at light, N ½ mile, L onto Raceway.

KidsEvents.com

A relatively new site, developed by local residents. They cover a wide area of children's events. A good place to get party ideas.

Nimble Thimble

19 Putnam Avenue, Port Chester, NY, 914.934.2934

Choose a project for your age group - for instance, make a fabric covered bulletin board or a vest. Parents can bring cake and ice cream. Ages: 5 and up.

Hours: Monday - Saturday, 10 am - 7 pm.

CHILDREN

PARTIES AWAY FROM HOME

Stamford Raceway
7 Hyde Street, Stamford, 316.8630
www.FlatOutFun.com
The three Slot Car racing tracks are "flat out fun" for beginners as well as seasoned racers.
Hours: Tuesday - Friday, Noon to 9:30 pm, Saturday 11 am to 9:30 pm, Sunday Noon to 7 pm.
Directions: Merritt Pwk N to exit 36, R on Route 106, R on Camp, L Hope, L on Hyde.

YWCA
259 East Putnam Avenue, 869.6501 x 235
www.ywcagreenwich.com
Rent a party room and/or hire one of their special instructors to teach the children activities such as swimming, gymnastics or climbing their rock wall. Parents provide the refreshments. All ages.
Hours: Parties are held during regular Y hours: weekdays, 6:30 am - 10 pm; Saturday, 7:30 am - 5 pm (summer Saturday hours are shorter).

YMCA
50 East Putnam Avenue, 869.1630
www.gwymca.org
Rent the gym, pool, roller blade or tennis court for your party with cake and presents in the Rendevous room. The Y can even provide a clown or magician. All ages.
Hours: weekdays, 5 am - 10 pm; Saturday, 6:30 am - 7 pm; Sunday, 8 am - 5 pm (summer hours may be shorter).

CHILDREN

PLAYGROUNDS

Town playgrounds are open from 9 am - 4 pm. From late June through early August, the Greenwich Department of Parks and Recreation conducts supervised activities at the playgrounds for children ages 7 to 15. There are a number of small playgrounds scattered throughout the town (Binney Park, Bible Street Park, Christiano Park, Eastern and Western Greenwich Civic Centers, Island Beach and Loughlin Avenue Park), however, only a few are worth a trip if you don't live in that area. Here are our favorites.

Bruce Park
60 acres, across from the Bruce Museum on Museum Drive. One of Greenwich's prettiest parks, with excellent play equipment.

Byram Park
30 acres, located on Ritch Avenue and Byram Shore Road in Byram. The park has an attractive beach area and the town's only public fresh water pool. (The playground is tucked behind the Byram Shore Boat Club.) How can you go wrong?

Greenwich Common
16 acres, located adjacent to Greenwich Avenue, with an entrance on Greenwich Avenue next to the Havemeyer Building (Board of Education). This is a wonderful place to rest during a busy shopping day and let your children play. The Common has a small but attractive playground area.

Public Elementary Schools
These playgrounds are well-kept and extensive. They are available to residents during the weekends and summer when school is not in session. For more information on the location of the elementary schools, see the Public Elementary School section under SCHOOLS.

Western Greenwich Civic Center
10 acres, located on the corner of Glenville Road and Pemberwick Road. This playground is a favorite with kids.

CHILDREN

PRESCHOOLER ACTIVITIES

Teddy Bear Clinic

Once a year (usually in September), the Greenwich Hospital invites young children and their teddy bears to lean about surgery, ambulances and health check-ups. Each teddy bear is given their own ID bracelet. Call 863.3627 for more information.

Tennis for Tots

Western Greenwich Civic Center   622-7821
A new and affordable way for youngsters (ages 3-7) to become future Andre Agassis!

TIP: KIDS SAFETY TRAINING

The Greenwich Safety Town is sponsored by the Junior League of Greenwich and the Red Cross. This full day program teaches kids (who are ready for kindergarten) about such matters as safety around strangers, household safety and how to cross the street. The program is conducted during the summer, but because its so popular, register your child before March.
Call the Junior League at 869-1979 for details.

CHILDREN

SCOUTING

Boy Scouts of America, Greenwich Council #67

63 Mason Street, 869.8424

www.bsa.scouting.org, www.scouts.com

This is the headquarters of the local chapter of the nonprofit organization dedicated to instilling ethical values in young people. The Scouts are fortunate to own the Seton Reservation, a large preserve located at 363 Riversville Road. It serves as the site for the Cub Scout day camp as well as many other scouting outdoor programs. Call to check on a troop near you. The chapter sponsors the following programs:

Programs open to boys: Tiger Cubs, age 6; Cub Scouts, ages 7 - 10; Boy Scouts, ages 11 - 18.

Programs open to boys and girls: Explorers, ages 14 - 20 (specialties: aviation, scuba, emergency rescue.)

The Greenwich office has a small store for uniforms. A larger selection is available at the Darien Sports Shop (1127 Post Road, Darien, CT, 203.655.2575), and the Connecticut-Yankee Council #72, Boy Scouts of America (in Norwalk, CT, exit 40A on the Merritt Parkway, 362 Main Avenue, 203.847.2445.

Hours: Greenwich Scouts office is open weekdays, 8:30 am - 4:30 pm.

Girl Scout Council of Southwestern Connecticut

529 Danbury Road, Wilton, CT, 800.882.5561, 203.762.5557

www.gsusa.org

This is the headquarters of the local chapter of the nonprofit organization dedicated to addressing girls' current interests and their future roles as women. The current Executive Director is Betsy Keefer; the Greenwich Unit Manager is Joan Karasick.

Programs: Daises, kindergarten; Brownies, grades 1 - 3; Junior Girl Scouts, grades 4 - 6; Cadettes, grades 7 - 9; Seniors, grades 9 - 12.

Uniforms are available from Best & Co. in Greenwich and from the Darien Sports Shop, 1127 Post Road, Darien, CT, 203.655.2575.

Hours: weekdays, 9 am - 5:30 pm, Thursday until 8:30 pm.

Indian Guides and Princesses

YMCA, 50 East Putnam Avenue, 869.1630

www.gwymca.org/indianpr.htm

Outings and campouts for fathers and their five- to ten-year-old children.

CHILDREN

SUMMER CAMPS

No need to travel to New Hampshire or Maine, the Greenwich area has all sorts of camps. For a more complete list, call Community Answers at 622.7979. Ask for their list of Summer Camps and Programs. It provides good information about everything from sailing programs to intensive educational programs. If your child is interested in a specific sport, check FITNESS & SPORTS for specialized camp information.

Allegra Summer Stock Performing Arts Camps
37 West Putnam Avenue, 629.9162
Drama, theater, jazz, tap and other fantastic art programs.

American Camping Association
New England Section, 800.446.4494
www.acacamps.org
A national non-profit educational organization that accredits children's summer camps. Call to get a copy of their directory.

Art Scampers
First Presbyterian Church, 37 Lafayette Place, 869.7782
Focus on art, music, drama, ages 3 - 6 years.
Audubon Center, 613 Riversville Road, 869.5272, ext. 227
For the little explorer in your home. A day camp with sessions such as Creepy Crawlies and Wetland Waders.

Audubon Summer Children's Programs
Audubon Center, 613 Riversville Road, 869.5272
www.GreenwichCenter.Audubon.org
Explorers Summer Children's Day Camp—one-week co-ed sessions grades K - 5. Wet and Wild and Nature Detectives. One week teens training in Ecological Research for grades 6 - 8.

CHILDREN

SUMMER CAMPS

Banksville Community House Summer Camp
12 Banksville Road, 622.9597
A perfect camp for those living in the Banksville area, featuring summer fun activities such as archery and swimming.

Bible Camps
St. Paul Evangelical Lutheran Church, 531.8466
Greenwich Baptist Church, 869.2437
Stanwich Congregational Church, 661.4420

Boy Scouts of America
Greenwich Council, 63 Mason Street, 869.8424
The Seton Reservation at 363 Riversville Road is a great treasure. Day camp is available for boys in grades 1 - 4 with no prior Scouting experience. The camp does a good job of teaching outdoor sports such as swimming, archery, canoeing and fishing.

Bruce Museum
(held at Greenwich Point), 869.0376
Weeklong summer workshops. Ages 6 - 9 years.

Brunswick School
100 Maher Avenue, Greenwich
Summer baseball camps for boys ages 6 - 12 as well as co-ed summer play camps for ages 3 - 5.

Camp Pelican
471 North Street, Greenwich, 869.4000
Contact: Pat Hellwig, 869.4242 or 914.232.5089
Established in 1965, this day camp provides instruction in a variety of outdoor and indoor activities. The camp begins in June and ends in August. Sessions are four to six weeks. Coed ages 3 -13. Capacity 500. The camp is located on the campus of Greenwich Catholic School.

Camp Simmons
Run by the Boys and Girls Club of Greenwich, 869.3224
Two-month session includes canoeing, swimming, field sports, archery, and nature hikes. Ages 6 - 18 years.

CHILDREN

SUMMER CAMPS

Camp Sunbeam
869.6600
Run by Christ Episcopal Church and Temple Sholom. Two 3-week sessions focus on crafts, sports, games and music for ages 5 - 8 years.

Computer Ed High-Tech Camps
1.888.226.6733
www.computercamps.com
Email: camp@computercamps.com
For the kid who can think of nothing but computers. Like-minded children come from all over the world to learn programming, computer graphics and rocketry. There are three camps - the closest is just outside Boston.

Connecticut All-Star Lacrosse Clinic
Held at Greenwich Country Day School, Old Church Road, 863.5675
Lacrosse for beginners and intermediate boys in grades 2 - 8.

Connecticut Children's Musical Theater
at Arch Street Teen Center, Arch Street, 852.9275
Co-ed day camp for ages 8 - 13. Children create a musical which they perform for their parents.

Country Day School
Old Church Road, 863.5600
Summer day camps for ages 4 - 12. Many programs for each age group.

Creative Summer at The Mead School
1095 Riverbank Road, Stamford 595-9500 x 653
For boys and girls ages 2 1/2 to 16 interested in dance, painting, design, drawing and more.

CHILDREN

SUMMER CAMPS

Department of Parks and Recreation
622.7830
There are a great variety of town-sponsored co-ed camps, such as Kamp Kairphree for ages 5-12 and the Music and Art Program for children 8-15 who have had at least one year of study with an instrument. Don't forget to ask for their program bulletin.
Baseball programs:
> Co-ed T-Ball for 5 & 6 year olds.
> Small Fry Baseball 7-9 year olds.

First Church Day Camp
First Congregational Church
108 Sound Beach Avenue, 637.5430
Co-ed day camp for ages 3-9. Beach activities, games, music and sports.

Gan Israel Camp
75 Mason Street, 629.9059
Run by Chabad Lubavitch of Greenwich, this co-ed July camp provides traditional camp activities for ages 20 months - 3 years, and 4 - 11 years.

Girls Inc. Summer Camp
At Western Greenwich Civic Center, 531.5699
Camp for 6 - 8th grade girls. Girls can sign up for individual weeks or longer sessions. The camp presents science and math in a fun atmosphere. Several campers have won science awards.

Greenwich Public Schools Summer Program
Western Middle School, 531.7977
Enrichment and review courses for all students from pre-K to grade 12.

Greenwich Sports Camp
869.4444
Held at the Greenwich Academy. Open to boys and girls ages 7 to 14, the camp offers 11 different sports including baseball, golf, lacrosse, soccer, tennis and volleyball.

CHILDREN

SUMMER CAMPS

In the Net Girls Basketball Camp
GHS Athletic Department, 625.8050
Directed by Liz Lawler, the Greenwich High School Girl's basketball coach, the camp introduces girls from first grade through middle school to basketball. The camp runs one week in the summer. Members of the GHS basketball team work as counselors.

Mad Science Summer Camp
888.381.9754.
www.MadScience.org/Connecticut
Sponsored by Mad Science and the Greenwich Department of Parks and Recreation. Programs for children ages 6 to 12.

Manhattanville College
2900 Purchase Street, Purchase, NY, 914.323.5214
The college (914.692.2200) provides a summer writing workshop for young people in grades 4 - 11, and hosts a number of sports camps, including soccer, basketball and tennis.

Performing Arts Conservatory
Convent of the Sacred Heart, 1177 King Street, 869.2924
Co-ed day camp for children entering grades 7 -10. Training in music and acting (plays by Shakespeare).

Purchase College
735 Anderson Hill Road, Purchase, NY, 914.251.6500
The State University of New York (SUNY) at Purchase offers a number of Summer Youth Programs in the Arts (art, music, acting) for ages 6 - 17. They have early drop-off and extended-day options.

Robin Hood Camp
Herrick Road, Brooksville, ME, 831-659-9143 (winter)
207.359.8313 (summer)
www.robinhoodcamp.com
One of the best all-around camps in the US. It has a strong Greenwich connection.

CHILDREN

SUMMER CAMPS

Sandpipers Beach Camp
637.3659
Sponsored by the Old Greenwich-Riverside Community center for children ages 3-10.

Silvermine School of Art
New Canaan, CT, 203.966.6668
Creative summer camp for the artistically inclined, ages 2 - 17. Learn painting, drawing, photography and sculpture on an attractive 4-acre campus.

Summer Camp Fair
Greenwich High School, 625.8000
http://www.greenwich.k12.ct.us/high/ghs/ghs.htm
Known as "Summerfare," this event is sponsored by the Greenwich High School PTA and draws hundreds of camps from around the USA. The fair is usually held in February.

Summer Camp Expo
Greenwich Academy, 625.8990   www.greenwichacademy.org
Their Summer Opportunity Fair is usually held at the end of January.

U.S. Academy of Gymnastics
6 Riverside Avenue, 637.3303
Tumble Bugs Day Camp.

Whitby School Summer Camp
969 Lake Avenue, 869.8464
Co-ed, ages 4-6. Montessori staff teaching gardening, cooking, arts and crafts and nature study.

Wideworld Children's Corner
521 East Putnam Avenue, 629.5567
A Japanese-English camp with festivals, water play and games. For children ages 3 - 6 years.

CHILDREN

SUMMER CAMPS

YMCA
50 East Putnam Avenue, 869.1630
www.gwymca.org
Summer Fun Clubs - four 2-week co-ed sessions begin at the end of
June. They include field trips, sports, and environmental education.

YWCA
259 East Putnam Avenue, 869.6501, ext. 225
www.ywcagreenwich.com
Camp Ta-Yi-To is a co-ed camp for grades K - 8; includes swimming
and tennis.

CLUBS/ORGANIZATIONS

COMMUNITY

Does this partial list of Community Clubs and Organizations give you an idea of the multitude of interests in Greenwich? The energy, enthusiasm and brilliance of individuals in each of these organizations is always remarkable, as is the astonishing abundance of good works they accomplish. For more information about these clubs and organization go to the web site: http://www.greenwich.lib.ct.us/ and click on Community Answers.

Acting Company of Greenwich
Lois Fern Hamilton, Artistic Director, 622.0774
For Reservations call 863.1919

American Association of University Women
Greenwich Branch
63 Northridge Road, Old Greenwich
Josephine Warde, President - 637.3422

American Legion
Greenwich Post 29
248 Glenville Road, 531.0109
Emile Smeriglio, Commander

American Pen Women (Connecticut Pioneer Branch of)
Membership Chairman, Connie Walton, 637.0213

American Red Cross
Greenwich Chapter
231 East Putnam Avenue, 869.8444
www.greenwich.ctredcross.org
Rosemary Calderato, Director

Archaeological Associates of Greenwich
33 Byram Drive Greenwich CT 06830,
869.0376 Bruce Museum
www.brucemuseum.org (click on "affiliates")
Nancy Bernard, Director

CLUBS/ORGANIZATIONS

COMMUNITY

Art Society of Old Greenwich
PO Box 103, Old Greenwich 06870, 637.9949
www.sidewalkartshow.com
Nancy Kuliuski 323.6108

Audubon Society of Greenwich
613 Riversville Road, 869.5272
www.greenwich.center.audubon.org
Tom Baptist, Executive Director of State Office ext. 222

Boys & Girls Club of Greenwich
4 Horseneck Lane, 869.3224
www.bgcg.org
Robert DeAngelo, Executive Director

Breast Cancer Alliance
15 East Putnam Avenue, Box 414, Greenwich 06830
www.breastcanceralliance.org
Suzanne Schroder Klein, Executive Director, 861.0014

Button and Bows
Bob Button, 637.4994
Peggi de la Cruz, 977.8627

Byram Garden Club
Byram Shubert Library
21 Mead Avenue, Byram
Jane Ellis, President - 532.1418

Children of the American Revolution
Mary Bush Society, Putnam Cottage
243 East Putnam Avenue
Contact: Katie Bacon, Senior Registrar - 637.6789

CLUBS/ORGANIZATIONS

COMMUNITY

Chinese Association of Fairfield County
PO Box 506, Riverside, CT 06878, 625.2715
Tak Eng, President - 637.5512

Church Women United of Greenwich
28 Whiffle Tree Lane, Riverside
Pat Brandt, President - 637.4870
Contact: Kate Bryner, Publicity - 869.6261

Common Threads Quilters
Greenwich Arts Center, Barbara Hicks, 329.8075

Council of Churches and Synagogues
461 Glenbrook Road, Stamford, CT, 348.2800
Rev. James Carter, Executive Director

Daughters of the American Revolution
Putnam Hill Chapter
243 East Putnam Avenue, 869.9697
Katie Bacon, Regent - 637.6789

Friends of Binney Park
Contact: Nancy Standard 637.9894

Friends of the Byram Shubert Library
Edith Bonizio, President, 532.1454

Friends of the Cos Cob Library
Cos Cob Library, 5 Sinawoy,
Maria Fulgieri, President, 622.6883, 629.0665

Friends of Greenwich Point
PO Box 711, Old Greenwich, 06870
Anne Orum, 869.7410

CLUBS/ORGANIZATIONS

COMMUNITY

Friends of the Greenwich Library
Susan Ferris, 625.6550, 622.7938
www.greenwich.lib.ct.us

Garden Club of Old Greenwich
11 Somerset Lane, Riverside
Pat jackson, President 637.4292
Pam Adam, Membership 637-4211

Garden Education Center
Bible Street, Cos Cob 869.9242
Christine Young, President

German Club of Greenwich
Freunde Deutscher Sprache
PO Box 7733, Greenwich
Elisabeth Patterson, President, 661.2133

Glenville Senior Citizens
Western Greenwich Civic Center
Thomas Roberto, President 661-9594

Green Fingers Garden Club
PO Box 4655, Greenwich 06830
Frankie Hollister, President - 622.8567

Greenwich Art Society
299 Greenwich Avenue, 629.1533
Mary Branch, President

Greenwich Daffodil Society
38 Perkins Road
Nancy B. Mott, President - 661.6142

CLUBS/ORGANIZATIONS
COMMUNITY

Greenwich Chamber of Commerce
21 West Putnam Avenue, 869.3500
www.greenwichchamber.com
Managing Director, Mary Ann Morrison

Greenwich Democratic Town Committee
PO Box 126, Greenwich 06836
Contact: George Von Tobel, Chairman - 629.9006

Greenwich Democratic Women's Club
Betsie Halkins, President, 45 Lockwood Avenue, Old Greenwich,
637.7550
Contact: Barbara Block - 637.3830

Greenwich Friends of Mission Wolf
661-0006 (Hotline at Audubon)
www.missionwolf.com

Greenwich Garden Club
PO Box 4896, Greenwich 06831
Leslie Lee, President 869.2178

Greenwich Green & Clean
Yantoro Community Center, 113 Pemberwick Road, 531.0006
Mary G. Hull, Executive Director

Greenwich Hospital Auxiliary
Greenwich Hospital, 5 Perryridge Road
auxiliary office: 863.3220
Medicare Assistance: 863-3334
Suzanne Rand, President
Contact: Marguerite Heithaus, Director of Volunteer Services,
863.3221

CLUBS/ORGANIZATIONS

COMMUNITY

Greenwich Jaycees
PO Box 232, Greenwich 06836
www.greenwichjaycees.org
Danielle Nash, President - 358.3134

Greenwich Kiwanis Club
PO Box 183, Greenwich 06836
Bill Dylewsky President - 975-8830, 531-9253

Greenwich Land Trust
PO Box 1152, Greenwich 06836-1152
www.gltrust.org
Ann Sawyer, Executive Director 629.2151

Greenwich Old Timers Athletic Association
PO Box 558, Greenwich 06836
David Theis, President - 869.4857

Greenwich Recycling Advisory Board (GRAB)
234 North Maple Avenue
Mary Hull, Chairman - 531.0006

Greenwich Republican Roundtable
17 Hustead Lane
Charles Glazer, Chairman - 629.4315

Greenwich Republican Town Committee
74 Greenwich Avenue, 869.2983
www.greenwichgop.com
David Hopper, Chair - (W) 629.1100

Greenwich Republican Women's Club
PO Box 335, Riverside, CT 06878
Mary Romeo, President, 698.2569

CLUBS/ORGANIZATIONS

COMMUNITY

Greenwich Riding and Trails Association, Inc.
PO Box 1403, Greenwich 06836,   661.3062
Walter L. Statton, President

Greenwich Seniors Club
Sheila Shea Russo, Executive Director - (W) 622.1500, (H) 531.4345
Contact: Rosemary Pugliese, Membership - 531.8600

Greenwich Women's Civic Club
PO Box 26, Greenwich 06836
Gwendolyn Petitt, President - 968.2821

Greenwich Woman's Club Gardeners
89 Maple Avenue, 869.2046
Valerie Anderson, President - 869-8965

Greenwich Women's Exchange
28 Sherwood Place, 869.0229
Helen Chester, Chairman and President - 869.4488

Greenwich World Hunger
PO Box 7444, Greenwich CT 06836
Irv Thode, 629.1131 or Sarah Boyle, 661.9771

Hadassah, Greenwich Chapter
Temple Sholom, 300 East Putnam Avenue
Fran Blaustein, Co-President - 622.0225
Felice Robinou, Co-President - 625.9666

Historical Society of the Town of Greenwich
39 Strickland Road, Cos Cob
www.hstg.org
Debra Mecky, Executive Director - 869.6899

CLUBS/ORGANIZATIONS

COMMUNITY

Hortulus
PO Box 4666, Greenwich, CT 06830
Wendy Serrell, President
Contact: Ann Lockyer - 661.9557

Japanese Volunteer Group (Kalmia)
c/o Japan Education Center
15 Ridgeway, 629.5922 ext. 2 or 3

Junior League of Greenwich
48 Maple Avenue, 869.1979
www.jlgreenwich,org
Susan Wohlforth, President
Contact: Lynn Benson, Office Manager

Knollwood Garden Club
PO Box 1666, Greenwich 06836
Friede Costigan, President - 869.5292

League of Women Voters of Greenwich
PO Box 604, Greenwich 06836-0604, 352.4700
www.lwvct.org/greenwich
Jo Ann Messina, President - 869.1464
Contact: Betsie Harkins, Membership Director

Lions Club of Greenwich
PO Box 1044, Greenwich 06836-1044
www.lionsclub.org
Robert Harris, President - 359.4611 ext 334
Contact Dave Noble - 661.2540

Lions Club of Old Greenwich
PO Box 215, Old Greenwich 06870
www.lionsclub.org
Phil Hahn, President - 637.5084

CLUBS/ORGANIZATIONS
COMMUNITY

Lions Club of Western Greenwich
www.lionsclub.org
Kevin Hamilton, President - 531.8499

National League of American Pen Women, Connecticut
8 Dartmouth Road, Cos Cob 06807
Catherine Bohrman, President - 629.8533
Connie Walton, Membership Chair - 637.7620

National League of American Pen Women, Greenwich
www.penwomen.org
108 Butternut Hollow Road, Greenwich
Anita Kiere, President - 869.4228

National Society of New England Women
365 Round Hill Road
Joan Ingersoll, President - 661.6314

NOW, Greenwich Chapter
PO Box 245, Cos Cob, CT 06807
www.now.org
Contact: Carolyn Hopley, Information - 622.1372

P.E.O. Sisterhood, Greenwich Chapter
www.peointernational.org
Kathy Rubenstein, President - 661.6264

Philoptochos
Contact Despina Fassuliotis, 661.5991

(American) Red Cross, Greenwich Chapter
231 East Putnam Avenue Greenwich CT 06830, 869.8444
www.greenwich.ctredcross.org

CLUBS/ORGANIZATIONS

COMMUNITY

Retired Men's Association
YMCA
50 East Putnam Avenue
Joseph Robinson, President - 698.2220

Riverside Garden Club
PO Box 11, Riverside 06878-0011
Terry Lubman, Membership - 637.8221

Rotary Club of Byram-Cos Cob
PO Box 4632, Valley Drive Station, Greenwich 06831
Tomas Menten, President - 622.0458

Rotary Club of Greenwich
PO Box 1375, Greenwich 06836
www.rotary.org
Marie Stacey, President - 637.4568

Round Hill Country Dances
Round Hill Community House
www.roundhill.net
Bernie Koser, President - 914.736.6489
For Information call 381.9509

Travel Club of Greenwich
Virginia Obrig, Program Chair - 661.4456

Trout Unlimited, Mianus Chapter
PO Box 663, Riverside CT 06878
(703) 522 0200 National Headquarters (Arlington VA)
Mike Law, President, 203.966.3364
www.mianustu.org   www.tu.org

UJA Federation of Greenwich
One Holly Hill Lane, Greenwich 06830-6080 , 622.1434
Pamela Zur, President

CLUBS/ORGANIZATIONS
COMMUNITY

United Way of Greenwich
1 Lafayette Court, 869.2221
Stuart Adelberg, President and C.P.O.

Veterans of Foreign Wars
Cos Cob Post 10112   PO Box 8, Cos Cob 06807
Vincent Mitchell, Commander - 326.0773

Veterans of Foreign Wars
Greenwich Post 1792
James Clifford, Quartermaster - 531.9557
Diane Larson, Commander - 531.9557

Woman's Club of Greenwich
89 Maple Avenue, 869.2046
Martha Kreger, President

YMCA
50 East Putnam Avenue, 869.1630
www.gwymca.org
John P. Eikrem, Executive Director
Contact: Pamela Hearn, Director of Development and Marketing

YWCA
259 East Putnam Avenue, 869.6501
www.ywcagreenwich.com
Rev. Brenda Stiers, Director

CLUBS/ORGANIZATIONS

COUNTRY CLUBS

Greenwich has a number of country clubs. Costs to join a country club vary from about $5,000 to $30,000 for the initiation fee with annual dues ranging from approximately $2,000 to $4,000. Country clubs with golf courses are typically the most expensive. Clubs with dining rooms usually require a quarterly food minimum. In addition, country clubs may have assessments for capital improvements. Membership in most private clubs requires a proposer and one or more seconders who are members. Therefore, the more members you know, the easier it is to join. Clubs which serve a particular area, such as Belle Haven or Milbrook, often give preference to area residents. The waiting period to join a club can be several years.

Bailiwick Club of Greenwich
Duncan Drive, 531.7591 (summer)
Bob Caie, Manager
Swimming and tennis.

Burning Tree Country Club
120 Perkins Road, 869.9004
Roger Loose, Manager
Dining, golf, swimming, tennis, paddle tennis.

Fairview Country Club
1241 King Street, 531.6200
Andrew Campbell, Manager
Dining, golf, tennis, paddle, swimming.

CLUBS/ORGANIZATIONS

COUNTRY CLUBS

Field Club
276 Lake Avenue, 869.1300
Martina A.Halsey, Manager
Dining, tennis (grass & indoor), squash, paddle, swimming.

Greenwich Country Club
19 Doubling Road, 869.1000
Jim Cirillo, Manager
Dining, golf, tennis, squash, paddle, swimming, skeet.

Innis Arden Golf Club
120 Tomac Avenue, Old Greenwich, 637.3677
Michael Ctanzaro, General Manager
Dining, golf, tennis, paddle, swimming.

Milbrook Club
61 Woodside Drive, 869.4540
John Zerega, Manager
Dining, golf, swimming, paddle, tennis.

Round Hill Club
33 Round Hill Club Road, 869.2350
Dennis Meermans, Manager
Dining, golf, swimming, tennis, skeet.

Stanwich Club
888 North Street, 869.0555
Peter Tunley, Manager
Dining, golf, swimming, tennis, paddle.

Tamarack Country Club
55 Locust Road, 531.7300
Tom Tuthill, Manager
Dining, golf, swimming, tennis.

CLUBS/ORGANIZATIONS
NEWCOMERS CLUBS

Several organizations are designed to help new residents make friends and feel welcome.

Chinese Association of Fairfield County
Contact: Tak Eng, 637.5512
Wide variety of social and educational programs. They publish a directory of Chinese-speaking resources for newcomers.

Greenwich Newcomer's & Neighbors Club
YWCA, 259 East Putnam Avenue, 869.6501
www.GreenwichNewcomers.com
Contact: Patty Capp: 522.1673; Christa Wetzel: 618.0598
The club has a comprehensive program of coffees, luncheons, dinners and special interest groups. Be sure to ask for their excellent newsletter. The Y playroom is available for baby-sitting during daytime events. A good resource whether you have lived in Greenwich for two weeks or twenty years.

International Club of the YWCA
YWCA, 259 East Putnam Avenue
Jackie Rothenberg, President - 622.0461
Founded in 1975, the club holds monthly functions to help women of all nationalities who are new to Greenwich make friends in the community. New members, including Americans, are welcome.

Old Greenwich-Riverside Newcomer's Club
PO Box 256, Old Greenwich, CT 06870
www.GreenwichNewcomers.com
Christina Crossman, President - 637.9958
The club is 37 years old and hosts a great variety of functions, from house renovation to gourmet dinners. They have events of interest to everyone, and they welcome new or established residents. Be sure to ask for their excellent newsletter.

CLUBS/ORGANIZATIONS

YACHT CLUBS

As one might expect for a town on the water, Greenwich has a number of excellent yacht and boating clubs. Many yacht clubs have long waiting lists (some as long as 12 years) but are considerably less expensive to join than a country club.

Belle Haven Club
100 Harbor Drive, 861.5353
Neil P. MacKenzie, Manager
Dining, boating, tennis, swimming. A combination yacht and country club.

Byram Shore Boat Club
PO Box 4335, Greenwich CT 06830
Byram Park, 531.9858 (clubhouse)
Frank Congiu Commodore - 531.6141
Mooring/docking adjacent to town park and beach.

Cos Cob Yacht Club
PO Box 155, Riverside CT 06878.
Walter X. Burns, Jr, Commodore - 661.5946
Social club for people interested in boating. Membership is by invitation. Meets the fourth Wednesday of the month at Ponus Yacht Club in Stamford.

CLUBS/ORGANIZATIONS

YACHT CLUBS

Greenwich Boat & Yacht Club

PO Box 40 Greenwich, CT 06830
Grass Island
Per Thompsen, Commodore - 869.6365
Club House, Mooring/docking and picnic areas.

Indian Harbor Yacht Club

710 Steamboat Road, 869.2484
www.indianharboryc.com
Thomas Nevin, Manager
Dining and boating facilities including mooring/docking.

Mianus River Boat & Yacht Club

98 Strickland Road Cos Cob, 869.4689
Jeff Downs, Commodore
Boat and yacht club open to any Greenwich resident. Meets the first
Monday of the month at 7:30 pm at the clubhouse. The clubhouse may
be rented for private functions by anyone who is sponsored by a member (but it is unavailable on weekends from May to September).
Accommodates a sit-down dinner for 75 people.

Old Greenwich Yacht Club

Tod's Driftway, Old Greenwich, 637.3074
John Ehlers, Commodore
Club house, launch and moorings are handled through the town hall.

Riverside Yacht Club

102 Club Road, Riverside, 637.1706
Gary Ashley, Manager
Dining, swimming and boating.

Rocky Point Club

Rocky Point Road, Old Greenwich, 637.2397
Doug Carlson, President
Clubhouse, mooring, salt water pool (Open in summer only).

COOKING SCHOOLS

Bella Cucina

New Canaan, CT, Carol Borelli, 203.966.4477

Established in 1996, the school has 1 - 6 session courses covering basic techniques and seasonal menus. The emphasis is on fine Italian cooking. Excursions to markets and restaurants, as well as travel programs to Italy. Courses conducted at the owner's home. Average class size ranges from 5 to 20 participants and costs vary from $45 to $270.

Complete Kitchen Cooking School

410 Main Street, Ridgefield, CT, 203.431.7722
www.TheCompleteKitchenLLC.com

A cooking store that provides a wealth of hands-on and demonstration cooking lessons provided by a variety of guest instructors. Although they have a store in Greenwich, the classes are usually held in Ridgefield. Classes are limited to 20. The average price is $40 - $70 per class.

Cucina Casalinga

Wilton CT, 203.762.0768
www.cucinacasalinga.com

Sally Maraventano has been teaching home-style Italian cooking for over 15 years. She has day-time and evening classes and can accommodate groups as large as 15 students. Classes cost about $85 per person (which includes dinner).

Ronnie Fein School of Creative Cooking

32 Heming Way, Stamford, 322.7114

Year-round cooking classes with an emphasis on ingredients, techniques and menus. She also has children's classes or will tailor a course to fit your needs. Hands-on classes are usually 4 people and cost $250 per session. She has been teaching cooking and writing food stories for the *Greenwich Time* for over 20 years.

COOKING

COOKING SCHOOLS

Foodsearch Cooking School

Ridgefield, CT, 203.438.0422

Karen Hansen also teaches at the New School and at New York University. Besides scheduled classes, she will custom-design classes. She conducts tours to France.

Greenwich Continuing Education

Greenwich High School, 625.7474, 7475

www.GreenwichSchools.org/gce

Well-priced, well-taught classes. Besides their specialized courses, they often have classes in basic cookery for beginners. Check the Culinary Arts section of their catalog.

Lauren Groveman's Kitchen

55 Prospect Avenue, Larchmont, NY, 914.834.1372

www.laurengroveman.com

Established in 1990, the school provides 5-session participation courses as well as individual classes for adults and young people. The emphasis is on techniques and the preparation of comfort foods, breads and appetizers. The average class size is 6. Cost is $450 for a five-session course and $100 for a specialty course.

Institute of Culinary Education

50 West 23rd Street, NY, NY, 800.522.4610, 212.847.0700

www.iceculinary.com

Although this school is in New York City, it has from time to time conducted courses in the Greenwich area. Founded by Peter Kump, it has been in business since 1975 and has established a large Greenwich following. The school provides hands-on courses and workshops from 5 to 25-hours. The emphasis is on techniques of fine cooking. The average class size is 12 for hands-on instruction and 30 for demonstrations. The school has a staff of 45 who operate from a 27,000 sq-ft facility with 9 kitchens. Hands-on classes range from $85 - $525. For additional cooking schools in New York City try www.ShawGuides.com.

CULTURE

INTRODUCTION

Rarely is a community so fully appreciative as Greenwich is of the value of the arts. Note the peaceful expressions on the faces in the audience of the Greenwich Symphony, or the joyful chatter of a family in the Bruce Museum, or the smiles surrounding the Grace Notes, and you may discover how many of our high-powered, busiest residents relax and refresh themselves.

For art museums see CULTURE, MUSEUMS; for art education see SCHOOLS, ADULT CONTINUING EDUCATION or CHILDREN, ENRICHMENT. Art galleries are listed under STORES.

ART

Art Society of Old Greenwich

Nancy Kuliuski, President, 323.6108

www.sidewalkshow.com

An organization of amateur and professional artists with membership open to everyone. We always enjoy their Sound Beach Avenue sidewalk art show in September.

Greenwich Arts Council

299 Greenwich Avenue, 622.3998

www.greenwicharts.org

Frank Juliano, executive director in combination with an outstanding board, is keeping this nonprofit organization dynamic. They are celebrating over twenty-five years of support for the arts. They manage the recently renovated Arts Center on the two top floors of the old Town Hall which houses two art galleries, a large dance studio, a small theater/recital hall and several artist studios. It is home to many Greenwich organizations, such as the Choral Society and the Art Society, as well as the Alliance Française. The Council publishes a newsletter with a good calendar of music and art events in town. The Council maintains a talent bank of all types of music and art teachers. It is also a good resource for classes as disparate as Tai Chi Chuan, classical ballet or acting. You can even rent a darkroom for black and white printing.

CULTURE

ART

Greenwich Art Society

299 Greenwich Avenue, 629.1533
Mary Branch, President
The Art Society has been stimulating interest in the arts since 1912.
Greenwich has many talented artists. While walking along Greenwich
Avenue, stop in the Greenwich Art Center to see the latest show.
Hours: weekdays, 10 am - 5 pm; Thursday until 7 pm;
Saturday, noon - 5 pm.

Union Church of Pocantico Hills

555 Bedford Road, North Tarrytown, NY, 914.631.8200, 2069
Stained glass windows created by Henri Matisse (1869-1954) and Marc
Chagall (1887-1985).
Hours: April - October, open daily except Tuesday, 11 am - 5 pm;
Saturdays, 10 am - 5 pm; Sundays, 2 pm - 5 pm.
Directions: I-95 to I-287 W, Exit 1; R on Rte 119 W, R on Rte 9 N;
R on Rte 448.

TIP: ART ON THE AVENUE
If you want to enjoy Greenwich Avenue at its best, do
not miss a stroll down the Avenue on the opening night
of this festival. The Greenwich Arts Council sponsors
this event in early May. Over 150 artists, retailers and
restaurants take part.
Call the Council at 622.3998 for the details.

CULTURE

MOVIES

Not many towns still have movie theaters left in their downtown area. Greenwich has two. Enjoy the luxury of strolling from a nice restaurant to one of these theaters. See Movie Phone under CULTURE, THEATER TICKETS for an easy way to buy your movie tickets. Also see CULTURE, VIDEO.

Clearview Twin Cinema
356 Greenwich Avenue, 869-6030

Crown Plaza Three
2 Railroad Avenue, 869-4030

Greenwich Library Friday Films
101 West Putnam Avenue, 622.7910
At 8 pm (doors open at 7:40) in the Cole Auditorium, the Library presents award-winning US and foreign films. Admission is free. Call to get a schedule and verify that a film is being shown.

Nearby Greenwich:

Crown Avon Two
272 Bedford Street, Stamford, CT, 324.9205

Crown Landmark Nine
5 Landmark Square, Stamford, CT, 324.3100

Crown Majestic Six
118 Summer Street, Stamford, CT, 323.1690
The newest theater in Stamford.

Crown Ridgeway Two
Ridgeway Shopping Center, 52 Sixth Street, Stamford, CT, 323.5000

CULTURE

MOVIES

Garden Cinemas

9 Isaac Street, Norwalk, CT 203.838.4504

Great movie theater for foreign movies you won't find in the area multiplexes. Unusual amenities: there's a small waiting area with leather couches and current magazines to read; there's a sound-proof area to leave children to play while you watch the movie; the theater has lots of leg room.

Directions: I-95 N to exit 16, L on East Ave, L on Wall, L on Isaac

IMAX Theater

At the Norwalk Aquarium, 10 North Water Street, SoNo, 203.852.0700

With a screen that is six stories high and eight stories wide, the visual effects are stunning. See full description under CHILDREN, FAMILY OUTINGS.

Hours: Open daily, 10 am - 5pm.

Rye Ridge Twin Cinema

1 Rye Ridge Plaza, Rye Brook, NY, 914.939.8177

State Cinema

990 Hope Street, Stamford, CT, 325.0250

One of the least-expensive theaters in the area. A good place to take a group of children and your best bet for avoiding long lines.

CULTURE
MOVIES: VIDEO & DVD

Residents of Greenwich campaigned against the establishment of a chain video store in town. As a result, the local video stores have survived and thrived.

Academy Video
80 East Putnam Avenue, 629.3260
A good selection in a convenient location with average service.
Hours: every day, 10 am - 10 pm.

Glenville Video
1 Glenville Street, 531.6030
A small store with a friendly staff who can help with your movie selection.
Hours: weekdays, 9 am - 9 pm, weekends, 10 am - 9 pm.

Video Station
160 Greenwich Avenue, 869.8543
A large selection with all the recent videos. A family run business. They know their movies. They can be extremely helpful if you are wondering what you should rent. The best selection of foreign films. They also have more than 1,100 DVDs for rent and for sale.
Hours: Monday - Sunday 9 am - 8 pm, Friday & Saturday until 9 pm.

CULTURE

MUSEUMS

Bruce Museum

1 Museum Drive, 869.0376

www.BruceMuseum.org

This year the Bruce attracted over 100,000 visitors to their 18 exciting exhibitions making the Bruce the second most popular museum in Connecticut. In addition, the Bruce sponsored over 50 lectures and gave educational programs to over 18,000 children. No wonder the Bruce is placed in the top 10% of US museums. The Museum sponsors two fairs in Bruce Park every year. The mid-May Craft Fair and the Columbus Day Arts Festival have juried artists from around the country and draw visitors from all over the area. When you become a member (which you should), you will be informed about their wonderful events.

There are a number of organizations affiliated with the Bruce.

> Astronomical Society of Greenwich, 869.6786 ext 338
> Connecticut Ceramics Study Circle, 869.9478
> Greenwich Antiques Society, 869.9531 or 661.7988
> Forum for World Affairs, 356.0340

Hours: Tuesday - Saturday, 10 am - 5 pm; Sunday, 1 am - 5 pm.

Bush-Holley House Museum

39 Strickland Road, Cos Cob, 869.6899

Home of the Historical Society, this is the place to learn about Greenwich history. They also have a good library and a shop with books on Greenwich history, as well as reproductions of 19th century children's toys and books. While you are there, pick up a list of their informative programs.

Hours: April - Dec: Wednesday - Friday, 12 - 4 pm; Saturday, 11 am - 4 pm; Sunday, 1 - 4 pm; Jan - March: Wednesday, 12 pm - 4 pm; Saturday, 11 am - 4 pm; Sunday 1 pm - 4 pm.

CULTURE

MUSEUMS

Donald M. Kendall Sculpture Gardens

At Pepsico, 700 Anderson Hill Road, Purchase, NY, 914.253.2000
One of the world's finest sculpture gardens is located right next to
Greenwich. The collection includes forty pieces by such 20th century
artists as Noguchi, Moore, Nevelson, and Calder. The sculptures are set
on 168 carefully landscaped acres. Pick up a map at the visitors parking
lot. There are some picnic tables.
Hours: every day from dawn to dusk, except for Saturday in August.
Directions: From Glenville, R on King, L at light on Anderson, L at light
into Pepsico.

Historical Society of the Town of Greenwich

39 Strickland Road, Cos Cob, CT, 869.6899
www.hstg.org
Their mission is to collect, preserve and disseminate the history of
Greenwich. The society conducts a wide variety of adult and children's
educational programs, exhibitions and workshops. Their extensive archives are open to anyone wanting to research town history. We sincerely appreciate this organization's dedication to preserving our
community's historical roots.

Katonah Museum of Art

Route 22 at Jay Street, Katonah, NY 914.232.9555
www.katonah-museum.org
The Museum offers an extensive range of activities to engage visitors
of all ages. Exhibitions present art from the past to the present. The
Museum's Learning Center is an interactive exhibition space in which
children can experience the fun of artistic exploration.
Hours: Tuesday, Thursday, Friday & Saturday, 10 am - 5 pm (Wednesday until 8pm); Sunday, noon - 5 pm.
Directions: I-684 to exit 6, East on Route 35 to Route 22, then South 1/
4 mile on Route 22 to the Museum on the left.

Museum Trips

Greenwich Continuing Education, 625.0141
One of the more popular programs offered are group trips to New York
City, Boston and other fine art museums.

CULTURE

MUSEUMS

Neuberger Museum
735 Anderson Hill Road, Purchase, NY, 914.251.6100
The museum is located on the 500-acre campus of the State University of New York (SUNY) at Purchase. It has 25,000 sq. feet of gallery space, a café, a store and an interactive learning center. It houses a well respected collection of modern art.
Hours: Closed Monday; Tuesday - Friday, 10 am - 4 pm; Saturday & Sunday, 11 am - 5 pm.
Directions: From Glenville, King Street N, L at light on Anderson, R at light into SUNY.

Putnam Cottage
243 East Putnam Avenue, 869.9697
Originally a tavern serving travelers along the Post Road, it is now a museum owned by the DAR. Each year on the last Sunday in February (1-3 pm) the Putnam Hill Revolutionary War battle is recreated. A definite must-see for adults and children alike.
Hours: April - December; Wednesday, Friday, Sunday, 1 pm - 4 pm. Special tours anytime.

Storm King Art Center
Old Pleasant Hill Road, Mountainville, NY, 845.534.3115
www.stormking.org
Take a walk or picnic in this leading outdoor sculpture museum with 120 masterworks set in a stunning 400-acre landscaped park. Great place to take the kids for a picnic. Open April 1 - November 15th.
Hours: 11 am - 5:30 pm; June, July & August open until 8 pm.
Directions: New York State Thruway, I-87 North to exit 16, Harriman; N on Route 32 for 10 miles; in Cornwall follow signs for the center.

CULTURE

THEATER/DANCE/MUSIC

Guide to Arts & Entertainment in Fairfield County

Published by *Greenwich Time*, 324.9799

This weekly guide provides a nice calendar of events as well as restaurant reviews.

Cameo Theater

Contact: Lori Feldman, 203.316.0262 or Pat Brandt, 637.4870

Theater company in its 20th season, performs at the First Congregational Church in Old Greenwich. A friendly group, open to anyone who is interested in acting or helping put on a show.

Caramoor Center for Music and Arts

Girdle Ridge Road, Katonah, NY, 914.232.5035, 1252

www.caramoor.com

Caramoor has wonderful music programs in a very intriguing setting. It should be on everyone's "must-do" list. For their evening performances, it is fashionable to bring a fancy picnic supper and eat on one of the lawns before the show. Caramoor has 100 acres of parklands and formal gardens. Most performances are open air, unless it rains. Mosquitoes are sparse but bringing some bug spray in the summer can't hurt. The main season is June through August although Caramoor provides fall, winter and spring indoor programs on a more limited schedule.

Directions: About 20 minutes from Greenwich. Take North Street N to the end (Bedford Village), R at the end, L on Route 22 N, R on Girdle Ridge Road; or I-684 N to exit 6, E on Rte 35, R on Rte 22 S.

Connecticut Playmakers

637-2298

Live theater open to adult participants from age 16. In addition to their major productions, the monthly meetings include dramatic presentations. The Playmakers Young People's Theater puts on a musical each summer. This is an enjoyable way for young people to meet each other and learn about the theater.

CULTURE
THEATER/DANCE/MUSIC

Emelin Theater
153 Library Lane, Mamaroneck, NY, 914.698.0098
Speakers, cabaret, jazz, classical music, musical theater, children's theater and more. Wonderful programs. Call for a catalog.
Directions: I-95 S to exit 18-A (Mamaroneck Ave), R on US 1, R on Library Lane.

Fairfield County Chorale
61 Unquowa Road, Fairfield, CT, 254.1333
scsu.ctstateu.edu/~Northcutt_J/chorale.html
Founded in 1963, the Chorale's repertoire consists of more than 100 classic works by composers from the 16th through the 20th century. Most performances are held at the Norwalk Concert Hall.

Fairfield Orchestra
50 Washington Street, Norwalk, CT
For information: 838.6995, for tickets: 622.5937
A well-respected, professional ensemble performing classical selections (usually in Norwalk). The Orchestra of the Old Fairfield Academy is the historical instrument affiliate. The Fairfield Orchestra is also known as the American Classical Orchestra.

Grace Notes
Contact: Anne Marcus, President, 683.0220, 869.8428
A women's "a cappella" singing group that has been entertaining Greenwich audiences for over thirty years. Singing with this group is a rewarding experience.

Greenwich Symphony Orchestra
869.2664
www.greenwichsym.org
This 90-member professional orchestra is in its forty-sixth season. They play consistently excellent music at a low ticket price. Ask for a CD of their music highlights. Concerts are Saturday evenings and Sunday afternoons at the High School. To inquire about the Symphony's Chamber Players, call 869.5734.

THEATER/DANCE/MUSIC

Greenwich Choral Society

PO Box 5, Greenwich, CT 06836-0005, 622.5136
Entering its seventy-sixth season, the society performs throughout the area during the winter months. Their annual Christmas concert held at Christ Church is a very popular event.

Long Wharf Theater

222 Sargent Drive, New Haven, CT, 203.787.4282, 800.782.8497
www.longwharf.org
Professional theater which produces traditional plays as well as plays by new playwrights. Over the last thirty-two years, Long Wharf has presented thirty-three world premiers, forty American premieres and twenty-three transfers to Broadway.
Directions: I-95 N to exit 46.

Palace Theater

61 Atlantic Street, Stamford, CT, 325.4466, 358.2305
www.onlyatsca.com
The Palace, along with the Rich Forum, is part of the Stamford Center for the Arts. The Palace is a 1,584-seat vaudeville theater that was acclaimed as "Connecticut's most magnificent" when it opened in 1927. The recently renovated Palace and the Rich Forum are a formidable duo.
Box Office Hours: weekdays, 10 am - 5 pm.
Directions: I-95 N to exit 8, L on Atlantic.

Rich Forum

307 Atlantic Street, Stamford, CT, 325.4466, 358.2305
www.onlyatsca.com
This theater has excellent facilities and an eclectic program of high quality events. Rich Forum, like the Palace, is committed to presenting the best of live theater, concerts, comedy and dance entertainment.
Box Office Hours: weekdays, 10 am - 5 pm.
Directions: I-95 N to exit 8, L on Atlantic.

CULTURE

THEATER/DANCE/MUSIC

Shubert Theater

247 College Street, New Haven, CT

www.Shubert.com

For tickets call Advantix, 800.228.6622

This not-for-profit theater is considered the crown jewel of downtown New Haven. Its productions are professional and well regarded. Some shows come directly from Broadway.

Box Office Hours: weekdays, 9 am - 9 pm, Saturday 9 am - 7 pm, Sundays Noon - 6 pm

Directions: I-95 N to Exit 47 "Downtown New Haven" to the Route 34 Connector. Take Exit 1 off Route 34 "Downtown New Haven", straight to the light and R on Church St. At third light, L on Chapel St. A the second light, L on College. The Schubert Theater is the second building on the Left. The parking garage entrance is just past the theater on your left.

SUNY at Purchase - Performing Arts Center

Anderson Hill Road, Purchase, NY, 914.251.6200

www.artscenter.org

The Performing Arts Center at the State University of New York at Purchase has wonderful music and dance performances, as well as plays. They have a number of summer offerings although the main season is September to May.

Directions: From Glenville, R on King Street, L at light on Anderson, R at light into SUNY Purchase.

Town Concerts and other summer events

622.7830

During July and August the Department of Parks and Recreation arranges free Tuesday afternoon and Wednesday evening concerts. In addition, the Fourth of July fireworks displays at the Greenwich High School and at Binney Park are always spectacular.

CULTURE
THEATER/DANCE/MUSIC

Westport Country Playhouse

25 Powers Court, Westport, CT, 203.227.4177

www.WestportPlayhouse.com

A six-play summer season starting in June. Very professional. Only a 20 minute trip. Good seats matter here. If you cannot get seats in the first fifteen orchestra rows or in the first 4 rows of the balcony consider another theater. They also have a children's series. While there, try dinner at the Splash Restaurant *(See the restaurant section)*.

Directions: I-95 N to Exit 17, L on Rt. 33, R on Rte 1, L on Powers Court, Playhouse on left.

Yale University Repertory Theater

149 Elm Stteet, New Haven, CT, 203.432.1234

www.yale.edu/drama/performance/conventions2.html

It is a drive—about an hour—but it's well worth it. Often as good as Broadway, but with much less hassle, better seats and lower prices. You can park right next to the theater for free. Subscribers can get front row seats.

Directions: I-95 N to exit 49, I-91 N to exit 3 (Trumbull Street). Stay in the middle lane and continue straight, L on Prospect Street (College Street), L on Elm.

TIP: SIDEWALK SALES

Greenwich residents eagerly await summer sidewalk sales. Expect a good time with bargains galore. Don't forget to go inside the stores - they are also full of incredible buys during these sales. Mid- July on Thursdays, Fridays and Saturdays in Central Greenwich and Old Greenwich.

CULTURE

TICKETS

Movie Phone

323-FILM (3456)

On Friday and Saturday nights, the demand for tickets is high and the lines can be very long—they often run out of tickets before you can get in. Call to hear previews and to buy your tickets in advance with your credit card. You should still arrive early for the best seating, but when you arrive you don't have to wait in the line. Just show your credit card and get your tickets.

When calling Movie Phone, their advertisements can sometimes be a nuisance. To get around this: press "*" to repeat or change your previous selection; "***" to start over; if you already know the theater you want, "#" plus the Theater Express Code will get you there immediately.

www.MovieLink.com

Purchase tickets for local theaters using the web. First choose New York City as your area, then choose Greenwich as your neighborhood. The same Express Codes used by Movie Phone apply here.

Café Rue

95 Railroad Avenue, 629.1056

They will buy tickets from Crown Plaza Three Theater (across the street) for those who dine there before the movie. Just call a couple of hours in advance and pay for your tickets with your dinner. (See description under RESTAURANTS).

Ticket Services

34 East Putnam Avenue, 661-5000

Private ticket services that can get you tickets for just about any event anywhere.

Ticket Affair/Ticket Box

www.TheTicketBox.com

869.9822, 800.331.9822

ENTERTAINING

CATERERS

These caterers have delicious food, they arrive on time and are dependable. As a result, they are often in high demand. Reserve early. For wine and other party foods, see FOOD STORES.

Abigail Kirsch Culinary Productions
914.631.3030
www.AbigailKirsch.com
Caterer of choice for many Greenwich residents when they are having a large party. Dear friends used Abigail for both daughter's weddings.

Aux Delices Events
1075 East Putnam Avenue, Riverside, 698.2085
www.AuxDelicesFoods.com
Debra Ponzek and Aux Delices are well-known for excellent food. They will cater or plan events of all types and sizes.

Eileen Grossman
Victorian teas and dinner parties, 323.5043
For an elegant event, be sure to give her a try.

Fjord Fisheries
137 River Road, Cos Cob, 661.5006
If you are invited to a clam bake or lobster party, chances are Fjord is the provider. They are a full-service caterer. You must try their salmon. From May through September, Fjord can cater a party of 40 to 120 on one of their four ships. Breakfast, lunch and dinner cruises lasting two to three hours are available.

Libby Cooke Catering
1 Boulder Avenue, Old Greenwich, 698.0545
Known for her fabulous presentations, she is equally competent with an intimate dinner party or a grand affair. You can sample her foods in her take-out shop.

ENTERTAINING

CATERERS

Patricia Blake Catering
Darien, CT, 203.661.9676
Many choices on her catering menu from comfort foods to exotic delicacies. She has an impressive repertoire of hors d'oeuvres. She especially enjoys customizing the menu to meet your needs.

Le Potager Catering
116 Woodbury Ave, Stamford, CT, 975.2546
Joseph Jenkins, one of New York City's upscale caterers, has moved to our area. He is receiving rave reviews for his tasteful, elegant parties.

Susan Morton
136 Hamilton Avenue, 661.8833
Susie has been serving up creative parties since 1984.

Watson's
201 Pemberwick Road, 532.0132
You will want to have a cocktail or dinner party just to have Sue Scully's good food. Large parties are her forte.

ENTERTAINING

PARTY PLANNERS

Hollywood Pop Gallery
372 Greenwich Avenue, 622.4057
www.hollywoodPop.com
A global event production company. They will create and coordinate every element of your event from amazing decorations to cutting edge entertainment. If you want your party to be remembered decades later, just give them a call. They put together about 200 adult and 1,000 children's parties a year.
Hours: weekdays, 10 am - 5 pm.

Winslow Associates
70 Hamilton Avenue, 869.6612
Judy Winslow organizes high-end political and social events. Call her for your special events. She recently organized one of the most memorable family reunions on record.

PARTY RENTALS

PM Amusements
36 Bush Avenue, Port Chester, 914.937.1188
This is the ultimate party rental source. If you want to turn your backyard into an amusement park or just rent a cotton candy machine, they have it all. Ask about sumo wrestling, a velcro wall, miniature golf, karaoke, clowns, inflatable rides, or perhaps just an Abe Lincoln or Mick Jagger look-a-like /impersonator. Call and ask for their catalog.
Hours: weekdays, 8 am - 5 pm; open sometimes on Saturday; call before going.
Directions: Post Road W to Main Street in Port Chester, R on Westchester, R on Haseco, R on Bush.

Smith Party Rentals
133 Mason Street, 869-9315
A good source for children's tables, chairs and other party needs, just as they are for adult parties. If they don't have it, you probably don't need it.
Hours: Monday - Saturday, 9 am - 5 pm.

PARTY SERVICES

Darien Lawn & Tree Care (DLTC)

Norwalk, CT, 203.866.1303

www.DLTCUSA.com   www.SnowManUSA.com

For your next winter party, if the temperature is 27F or lower and you have a good source of water, rent a snow maker or have Jonathan Sweeney come and make snow for you, just like he does for the movies. 10-feet of snow should do the trick for most parties.

Fjord Charters

203.622.4020

Fjord, sails from Cos Cob or just about any port in Long Island Sound. They have three very distinctive luxury boats with seating for 65 to 120 guests for dinner. A great way to entertain.

Greenwich Police

622.8015

If you are having a large party, consider hiring an off-duty policemen to help your guests know where to park safely. Be sure to call well in advance and to confirm back that someone has signed-up to help you.

TIP: MAKING FRIENDS

If you are new to town or a long term resident and want to have an easy, fun way to meet others, join one of the two newcomers clubs. For details see www.GreenwichNewcomers.com.

FITNESS & SPORTS
INTRODUCTION

Fans and players of almost every imaginable sport live in Greenwich. Paddle tennis was even invented in Greenwich. Best of all, whether you are a professional or an amateur, finding a place to fish, skate, golf, sail or play ball is easy in our town.

ARCHERY

Cos Cob Archery Club
205 Bible Street, 625.9421 or Bob Harris, 869.6137
Twenty-four regular targets—members must have their own equipment and be over 18. Members have a key to the range and can practice any time. To join, visit the range Saturday or Sunday or attend the meeting on the second Wednesday of each month at 7:30 pm.

BADMINTON

Greenwich Badminton Club
Contact: Steve Edson, 637.2623
An affiliate of the US Badminton Association, www.usabadminton.org, they play at the YWCA.

YWCA
259 East Putnam Avenue, 869.6501
The Y provides supervised round robin youth badminton for all skill levels on Tuesday and Thursday evenings. The Y hosts tournaments sanctioned by the US Badminton Association.

FITNESS & SPORTS

BASEBALL

Babe Ruth League

Contact: Vinnie Gullotta, for the Bambino Division, 869.4132
Tina Carlucci, for the Junior Division, 531.9223
Bob Spaeth, for the Senior Division, 661.2386
Nonprofit organization sponsoring baseball. The Bambino division is for children 10 to 12; Junior division is for children 13 to 15; Senior division is for ages 16-18. Teams play from late May through mid-July at the Greenwich High School and Julian Curtiss Elementary School. Registration is in early April.

Blue Fish Professional Baseball

Listed as "Bridgeport Bluefish" under CHILDREN, FAMILY OUTINGS.

Brunswick Baseball Camp

Brunswick School, 100 Maher Avenue, 622.5800
The school offers six one-week baseball camps for boys ages 7 to 13.

Cos Cob Athletic Club

Contact Toni Natale, 869.0281
This community organization sponsors spring co-ed T-Ball for beginners in grades K-2.

FITNESS & SPORTS

BASEBALL

Greenwich Department of Parks and Recreation Programs

Town Hall, 101 Field Point Road, 622.7830

Indoor baseball clinics January through March, at Dundee School for children ages 7 to 13. Co-ed spring outdoor clinics for Small-Fry age 7; Midget for age 8. Doyle Baseball School for ages 7-12, during school vacation in April; July & August co-ed baseball league for ages 9-12.

Pro Batter Training Center

327 Main Avenue, Norwalk, CT, 203.847.3700

www.welovethisgame.com

Located in a warehouse, this indoor baseball/softball training center can provide challenging batting practice for the beginning to the advanced player. Pro Batter can also provide expert batting and pitching instruction. During the summer the facility is relatively unused. During the winter it can be quite busy.

Summer hours: weekdays, noon - 9 pm; Weekends, 9 am-9 pm.

Directions: I-95 N to exit 15; Route 7 N to exit 2 (New Canaan Avenue); L off the Ramp; L on Main.

Old Greenwich-Riverside Community Center Programs

90 Harding Road, 637.3659

They sponsor a variety of baseball and softball teams and instruction programs for girls and boys from kindergarten through 8th grade. Evaluations are usually in March.

Uniforms and Equipment

See FITNESS & SPORT, TEAM SPORTS EQUIPMENT.

YMCA Baseball Programs

50 East Putnam Avenue, 869.1630

The Y provides sessions for boys & girls, ages 4 - 5, 7 and 6 - 8 to learn the fundamentals of baseball, as well as clinics for children in grades 1-5.

BASKETBALL

Business People's Lunch Time Pick-Up Basketball
At the Greenwich Civic Center, call 637.4583.

Greenwich Basketball Association
Contact Joe Curreri at 661.4641
Now in its 6th season, the Association is a town-wide instructional and competitive basketball program for 5th to 10th graders. It is designed to encourage and stimulate each child to build basketball skills. Players on high school teams are prohibited from league involvement. Registration and evaluation start in October.

Hoop Start USA, Summer Basketball Camp
800.771.3555, 637.4583
Sponsored by the Greenwich Parks and Recreation Department and run at the Greenwich Civic Center, it provides high quality instruction for boys and girls, Pre-K through the 5th grade. Camps begin in June.

Men's Basketball League
Call 622.7830 for information.
A recreation program from January through March at the Greenwich Civic Center.

FITNESS & SPORTS

BASKETBALL

OGRCC Basketball Programs

Old Greenwich - Riverside Community Center,
90 Harding Road, 637.3659

Starting in October, OGRCC sponsors a number of basketball programs for young children through adults: Youth Basketball for boys and girls in the 3rd and 4th grades; Boys' Basketball and Girls' Basketball for 5th to 8th graders; Adult Pick-Up Basketball for 18 and over.

Parks and Recreation Basketball

Greenwich Parks and Recreation Department, 622.7830

Co-Ed Clinics, K to 6th grade at the Glenville and Dundee Schools.
Girls' Clinic, K to 6th grade at the Dundee School.
Men's League at the Central and Eastern Middle Schools.

Uniforms and Equipment

See FITNESS & SPORTS, TEAM SPORTS EQUIPMENT.

YMCA Programs

50 East Putnam Avenue, 869.1630

The Y provides clinics in Basketball for children in grades 1 - 5. They also sponsor A and B levels and an Adult Summer Outdoor Basketball League for ages 19 and up.

FITNESS & SPORTS

BICYCLING

Connecticut Department of Transportation
2800 Berlin Turnpike, PO Box 317564
Newington, CT 06131-7564.
The Connecticut Bicycle Map is published by the State. Write for a copy.

Connecticut Bicycle Newsletter
PO Box 121, Middletown, CT 06457
Published seasonally by the Coalition of Connecticut Bicyclists.

Greenwich Department of Parks & Recreation
622.7830
A tour map/guide of the 7.5-mile town bike route is available at the Recreation Division Office.

Sound Cyclists
203.840.1757
www.SoundCyclists.com
This social cycling club offers, at no cost, rides for all levels of ability led by experienced cyclists. Routes are along scenic coast lines and country roads and vary from 12 miles to 60+ miles.

Road Hogs
17 East Putnam Avenue, 661.0142, 977.0259
www.roadhogs.org
They conduct classes for runners, cyclists and swimmers, of all ages and abilities. Entry forms for the latest races are available here at Threads and Treads which is a good source for biking, swimming and running attire.
Hours: Monday - Saturday, 9:30 am - 5:30 pm

FITNESS & SPORTS

BOATING

Boat Master Services
Yacht Haven Marina, Washington Blvd, Stamford, CT, 203.348.1441
You can trust your treasure to this full-service boat cleaning company.

Greenwich Community Sailing
Tod's Driftway, Old Greenwich, 698.0599
CT approved boating certificate courses.

Greenwich Marine Facilities
622.7818
Assigns boat moorings for the town. To apply for a slip (as always, bring in a utility bill as proof of residency and a photo ID) you must own a boat and know the vessel's length, draft and beam. Boats are categorized as sail or power and over or under 20 feet; 20 feet and over receive deep-water moorings. After registering, you are put on a waiting list. The list is never short, but the amount of time varies with the vessel's type and size, as well as the location you request. The town has moorings at Greenwich Point, Cos Cob, Grass Island and Byram.

Greenwich Power Squadron
www.captain harbor.org
The Power Squadron is an all-volunteer civic organization with 200 Greenwich members; its present commander is Martin Mattler (637.0615). The Squadron's primary goal is education and boating safety—both sailing and power boating. The Squadron teaches two courses at the Greenwich High School through the Continuing Education program (625.7474) and depending upon demand, runs additional courses throughout the year. All boaters—even jet skiers—must have a Connecticut Boating License. The Power Squadron course qualifies you for your Connecticut license. This course is the first step for anyone who wants to enjoy the miles of coastline available to Greenwich residents.

Indian Harbor Yacht Club
710 Steamboat Road, 869.2484
One of the few private clubs with a sailing program open to the public. The program has such a good reputation that it is usually filled by February.

FITNESS & SPORTS

BOATING

John Kantor's Longshore Sailing School

Westport, CT, 203.226.4646

www.longshoresailingschool.com

If you or your children (ages 9-16) want to learn to sail and can't get into one of the Greenwich programs, try this school in Westport. It provides instruction from basic sailing to racing techniques. Register in February for two week sessions blending fun and substance. This year you can learn to race model sailboats at their new radio-controlled laser sailing class.

Old Greenwich Yacht Club

Greenwich Point, Old Greenwich, 637.3074

This club is open to all residents with beach cards. It has deep water moorings as well as Mercury sailboats for member use. The club provides sailing lessons on weekends and trophy races during the summer.

See the section on CLUBS for details on other yacht clubs.

Sound Sailing Center

South Norwalk, CT, 203.838.1110

Selected to manage the Old Greenwich Yacht Club sailing program, SSC focuses on adult education at its Norwalk Harbor facility.

After hours, call 203.454.4394.

Yachting Magazine

203.299.5900

www.yachtingmag.com

Published in Norwalk, this is the magazine for those who really want to get in the sailing swing.

FITNESS & SPORTS

BRIDGE

Lest you wonder why bridge is in this section, we regard it as fitness for the brain.

YWCA

259 East Putnam Avenue, 869.6501

The Y provides a variety of bridge lessons from beginning to advanced. Each Monday at noon, up to 100 serious players gather at the Y to participate in three and a half hours of duplicate or tournament bridge, played under the oversight of Steve Becker, who writes a syndicated bridge column. The game is franchised by the American Contract Bridge League and players can earn master points toward becoming life masters.

TIP: KAYAK/CANOE GUIDE

SWRPA (South Western Regional Planning Agency) publishes a full-color laminated guide to help you find your way around Norwalk's 23-island archipelago. SWRPA is located at 888 Washington Blvd in Stamford. Call 316.5190 for a copy.

FITNESS & SPORTS

CANOEING/KAYAKING

The Mianus River in Greenwich is a good place to practice canoeing. There is no need to worry if you fall in - the water is very clean. For the more adventurous, the Housatonic River has class I and II rapids, and is a center for trips and instruction. Outfitters come and go, but check out the following:

Clarke Outdoors
West Cornwall, CT, 860.672.6365
www.clarkeoutdoors.com

Kittatinny Canoes
Dingmans Ferry, PA, 800.356.2852, 570.828.2338
www.kittatinny.com
Canoeing, kayaking or rafting the Delaware. Calm water for families or beginners, white water for experts.

North American Whitewater
Kent, CT, 800.727.4379
www.nawhitewater.com

CROQUET

Greenwich Croquet Club
Greenwich has enjoyed an active Croquet Club for many years. William Campbell (661.9122) is the contact person. The Club is open to everyone and plays on the Bruce Park Green. Besides providing instruction, the Club holds the Greenwich Invitational Tournament every July 4th, and in August, hosts the Connecticut State Championship.

FITNESS & SPORTS

FISHING

Greenwich is ideally located on the Long Island Sound for excellent salt water fishing from May to December. Going East or West at different times of the year provides a multi-species catch including Striped Bass, Bluefish, Fluke, Porgies and Blackfish. Light spin, fly or bait tackle is the most fun. Freshwater fishing for Trout and Bass is good in the Mianus River. Fishing in reservoirs is prohibited. Blue ribbon trout streams in CT and NY are within a 90 minute drive. The resources below can help you. Also see fishing stores under SHOPPING. They provide more than just equipment.

Connecticut Angler's Guide
Connecticut Department of Environmental Protection
860.424.FISH
This guide should come with your license. It provides a summary of the rules and regulations governing sport fishing in Connecticut, descriptions of places to fish, the kinds of fish found there, and license information.

Fishing Licenses
Licenses can be obtained from the Town Clerk's office, 622.7897

Mianus River Park
Merrybrook Road (Cognewaugh Road), 622.7814
Good trout fishing. Be sure you have your license, they do check.
See section on PARKS & RECREATION, PARKS & NATURE PRESERVES for directions.

Sound Fishing Charters
Contact: Kevin Reynolds, 622.0522
In business since 1997, they plan four-hour to all-day fishing trips for groups up to six, complete with rods and bait. Call several weeks in advance for weekend trips.

Trout Unlimited, Mianus Chapter
Mike Law, President, 203.966.3364
Non-profit organization dedicated to preserving water quality. Classes in fly-fishing and fly-tying.

FITNESS & SPORTS

EXERCISE

Dynamic Martial Arts

202 Field Point Road, 629.4666

Kick boxing is the hot new way to exercise, especially for women. This is a workout that will leave your muscles screaming and you asking for more. United Studios combines aerobic boxing with weights and floor stretches for a terrific all-around activity. Call for hours.

Greenwich Fitness Center

1 Fawcett Place, 869.6189

Your standard, well-equipped fitness center with classes and weight rooms. Summer members welcome. Initiation fee approximately $200.
Hours: Monday - Thursday, 6 am - 9:00 pm; Friday, 6 am - 8:30 pm, Saturday, 7:45 am - 4:30 pm; Sunday, 9 am - 3 pm.

NY Sports Club

6 Liberty Way, 869.1253

In addition to a 6,000 sq. ft. state-of-the-art fitness center, the aerobics and Spinning™ studios offer classes seven days a week. Medically-based health and wellness programs include nutrition, massage, personal training and a Medicare certified physical therapy department. Childcare available. Initiation fee appromately $100 - 650.
Hours: weekdays, 6 am - 9:30 pm; Saturday, 8 am - 5 pm; Sunday, 8 am - 4 pm.

Pumping Iron

209 Bruce Park Avenue, 203.661.5017

www.PumpingIronGreenwich.com

A lot of independent personal trainers use this gym.
Hours: Monday - Thursday, 5:30 am - 10 pm; Friday, 5:30 am - 9 pm; Saturday, 7 am - 5 pm; Sunday, 8 am - 1 pm.

FITNESS & SPORTS

EXERCISE

Sportsplex

49 Brownhouse Road, Stamford, CT, 358.0066

On the border of Stamford and Old Greenwich is a complete training facility for adults and children. Morning programs for pre-schoolers and after-school programs for ages 6-8. Supervised nursery for children. In addition to machines, and spinning, they have an Olympic length pool, four squash courts and one racquetball court. Swimming and squash lessons are available. The aerobics center has a specially designed exercise floor. Call for an enthusiastic tour.

Hours: weekdays, 5:30 am - 10 pm; Saturday 7 am - 8 pm, Sunday 8 am - 8 pm. (Different summer hours).

Thompson Method Exercise Classes

222 Mill Street, 531.8762

Thompson Method classes work on stretching, strength and stamina (including combinations). Associates who attend the school swear by it. The cost for six months is $1,100, although there are a variety of different plans at different rates.

Velocity

280 Railroad Avenue, 552.0098

www.velocitygym.com

Studio cycling is a hot trend in cardiovascular training. Run by Olympic competitor Darcy Ramsey, Spin Gym cyclists feel better and have a great time.

Hours: Monday, Wednesday & Friday, 6 am - 6:15 pm;
Tuesday & Thursday, 8:15 am - 7 pm; Weekends, 8 am - 10:20 pm.

World Gym

1333 East Putnam Avenue, 637.3906

Newly opened in the former Caldor building, they intend to be one of the least expensive in town. No one in our group has tested them, please let us know what you think.

Hours: Monday - Thursday, 5 am - 10 pm; Friday, 5 am - 9 pm; Saturday, 8 am - 6 pm; Sunday, 8 am - 5 pm.

FITNESS & SPORTS

EXERCISE

YMCA

50 East Putnam Avenue, 869.1630

www.gwymca.org

Renovated facility with an impressive weight room. The Y also provides aerobics, swimming, studio cycling, tennis, basketball, yoga, etc. Nice indoor track. Good outdoor tennis courts. Both Ys are open to men and women. You should consider joining, but you don't have to be a member to use their facilities.

A guest pass is $15.

Hours: weekdays, 5 am - 10 pm; Saturday, 6:30 am - 7 pm; Sunday, 8 am - 5 pm.

YWCA

259 East Putnam Avenue, 869.6501

www.ywcagreenwich.com

Gymnasium, climbing wall, badminton, tennis, racquet ball, weight room, classes, etc. Very good indoor pool and swimming programs.

Hours: weekdays, 6:30 am - 10 pm; Saturday, 7 am - 5 pm; Closed on Sunday.

FITNESS & SPORTS

FOOTBALL

Cos Cob Athletic Club
Contact: Toni Natale, 869.0281
A community organization sponsoring midget football teams for ages 8 - 13.

Gateway Youth Football League of Greenwich
Contact Bill Dunster 625.0842 or Bob Patton 655-3680
Town-wide instructional/competitive tackle football league for children ages 8 -13. Registration takes place in August. The season runs from September to November. Practices are held 2 - 3 times a week. Games are on Sunday.

Uniforms and Equipment
See SHOPPING

YMCA Programs
50 East Putnam Avenue, 869.1630

FITNESS & SPORTS

GOLF

Public Golf Courses

There are a number of nearby courses open to non-residents. Some of these have limited times for non-residents; the greens fees listed are for weekday/weekend. However, many facilities have discounts for seniors, juniors, early morning or late afternoon play, or for 9-hole rounds. If you like the course, check out their policy on season passes. In any event, be sure to book before you go.

www.ctgolfer.com

www.co.westchester.ny.us/parks

Brennan

451 Stillwater Road, Stamford, CT, 324.4185

Par 71, fee $33/$38. You can reserve seven days in advance.

Griffith Harris Memorial Golf Course

1300 King Street, 531.7200, 6944, 7261.

www.golfweb.com/gwid/15825.html

Open only to town residents (including tenants). This par 71, 18-hole golf course designed by Robert Trent Jones has a club house, pro shop, putting green and driving range. Call for details about obtaining a membership card. You will need to bring proof of Greenwich residency (such as a current phone bill) and a photo ID (such as a driver's license). Greens fees for adult members are $15/$16 for 18 holes. Membership is $75 for an adult permanent resident or $135 for a summer resident. Bring a guest.

Maple Moor

1128 North Street, White Plains, NY, 914.995.9200

automated reservations: 914.995.4653

Par 71, fee $39/$44. You can reserve seven days in advance.

Oak Hills

165 Fillow Street, Norwalk, CT, 203.838.1015

Par 71, fee weekdays: $35 / after 4 pm $23, weekends and holidays:$40. You can reserve seven days ahead for weekdays only.

GOLF

Pound Ridge Golf Course

Route 137, Pound Ridge, NY, 914.764.5771

9 holes, Par 35, Fee $25/$40. On weekends, non-members can play after 1 pm. A cart must be rented on the weekends. Cart rental is about $25.

Richter Park Golf Course

100 Aunt Hack Road, Danbury, CT
203.792.2552, 748.5743, 792.2550, ext. 11.
www.RichterPark.com
Considered to be the number 1 public course in Connecticut. 18-holes, weekday starting times can be reserved 3 days in advance, slots start at 9 am. Greens fees, $48 before 4 pm, $30 after.

Ridgefield

545 Ridgebury Road, Ridgefield, CT, 203.748.7008
Par 70, Fee $40 weekdays, $45 weekends. You can reserve up to two days ahead for weekends.

Saxon Woods

Old Mamaroneck Road, Scarsdale, NY, 914.231.3461
Automated reservations: 203.995.4653
Par 71, fee $39/$44. You can reserve up to seven days ahead.

Sterling Farms

1349 Newfield Avenue, Stamford, CT, 461.9090
Automated reservations: 203.995.4653
Par 72, Fee $30/$45. On weekends, non-residents can play after 2:30 pm. You can reserve up to seven days in advance.

Vails Grove

Peach Lake, North Salem, NY, 845.669.5721
Par 66 (9-hole, double-tee). Fee $20/$20.
On weekends, non-members can play after 1 pm.

FITNESS & SPORTS

GOLF PRACTICE

If you need a little practice before playing, use the golf range at Griffith Harris Memorial Golf Course or one of these:

Golf Training Center in Norwalk

145 Main Street, Norwalk, CT, 203.847.8008
www.golftraining.com
They provide indoor practice for your pitching and putting techniques, including driving bays with computer replay, virtual reality golf and exercise areas.
Hours: Monday - Thursday, 8 am - 10 pm; Friday, 8 am - 8 pm;
Saturday, 8 am - 6 pm; Sunday, 8 am - 6 pm.
Directions: I-95 N to exit 15, Rte 7 N to exit 2, L at bottom of ramp, R on Main.

Nike Golf Schools and Junior Camps

800.645.3226
www.us-sportscamps.com
Nike sponsors a great number of adult and junior golf camps. The closest are Williams College, Williamstown, MA; Stowe, VT; and Loomis Chaffee, Windsor, CT.

Westchester Golf Range

701 Dobbs Ferry Road, White Plains, NY, 914.592.6553.
You can practice here until late.
Hours: Open every day, 8:30 am - 9 pm.
Directions: I-287 W to exit 3, Sprain Brook Pkw S to Rte 100B.

FITNESS & SPORTS

HOCKEY

Department of Parks and Recreation Ice Hockey Programs

At Dorothy Hamill Skating Rink, 622.7830

Prep League for boys and girls ages 13 and 14. Junior Hockey League ages 15 to 17. Sunday evening games, weekly practices. High school varsity participants are not allowed.

Department of Parks and Recreation Field Hockey Programs

Pemberwick Park, Moshier Street & Pemberwick Road

Contact: Claudia Collins, Recreation Supervisor, 622.7830

Co-ed field hockey clinics for grades 2-8 on Saturday mornings from late September through October.

Dorothy Hamill Skating Rink

Sherman Avenue, 531.8560, September - March; 622.7830, off-season.

An excellent municipal skating facility for Greenwich residents and their guests. You will need proof of residency such as a beach card. The Rink offers a full schedule of ice hockey programs for children, teens and adults.

Hours: September - March, weekends, 2 pm - 4 pm. Daily schedules are available.

Directions: US 1 W, L on Western Junior Highway, R on Henry, R on Sherman Avenue.

Greenwich Blues Youth Ice Hockey Association

PO Box 1107, Greenwich, CT 06836

Contact: Joe Rogers, 698.0542

Non-profit organization sponsoring competitive travel teams for boys and girls: Mites, under age 9; Squirts, 9-11; Peewees, 11-13; Bantam, 13-15. Dorothy Hamill Rink is their home rink. Season is from September through March, tryouts are in early September.

FITNESS & SPORTS

HOCKEY

Old Greenwich-Riverside Community Center In-Line Roller Hockey
90 Harding Road, Old Greenwich, 637.3659
Adult pick-up roller hockey as well as spring and summer instruction and games for boys and girls ages 6 - 14. Call for times and details.

Stamford Twin Rinks
1063 Hope Street, Stamford 968.9000
www.icecenter.com
They have a wide variety of programs for all level and interests.

Uniforms and Equipment
See SHOPPING.

Windy Hill Skating Club
Linda Myder, Membership Chair, 531.7774
Non-profit skating club affiliated with the US Figure Skating Association. Membership is open to all figure skaters who have progressed beyond "Basic 6". Home ice is the Dorothy Hamill Rink.

YMCA Programs
50 East Putnam Avenue, 869.1630
In-line skating and hockey instruction for children and adults. Roller hockey for children ages 6 - 14.

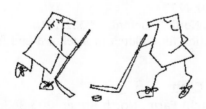

FITNESS & SPORTS

HORSEBACK RIDING

Picture fall leaves, stone walls and a rider on a handsome horse on a scenic woodland trail. Yes, this is Greenwich. Where we have over 150 miles of riding trails which connect to the 100 miles of trails in Stamford. For insurance reason, most stables will not rent horses for unaccompanied trail rides unless you have been taking a series of lessons and they know how you ride.

Arcadia Farm

69 Stone Hill Road, Bedford, (North Salem) NY, 914.234.6706
Set on 100 acres with indoor and outdoor riding areas, they give lessons from beginner to advanced.
Directions: North St. to the end, R onto Rte 22. Go thru Bedford Village, the road will bear L. R onto Rte 121. Go 2 miles, R onto Rte 137. The farm is 1/4 mile on the R. Sign says Coker Farm.

Back Barn Farm

203 Greenwich Road, Bedford, NY 914.234.6692
Boarding, lessons both indoor and outdoor.

Country Lane Farm

39 John Street, 629.4723
175 Ingleside Drive, North Stamford, CT 322.1115
Professional instruction for children in a relaxed and friendly atmosphere.

Greenwich Polo Club

Conyers (White Birch) Farm, North Street, 203.863.1213
People interested in playing polo should call the club for information about membership and events.

FITNESS & SPORTS

HORSEBACK RIDING

Greenwich Pony Club

Contact: Nancy Fertig, 661.6878

Greenwich chapter of a national non-profit organization which promotes horse management and equestrian skills for young people, ages 8-21. You provide the pony or horse.

Greenwich Riding and Trails Association

PO Box 1403, Greenwich 06836, 661.3062

Greenwich has an extensive trail network which you can take advantage of if you own your own horse. This nearly 100 year-old organization maintains 150 miles of horse trails in town and devotes its resources to conservation and open space. For information and help, call them. A great organization to join.

Kelsey Farm

1016 Lake Avenue, Greenwich, CT 06831, 869.5595

Run by Easy Kelsey, the stable is very active in the Greenwich Riding and Trails association. There is an indoor ring.

Lionshare Farm

404 Taconic Road, 869.4649, 552.0677

www.lionsharefarm.com

An excellent riding academy with programs for children and adults. The farm, owned by Peter Leone, an Olympic silver medalist, has two indoor rings and an outdoor ring, as well as access to the Greenwich trails. It is the premier show jumping stable in the Greenwich area. This is the first place to go if you want to buy a jumper.

On The Go Farms

1145 King Street, 532.4727

A friendly stable, focused on safety, with horses that are well-cared-for. Participants like the comradery.

FITNESS & SPORTS

HORSEBACK RIDING

Ox Ridge Hunt Club

512 Middlesex Road, Darien, CT, 203.655.2559

www.oxridge.com

There are many places to learn to ride, but serious riders will like Ox Ridge. This private hunt club offers riding lessons to the public. They have good horses, indoor and outdoor facilities and top instructors. Directions: Merritt Pwy exit 37, R onto Rte 124S. Stay on for 1.5 miles. At rotary, R onto Middlesex. At stop sign, L. Entrance on L.

Pegasus Therapeutic Riding Inc

Based at Kelsey Farm, call Florence Asch 869.5150 or 356.9504

www.pegasustr.org

Non profit organization provides riding as therapy for disabled children and adults

Stratford Stables

120 Cottage Avenue, Purchase NY, 914.686-3691, 939-9294

Lessons for beginners through advanced, with a specialty in training for show.

Windswept Farms

107 June Road, Stamford, CT, 322.4984

Windswept, a stable with a warm family atmosphere, is owned by Bill and Mona Raymond, who have been in the horse business for over thirty years. Bill used to ride in Rodeos and Mona is an expert in English riding and jumping. Both Western and English saddles are available. They give outdoor riding lessons for boys and girls 6-17. No previous riding experience is required. Located at the Greenwich/Stamford border, the stable has access to the Greenwich trail system. Their June through August pony summer camp is extremely popular. Sign up early. Campers have fun riding, learning horse etiquette and how to tack and clean their horses. The day often finishes with a dip in the swimming hole.

Directions: Merritt Pkw exit 33, go straight. R at intersection. R at next intersection. Go over parkway bridge, turn L onto Riverbank. Second L onto June Rd. Go over bridge. Farm is on the R.

FITNESS & SPORTS

ICE SKATING

Binney Pond
Sound Beach Avenue, Old Greenwich
This is the prettiest pond for skating and it is town-tested for safety.

Dorothy Hamill Skating Rink
531.8560 - Mid-Sept through Mid-March
622.7830 during the off season
www.greenwichct.org
We expect more Dorothy Hamill's to graduate from this rink!
Ask about figure skating lessons and hockey clubs.

Mianus River
Park off of Valley Road, bring your skates and hockey sticks (a shovel, too!)

Skating Club
Cardinal Road, 622.9583
The Skating Club, set inconspicuously off Fairfield Road, has an outdoor rink and offers a strong skating program for children. Because of its small membership, it is one of the more difficult clubs to join.

Stamford Twin Rinks
1063 Hope Street, Stamford 968.9000
www.icecenter.com
They have a wide variety of programs for all level and interests.

Windy Hill Skating Club
Linda Myder, Membership Chair, 531.7774
Non-profit skating club affiliated with the US Figure Skating Association. Membership is open to all figure skaters who have progressed beyond "Basic 6". Home ice is the Dorothy Hamill Rink.

FITNESS & SPORTS

KARATE

Old Greenwich School of Karate
242 Sound Beach Avenue, 698.1057, 637.2685
Ages 4 and up.

Dynamic Martial Arts
202 Field Point Road, 629.4666

LACROSSE

NOTE: Bridgeport Barrage major League Lacrosse is listed in CHILDREN, FAMILY OUTINGS.

Gilman Lacrosse Camps
877.536.2267, 203.834.7597
www.gilmanlacrosse.com
Summer camps in Westport for boys and girls, grades 1 - 11.

Greenwich Youth Lacrosse
www.gyl.idsite.com, www.eteamz.com
PO Box 4627, Greenwich, CT 06831-0412, 352.3933
Contact: Tim Connor, 352.3271 (boys), 352.3273 (girls)
A non-profit organization sponsoring lacrosse teams. House League for boys and girls in grades 1 - 6; Travel teams for boys and girls in grades 3 - 4 and 5 - 6. Boys travel teams for grades 7 - 8. Registration is usually in March.

Women's Summer Lacrosse League
Sponsored by the Greenwich Academy.
Contact: Angela Tammaro, 625.8959
Women's lacrosse league playing evenings from mid-June through July. Membership is open to any player who has completed grade 9.

Uniforms and Equipment
See SHOPPING.

FITNESS & SPORTS

PADDLE TENNIS

Loughlin Avenue Park
Loughlin Avenue, Cos Cob
This 6-acre park has the town's only paddle tennis courts. The courts are lighted and open year-round. A small playground adjoins the tennis and paddle tennis courts. Call the Department of Parks & Recreation (622.7830) for a card to use the courts and for information on using the lights.

POLO

Greenwich Polo
Conyers (White Birch) Farms, North Street, 203.454.9604
Greenwich has a world-class polo facility. Most summer Sundays you can watch a good polo match in a beautiful setting. Matches begin at 3 pm, the gates open at 1 pm. General admission is $20 per car.

RACING - AUTO

Lime Rock Park

Lakeville, CT, 800.Race.LRP   www.limerock.com

About two hours north of Greenwich is the Lime Rock Race Track. The track is closed on Sundays, but most Saturdays (from early April to November) there are formula and sports car races. Lime Rock has no grandstands, and therefore there is no formal ticket system. Call to find out about the race schedule or to get a copy of their free newspaper, Track Record. The biggest race days are usually Memorial Day and Labor Day.

Overland Experts

Hadlyme, CT (near Essex and Old Lyme), 877.931.3343
www.OverlandExperts.com

4WD on and off-road driving instruction as well as international expeditions.

Skip Barber Racing School

Lime Rock Park, Lakeville, CT, 860.435.1300, 800.221.1131
www.skipbarber.com

Skip Barber is the largest racing school in the country. If you have always wanted to learn to race, this is the place to learn. Two basic driving courses are offered, with a lot of variations for each course: Advanced Driving School—one and two-day courses driving three different cars supplied by the school; Racing School—three hours to eight days. The school supplies the formula cars.

FITNESS & SPORTS

ROCK CLIMBING

Go Vertical

727 Canal Street, Stamford, CT, 358.8767

www.govertical.com

8,000 square feet of safe, challenging, indoor climbing surfaces, with on-site equipment. Lessons for beginners aged 13 and over. All necessary equipment can be rented. Be sure to call in advance if you are a beginner.

Hours: weekdays, 10 am - 10 pm;

weekends, 10 am - 8 pm.

Directions: I-95 N to exit 8. R on Canal (2nd Light).

YWCA

259 East Putnam Avenue, 869.6501

The Y provides training workshops for beginning climbers.

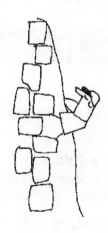

FITNESS & SPORTS

ROLLER SKATING

See FITNESS & SPORTS, HOCKEY.
For skate boards and in-line skates, try Chili Bears or Rink & Racquet.

Eastern Civic Center
90 Harding Road, Old Greenwich, 637.4583
The Greenwich Civic Center offers roller skating from October - April.
Call for details.

Stamford Skate Park
81 Camp Avenue, Stamford, CT, 322.2673
In-line skating, skate boarding, BMX biking, batting cages, arcade.
Hours: Tuesday - Thursday, 3 pm - 8 pm; Friday, 3 pm - 10 pm; Saturday, noon - 10 pm; Sunday, noon - 6 pm.
Directions: Merritt Pkw N to exit 36, R on Rte. 106, second light R on Camp.

Greenwich Skateboard Park
Skateboard enthusiasts will soon have their own skateboarding park thanks to the Junior League of Greenwich, who wanted a safe place for people to skate. This 7,754 square-foot skate park will be located at the Roger Sherman Baldwin Park.

RUNNING

Babcock Preserve
North Street, 622.7824
Two miles north of the Merritt Parkway, 297-acres of well-marked running trails.

Greenwich Point (Tod's Point)
Entrance at the south end of Shore Road in Old Greenwich.
This 147- acre beach has lots of jogging and biking trails.

Jim Fixx Memorial Day Race
Greenwich Recreation Office, 622.7830
This five-mile race, which starts and ends on Greenwich Avenue, begins the running season. If you run in no other event, you should consider it. It is always well-attended and attracts a great variety of talented and not-so-talented runners.

FITNESS & SPORTS

SOCCER

Connecticut Junior Soccer Association
New Britain, CT, 860.224.2572
www.cjsa.org
To check up on the latest programs call or visit their web site.

Greenwich Soccer Association
PO Box 1535, Greenwich, CT 06830, 352.5864
They field girls' and boys' travel soccer teams for ages 9 to 14. They play travel teams from other Fairfield County towns on Sunday afternoons. Tryouts are required and usually begin in November for the spring season.

Greenwich Soccer Club
PO Box 332, Cos Cob, CT 06807, 661.2620, 863.1936
The Greenwich Soccer Club is a volunteer based, all-inclusive, recreational and instructional program with a firm commitment to safety, fun and fairness. The GSC is a town-wide recreational program open to every boy and girl, ages 6 - 14, who either resides in or attends school in town. In the fall, over 1,700 boys and girls participate on Saturdays (coached by some 350 parent volunteers) with mid-week clinics taught by professional instructors. There are separate leagues for the boys and girls. The GSC is a privately funded, non-profit community service organization founded in 1976. Ken Irvine is the President.

Indoor Soccer
Greenwich Parks and Recreation, 622.7830
Winter co-ed training for children K - 6th grade. Limited to twenty-five children, so apply early. Registration by mail only: Greenwich Parks & Recreation, Recreation Division, 101 Field Point Road, Greenwich, CT 06836-2540.

Old Greenwich-Riverside Soccer Association
637.6776
Part of the Old Greenwich-Riverside Community Center and the Connecticut Junior Soccer Association, the club provides a comprehensive soccer program for over 700 youngsters who just wish to play for fun, as well as for those who wish to compete.

FITNESS & SPORTS

SOCCER

Uniforms and Equipment
See SHOPPING

YMCA
50 East Putnam Avenue, 869.7252

www.gwymca.org

The Y provides spring training in the basics for youngsters ages 4 - 5 and 6 - 8. The emphasis is on sportsmanship and having fun.

SHOOTING

Cos Cob Revolver & Rifle Club
451 Steamboat Road, 622.9508

www.ccrr.com

For those looking for a safe way to practice target shooting, this Greenwich club (despite its Cos Cob name), just across from the train station, has terrific facilities and a very helpful membership (including the Greenwich Police, many of whom practice here). To join, call and listen to the recorded announcement. Usually, all you have to do is attend a meeting (the second Wednesday of each month at 8 pm). To transport a gun to and from the club you need a Connecticut handgun license, which they can help you obtain.

FITNESS & SPORTS

SKIING

Old Greenwich-Riverside Community Center
90 Harding Road, 637.3659
Day ski trips for members in grades 5-8.

St. Paul's Episcopal Church
200 Riverside Avenue, 637.2447
Skate and ski swap for growing children. Call for details and dates.

There are a great variety of ski areas in the Northeast. For fun on the slopes try some of the following areas:

LOCAL FAMILY SKI AREAS

Hunter
Hunter, NY, 518.263.4223   1.888.486.8376
www.huntermtn.com
Difficulty: Beginner, Intermediate, Advanced.
Size: 12 lifts, 53 trails, snowmaking, snowtubing.
Distance: 2.5 hrs, I-87 N exit 20, Rte 32 N, Rte 23A W.

Mohawk
Cornwall, CT, 860.672.6100, 800.895.5222
www.mohawkmtn.com
Difficulty: Beginner & Intermediate.
Size: 5 lifts, 24 trails, snowmaking, night skiing.
Distance: 1.5 hrs, I-95 N to Rte 8 N to exit 44.
At the second light, left onto Rte 4 W (about 20 minutes).

FITNESS & SPORTS

SKIING

Mount Southington
Southington, CT, 860.628.0954
For snow conditions call 860.628.7669
www.MountSouthington.com
Difficulty: Beginner & Intermediate.
Size: 7 lifts, 14 trails, snowmaking, night skiing.
Distance: 2 hrs, I-84 N exit 30.

Powder Ridge
Middlefield, CT, 877.754.7434, 860.349.3454
www.powderridgect.com
Difficulty: Beginner & Intermediate, snowtubing.
Size: 7 lifts (2 for tubing), 5 wide runs, 14 trails, night skiing.
Distance: 45 minutes, Merritt Pkw N exit 67.

Windham
Windham, NY, 518.734.4300, 800.754.9463
www.skiwindham.com
Difficulty: Beginner, Intermediate & Expert.
Size: 33 trails, 7 lifts, snowmaking.
Distance: 2.5 hrs, I-87 N exit 21, Rte 23 W.

Winding Trails Cross Country Ski Center
Farmington, CT, 860.677.8458
www.WindingTrails.com
Difficulty: Beginner, Intermediate.
Size: 20 Kilometers of trails.
Distance: 2.5 hrs, I-84 N exit 39, Rte 4 W.

FITNESS & SPORTS

SKIING

LARGE REGIONAL SKI AREAS
CATERING TO FAMILIES
These areas also have extensive summer family activities.
Check their web sites for details.

Killington
Killington, VT, 800.621.6867
www.killington.com

Mount Snow
Dover, VT, 802.464.2151, 800.245.7669
www.mountsnow.com

Stowe
Stowe, VT, 802.253.3000, 800.253.4754, 8562
www.Stowe.com

Stratton
South Londonderry, VT, 802.297.2200, 800.787.8866
www.stratton.com

FITNESS & SPORTS
SQUASH

Field Club
276 Lake Avenue, 869.1309
A private club which offers a weekly Junior Summer Squash Camp often open to the public. They have international singles and doubles courts.

Greenwich Academy Squash Training Camp
200 North Maple Avenue, 625.8900 x 7287
During the summer, the Academy uses their five international squash courts to provide training for children in grades 5 and above.

Sportsplex
49 Brownhouse Road, Stamford, CT, 358.0066
Right on the border of Old Greenwich and Stamford. The Sportsplex provides a complete training center, including four hardball squash courts, one racquetball court and squash instructions.

FITNESS & SPORTS

SWIMMING

For Greenwich Beaches see PARKS & RECREATION, BEACHES.

Department of Parks and Recreation
622.7830
They organize Family Swims at Greenwich High School.

Greenwich Youth Water Polo League (GYWP)
P.O. Box 38 Cos Cob, 352.3405 (recording)
Founded by the coaches of the Greenwich High School water polo team.
The GHS has one of the strongest programs on the Eastern seaboard.
This league is for boys and girls ages 9 to 15 who want to learn to play
water polo.

Nike Swim Camps
800.645.3226
www.us-sportscamps.com
Nike runs a number of swim camps around the country for boys and
girls ages 10 to 18. The Peddie School program (June and July) in
Hightstown, NJ is the closest.

Town Swim Team: The Dolphins
In addition to the high school swim team, the town has a superior
competition swim team, the Dolphins (YWCA - 869.6501). The Dolphins are for serious swimmers. Kids start early: swim practice is every day, with meets held on most Sundays. All that is required to join
is parental consent and the ability not to sink. Some children start as
early as four.

FITNESS & SPORTS

SWIMMING

YMCA Programs

50 East Putnam Avenue, 869.1630

Skippers - for parents and babies 6 months to 2 years.

Perch - for ages 2 - 3. Children, with help of parent, propel themselves using flotation aids.

Progressive youth lessons: Polliwog, Guppy, Minnow, Fish, Flying Fish, Shark, for ages 5-12.

Private swimming lessons are available.

Marlins Swim Team, ages 5-18, September to March.

YWCA Programs

259 East Putnam Avenue, 869.6501

Aqua Babies - for parents and babies 6 months to 3 years;

Aqua Tots/Kids - for ages 2½ to 4 years who are ready to participate without the parent. Both are ideal introductions to swimming and safety in and around the water. Junior Aquatics - K to 12 years. Progressive learn-to- swim lessons.

Dolphins Swim Team - K to high school - competitive technique instruction. Private swimming lessons are available.

TIP: SPORT TRAINING CLASSES

When you are looking for a good sports program, there are three places you should call or visit: The Department of Parks & Recreation at Town Hall (622.7830), the YWCA (869.6501) and the YMCA (869.1630). They all have a multitude of great programs. In this guide we have only been able to list a few.

FITNESS & SPORTS

TENNIS

Greenwich Racquet Club
1 River Road, Cos Cob, 661.0606
4 indoor Har-Tru courts. They have good instruction and adult clinics.

Greenwich Tennis Headquarters
54 Bible Street, Cos Cob, 661.0182
There are 38 all-weather courts available throughout Greenwich, as well as a paddle tennis court location. The town runs junior and adult clinics for all levels and provides private lessons. It also sponsors a junior and adult town tennis tournament which attracts some very good players. Call for information, a map of the courts and a tennis permit.

Grand Slam
1 Bedford-Banksville Road, Bedford, NY, 914.234.9206
Five Har-Tru courts, five hard surface (Deco Turf II) courts. During the winter, eight are indoor, during the summer, five are outside. Excellent junior and adult programs including USTA League Play.

Nike Adult and Junior Tennis Camps
800.645.3226   www.us-sportscamps.com
Nike sponsors a great number of adult and junior tennis camps. The closest are: Amherst College, Amherst, MA;
Loomis-Chaffee, Windsor, CT; Peddie School, Hightstown, NJ;
Lawrenceville School, Lawrenceville, NJ.

Old Greenwich Tennis Academy
151 Sound Beach Avenue, 637.3398
5 indoor Har-Tru courts. Mainly used by groups who contract for court time. Open September to May.

Personal Pro Services
May - October, Greenwich, 962.2673;
November - April, Scottsdale, Arizona, 480.575.9702.
email: personalpro@earthlink.net
Tim Richardson is a USPTA Pro 1 tennis instructor. During the playing season, Tim will help you perfect your tennis game in the privacy of your own court and on your own schedule. Tim has been teaching on private Greenwich courts for almost 20 years.

FITNESS & SPORTS

TENNIS

Sound Shore Tennis
303 Post Road, Port Chester, NY, 914.939.1300
Twelve indoor hard surface courts. Open September to May and rain-only weekends after May.

Wire Mill Racquet Club
578 Wire Mill Road, Stamford, CT, 329.9221
Just off exit 35 of the Merritt Parkway, Wire Mill (four outdoor red clay courts) is owned by the pros who teach in the winter at the Greenwich Racquet Club. Inexpensive to join.

YMCA Programs
50 East Putnam Avenue, 869.1630
The Y provides a number of tennis clinics as well as private lessons for women, men and children, from beginner to advanced.

YWCA Programs
259 East Putnam Avenue, 869.6501
Beginner and intermediate lessons for adults and children as young as six.

FITNESS & SPORTS

VOLLEYBALL

Department of Parks and Recreation Volleyball Programs

Contact: Frank Gabriele, 622.7830

The town sponsors adult co-ed volleyball games at the Western Greenwich Civic Center in Glenville. They also sponsor the Greenwich Volleyball League, an adult, winter co-ed volleyball league for A and B flight teams. They play at Glenville Elementary School on Tuesday & Thursday nights. Greenwich residents 16 years and older may participate.

Nike Volleyball Camps

800.645.322

www.us-sportscamps.com

Nike sponsors a number of volleyball camps around the country for ages 13 to 18. The closest camp is at Cornell University, Ithaca, NY.

Uniforms and Equipment

See FITNESS & SPORTS, TEAM SPORTS EQUIPMENT.

YMCA Volleyball Programs

50 East Putnam Avenue, 869.1630

The Y sponsors informal, co-ed volleyball games for adults.

FITNESS & SPORTS

WALKING

Audubon Guidebook to Walking Trails

A 63-page guide to 26 area walking trails is available from the Greenwich Audubon Society, PO Box 7487, Greenwich, CT 06831.

Audubon Center

613 Riversville Road, 869.5272

www.audubon.org

280 acres of well-kept trails, a delightful place to walk. The entrance is on the corner of Riversville Road and John Street.

Babcock Preserve

North Street, Greenwich

297 acres stretching between North Street and Lake Avenue. The entrance is on North Street about 2 miles north of the Merritt Parkway. An extensive network of trails which range in length from 1 to 3.5 miles.

Greenwich Point

Shore Road, Old Greenwich

147 acres at the end of Sound Beach Avenue. Greenwich Point is a popular spot for water sports, as well as walking, bicycle riding, roller blading and running. A network of trails leads along the changing coastline and through the woods. A trail guide is available at the Seaside Center of the Bruce Museum. During the summer a beach pass is required.

Mianus River Park

Cognewaugh Road, Cos Cob

220 acres stretching from Greenwich into Stamford. The entrance is ½ mile east of Stanwich Road on Cognewaugh Road. The two trails of most interest are the Pond Trail and the Oak Trail.

Montgomery Pinetum

Bible Street, Cos Cob

91 acres, just off of Bible Street in Cos Cob. The entrance is on the west side directly opposite Clover Place. Obtain a map and tree guide from the Garden Center office, then enjoy the extraordinary diversity of trees and plantings. One path leads to the 22-acre Greenwich Audubon Society's Mildred Bedard Caldwell Wildlife Sanctuary.

Greenwich Continuing Education
At Greenwich High School, 625.7474, 625.0141
Beginning and advanced yoga courses as well as t'ai chi ch'uan classes.

Greenwich Health at Greenwich Hospital
25 Valley Drive 863.4277, 1.888.305.9253
They offer a number of wellness programs including yoga and t'ai chi ch'uan classes.
Hours: weekdays, 9 am - 5 pm.

Old Greenwich-Riverside Community Center
90 Harding Road, Old Greenwich, 637.3659
They offer a beginning yoga program.

Pilates Method
www.pilates-studio.com
If you hear your friends talking about "Powerhouses" and "alignment", they may be enrolled in a Pilates program. Classes are taught at the Sportsplex and YWCA among others.

YMCA
50 East Putnam Avenue, 869.1630
www.gwymca.org
The Y offers a beginning course in yoga techniques to reduce stress.

YWCA
259 East Putnam Avenue, 869.6501
wwww.ywcagreenwich.com
The Y offers yoga programs for all levels.

FLOWERS & GARDENS

The Greenwich Department of Parks has a green thumb and together with the talents of garden club volunteers (who you will see gardening on many of the town's intersections) make Greenwich so beautiful.

Gateway Greenery

Jeffery Doty, Greenwich, CT 531.4505

Jeff is an expert on plants and gardens. He worked for over 12 years at a local garden center before branching out on his own. He is just the person you need when your indoor plants need rejuvenating. He will watch your home and care for your plants while you are away. Ask him about his line of beautiful orchids and if you are too busy to decorate for the holidays, call Jeff. He will not only put your tree up, he will take it down afterwards.

Garden Education Center

Montgomery Pinetum, Bible Street, Cos Cob, 869.9242
www.gecgreenwich.org

The Center's horticulture buildings provide classrooms and workrooms for a variety of programs and lectures. Founded in 1957, the center is not only a strong educational facility, but also provides a good framework for new residents to make friends.

Hours: Closed during the summer. Open September 1 to Memorial Day; weekdays, 9 am - 3:30 pm; in October and December, also Saturday, 10 am - 3 pm.

New York Botanical Gardens

Bronx, NY, 718.817.8705   www.nybg.org

Greenwich garden enthusiasts know their way to the NY Botanical Gardens. The gardens have recently undergone a $25 million renovation and are considered the best in the country.

Hours: Tuesday - Sunday, 10 am - 6 pm. Wednesdays are free.

Directions: (30 minutes) Merritt/Hutchinson Pkw S to exit 15; Cross County Pkw W to exit 6; Bronx River Pkw S to exit 8W (Mosholu Pkw); at second light, L into Garden.

Loretta Stagen Floral Designs

81 Commerce Street, Stamford, CT 323.3544
www.lorettastagen.com

Innovative flower arrangements and party decorations for corporate events and weddings. She also offers classes and workshops in flower arranging. For five or more students, she will create a special class in their area of interest. Her web site has links to wedding sites.

FLOWERS & GARDENS

GARDEN CLUBS

Byram Garden Club
Byram Shubert Library
21 Mead Avenue, Byram
Jane Eillis, President 532-1418

Friends of Binney Park
Nancy Standard - 637.9894

Garden Club of Old Greenwich
PO Box 448, Old Greenwich 06870
Pat Jackson, President, 637.4292
Membership by invitation.

Green Fingers Garden Club
PO Box 4655, Greenwich 06830
Frankie Hollister, President - 622.8567
Membership by invitation.

Greenwich Daffodil Society
38 Perkins Road
Nancy B. Mott, President - 661.6142

Greenwich Garden Club
PO Box 4896, Greenwich 06831
Leslie Lee, President
Membership by invitation.

Greenwich Green & Clean
Yantoro Community Center, 113 Pemberwick Road, 531.0006
Mary G. Hull, Executive Director

Greenwich Woman's Club Gardeners
89 Maple Avenue, 869.2046
Valerie Anderson, President - 869.8965

FLOWERS & GARDENS

GARDEN CLUBS

Hortulus
PO Box 4666, Greenwich, CT 06830
Wendy Serrell, President 661.2498
Membership by invitation.

Knollwood Garden Club
PO Box 1666, 06836
Frieve Costigan 869.5292
Membership by invitation.

Riverside Garden Club
PO Box 11, Riverside 06878-0011
TLinda Lund, President, 698.1936
Membership by invitation.

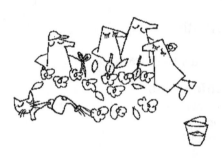

TIP: TOUR GREENWICH GARDENS
Each year in June, the Garden Education Center organizes a
tour of some of Greenwich's most special, private gardens.
Call 869-9242 for details.

GAMBLING

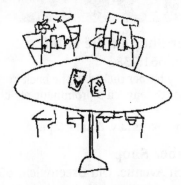

Gambling has come to Connecticut and our two casinos are closer and more attractive than those in Atlantic City, NJ. The casinos are very close to each other. For bus transportation call Dattco, 888.770.0140. For more information on the area see HOTELS & INNS, WORTH A VISIT.

Foxwoods Resort Casino

800.369.9663

www.foxwoods.com

Just seven miles from Mystic, CT, this resort is owned by the Mashantucket Pequot Tribal Nations. It is the largest hotel complex in the Northeast. The 312-room Grand Pequot Tower is very comfortable, and—in addition to an array of restaurants, entertainment and, of course, gaming tables—there is a golf club.

Directions: I-95 N to exit 92, West on Rte 2. About 2.5 hours from Greenwich.

Mohegan Sun

860.204.8000

www.MoheganSun.com

www.sunint.com

Somewhat smaller than Foxwoods, this casino still has over 192 gaming tables and 3,000 slot machines. The casino is owned by the Mohegan Nation and Sun International. The Mohegan Sun complex reflects the culture and history of the Mohegan Nation. Many people prefer its Native American theme decoration.

Directions: 95 N to exit 76, 395 N to exit 79 A, Rte. 2A less than 2 miles to Mohegan Sun Boulevard. About 2 hours from Greenwich.

GROOMING

BARBERS

Benford Barber Shop at the Palm
20 Church Street, 661.7383
This out-of-the-way barber tucked in the back of the Palm Barber Shop is used by many of Greenwich's prominent residents. Haircuts are by appointment.
Hours: Wednesday - Saturday, 8 am - 5 pm.

Off-Center Barber Shop
259 Sound Beach Avenue, Old Greenwich, 637.1313
An Old Greenwich institution. Kids love haircuts in the Jeep.
Hours: Monday -Wednesday, 8 am - 6 pm; Thursday, 8 am - 7:30 pm; Friday 8 am - 5 pm; Saturday, 8 am - 5 pm (summer until 2 pm); appointments on Sunday by request.

Subway Barber Shop
315 Greenwich Avenue, 869.3263
They cater to children.
Hours: Monday - Saturday (closed Wednesday), 8 am - 5 pm.

DAY SPAS

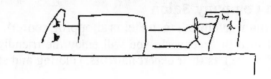

(The) Greenhouse Spa

44-48 West Putnam Avenue, 622.0300
Full-service menu for men and women includes facials, massages, body treatments, hair removal and make-up.
Hours: Monday - Wednesday, 9 am - 5 pm; Thursday, 9 am - 7 pm; Friday & Saturday, 8 am - 5 pm.

Harmony

270 Mason Street, 861.7338.
Considered a "real find", this tiny day spa is just the place for an excellent facial, eyelash tints, waxing, microderm abrasion or a relaxing Reiki facial treatment.
Hours: Monday - Saturday, 9 am - 5 pm.

Noelle Spa for Beauty and Wellness

1100 High Ridge Road, Stamford, Ct, 322.3445
Complete day spa with a great variety of services from hair care to facials, massages and nails.
Hours: Monday, 8:15 am - 5:30 pm; Tuesday & Thursday, 8:15 am - 8 pm; Wednesday, 8:15 am - 5:30 pm; Friday, 8:15 am - 6 pm; Saturday, 8:15 am - 5 pm; Sunday, 9:30 am - 6 pm.
Directions: Merritt Parkway to exit 35 (High Ridge Road). Take a right off of the exit. Noelle is immediately on the right.

Serenity Health & Wellness Center

116 East Putnam Avenue, 629.9000
Veronica, formerly of the Greenhouse, opened this comfortable day spa offering skin care, body treatments, Ayurvedic treatments, message and waxing. If you wish to restore your spirit, let them pamper you.
Hours: Monday, Wednesday & Friday, 9 am - 6 pm; Tuesday, 9 am - 7 pm; Thursday, 9 am - 8 pm; Saturday, 9 am - 5 pm.

GROOMING

HAIR SALONS

Carlo and Company Salon
70 East Putnam Avenue (Fresh Fields shopping center), 869.2300
Long established in Greenwich, you will enjoy the friendly, attentive atmosphere as well as their expert haircuts, coloring and styling.

Enzo Ricco Bene Salon
1800 E. Putnam Avenue(at the Hyatt), Old Greenwich, 698.4141
This attractive salon located off the lobby of the Hyatt Regency Hotel offers a pleasant and talented staff of colorists and stylists. For easiest access use the free valet parking.
Hours: Monday & Saturday, 8 am - 5 pm ; Tuesday, 8 am - 7 pm; Wednesday & Friday, 8 am - 6 pm; Thursday, 8 am - 8 pm.

Hopscotch
144 Mason Street, 661.0107
A cutting edge high-tech salon catering to a fashionable clientele. People come from New York City to go here.
Hours: Monday - Saturday, 8:30 am - 5 pm (Saturday to 4:30).

Lane's Hair Stylists
18 Greenwich Avenue, 622.9566
Old-fashioned beauty shop, serving men, women and children. Good place for a haircut. No appointments.
Hours: Monday - Thursday, 9 am - 5 pm;
Friday and Saturday, 9 am - 8 pm

Visible Changes
204 Sound Beach Avenue, Old Greenwich, 637.9154
If you've seen a great haircut—it's likely to have been cut here.
Hours: Tuesday - Saturday, 9 am - 6 pm.
(Tuesday & Thursday, until 8 pm).

GROOMING

NAIL SALONS

Nails by Empy
138 Hamilton Avenue, 661-6625
By appointment.
Hours: weekdays, 9 am - 6 pm; Saturday 9 am - 4 pm.

Nails R Us
1 Havemeyer Lane, Old Greenwich, 698.3320
By appointment or walk-in.
Hours: Monday - Saturday, 9:30 am - 7 pm; Sunday, 10 am - 5:30 pm.

Tiffany Nails
349 Greenwich Avenue, 661.3838
Walk-ins only.
Hours: Monday - Saturday, 9:30 am - 7 pm; Sunday 10 am - 5:30 pm.

HEALTH

MEDICAL CARE

IN AN EMERGENCY, DIAL 911

Access Ambulance

1111 East Putnam Avenue Riverside , 637.2351 for dispatch

Private, for-profit, non-emergency ambulance service operated by GEMS. It provides transportation between patients' homes and medical facilities such as hospitals, nursing homes, and cancer centers.

Burke Rehabilitation Hospital

785 Mamaroneck Avenue, White Plains, NY 914.597.2500

www.burke.org

A nearby 60-acre private, not-for-profit, facility specializing in inpatient and outpatient multi-disciplinary physical rehabilitation and research. They have a national reputation for their tailored programs to lessen disability and dependence resulting from disease or injury.

Connecticut Magazine Survey of Top Doctors and Hospitals in Connecticut

www.ConnecticutMag.com

Convenient Medical Care

1200 East Putnam Avenue, Old Greenwich, 698.1419

Walk-in clinic. Quick and efficient for minor injuries and ailments.

Copeland Optometrists

203 South Ridge Street, Rye Brook, NY, 914.939.0830

For years, they were just over the border in Port Chester, but recently they moved another 5 minutes away to Rye Brook. Nevertheless we followed them because of their reliable, caring service. Owned and operated by the Copeland Family, you can count on a good eye examination, the correct prescription and a set of fashionable glasses or contact lens at a reasonable price.

Hours: weekdays, 9 am - 6 pm (Wednesday until 1 pm, Thursday until 9 pm); Saturday, 9 am - 5 pm.

Directions: Rte 1 S through Main St, R on Westchester, L on Bowman, L on South Ridge.

HEALTH

MEDICAL CARE

Greenwich Emergency Medical Service (GEMS)

637.7505 (general information)

GEMS has six ambulances, 11 paramedics and 12 full time EMTs. GEMS also provides programs in CPR and basic first-aid. GEMS ambulances have the latest equipment and well trained Emergency Medical Technicians and paramedics. Once you call 911, their computer-aided dispatch system allows them to reach 75% of patients within 5-minutes and 95% with 8-minutes. Greenwich is lucky to have such a coordinated ambulance organization. GEMS also operates a for-profit non-emergency ambulance service called Access Ambulance, listed separately.

Greenwich Hospital

5 Perryridge Road, 863.3000

www.greenhosp.org

Greenwich Hospital is a 160-bed, nonprofit, community teaching hospital, affiliated with Yale-New Haven Hospital. The Hospital has a new, 350,000-square-foot facility that is the model for advanced health care. The rooms in this new area are carefully designed to make the patient feel comfortable. As a result, many feel it's more like staying at a fine hotel than a hospital. Even the intensive care unit has woodland views and amazing amenities. Word is spreading fast that this is the most comfortable place to have your baby.

Greenwich Hospital has a wonderful **emergency room: 863.3637**.

The hospital has a Consumer Health Reference Center, call 863.3285 weekdays 8:30 am - 4:45 pm for information.

Greenwich Physical Therapy Center

1171 East Putnam Avenue, Riverside, 637.1700

An independent (non-physician owned) physical therapy center specializing in orthopedic and sports related injuries. The director has worked extensively with the NY Rangers hockey team. Everyone raves about them and for good reason.

Hours: Monday, Wednesday, Friday, 7 am - 4 pm, Tuesday & Thursday 9 am - 7 pm.

HEALTH

MEDICAL CARE

HealthGain.Org

65 High Ridge Road, Stamford, 637.3417

www.HealthGain.org

The Director, Peter Flierl, was the former director of Greenwich Health at Greenwich Hospital. Health Gain is an independent resource center providing heath care professionals in the Western and Eastern traditions.

Hospital for Special Surgery

535 East 70th Street, NYC, www.hss.edu

143 Sound Beach Avenue, Old Greenwich, 698.8887

Top ranked hospital for bone, joint or muscle problems. Greenwich office provides diagnostic services as well as pre- and post-operative tests.

Peak Wellness

50 Holly Hill Lane, 625.9608

Company offers a wide range of health services on a one-to-one basis. The most common problem they deal with is obesity. They help many overcome their lack of interest in diet and exercise.

Physician Referral Service

863.3627 or 888.357.2409

Sponsored by Greenwich Hospital, this service is available weekdays between 8:30 am and 4:30 pm. They will find the doctor with the qualifications you are looking for and will even make your first appointment.

Silver Hill Hospital

208 Valley Road, New Canaan, CT 800.899.4455

www.SilverHillHospital.com

A private, not for profit, full service psychiatric and substance abuse hospital, providing inpatient, outpatient, partial hospital programs and transitional care. Anonymity is important. Many celebrities have quietly restored their health here.

HEALTH

MEDICAL CARE

Westchester Medical Center
Valhalla, NY 914.493.7000
www.wcmc.com
Connected with the New York Medical College, their Trauma Center and Children's Hospital are renowned.

Yale-New Haven Hospital
20 York St, New Haven, 203.688.2000
This private, not for profit hospital, is the teaching hospital for Yale University School of Medicine. It is considered one of the premier hospitals in the area. Greenwich Hospital, is affiliated with this hospital.

MEDICAL CLAIMS

National Medical Claims Service
363.0140
They have moved to Stamford, but are still a Greenwich family business. They are one of the few companies in the country that will take on the whole process of filing and collecting medical claims for you.

TIP: MEDICARE ASSISTANCE
If you are having problems with medical claims, the Greenwich Hospital Auxiliary offers free help on Wednesdays and Fridays from noon to 2:30 in room 1-124 in the new hospital. Call 863-3334.

HEALTH

VOLUNTEER OPPORTUNITIES

See also CLUBS/ORGANIZATIONS

American Red Cross
Greenwich Chapter
231 East Putnam Avenue, 869.8444
Rosemary Calderato, Director

Greenwich Hospital Auxiliary
Greenwich Hospital
5 Perryridge Road
863.3220 - auxiliary office
863.3334 - Medicare Assistance
Suzanne Rand, President
Contact: Marguerite Heithaus, Director of Volunteer Services - 863.3221

Volunteer Center
62 Palmer's Hill Road, Stamford, CT, 348-7714
A nonprofit organization which will help you find a good place to volunteer your talents.

HOME

DRY CLEANING

Berger Cleaners
282 Mason Street, 869.7650
A good choice for your curtains and draperies.
Hours: weekdays, 7 am - 6 pm; Saturday, 8 am - 3 pm.

Cleaner Option Dry Cleaners
1081 East Putnam Avenue, 637.1710
A perfect choice for your everyday dry cleaning and laundry. Excellent service at good prices. Free pick-up and delivery.
Hours: No real storefront hours, just leave a message on their answering machine.

Thomas Dry Cleaning and Chinese Hand Laundry
68 Lewis Street, 869.9420
A good choice for fine linens and table cloths.
Hours: weekdays, 7:30 am - 7 pm; Saturday, 7:30 - 6 pm.

Triple S Carpet and Drapery Cleaners
400 West Main Street (Post Road), Stamford, CT, 327.7471
They clean draperies and upholstery and will come to the house to clean rugs and upholstery. They do a great job of cleaning and/or repairing rugs.
Hours: weekdays, 8 am - 5:30 pm; Saturday, 8 am - 1:30 pm.

HOME

MOVING

Alexander Services
Call Shawn Alexander at 888.656.6838, 203.324.4012.
They are the mover of choice for many antique shops.

Callahan Brothers
133 Post Road, Cos Cob, 869.2239
They are the local agent for North American Van Lines and have been a fixture in Greenwich for many years. When you need to move across the country or across the world, give them a call.

Joe Mancuso Moving
Joe Mancuso, 914.937.2178
An excellent resource when you are making a local move.

Tilford Piano Movers
Days:203.426.8625, evenings after 7 pm: 203-743.6107
They specialize in local and long distance piano moving.

Young Man with Van
Contact: Oliver Wright, 203.866.3608, 203.760.0156
cell: 203.820.6668
Oliver is a good resource for moving small items.

SEE AUTOMOBILES / VEHICLE RENTALS

HOME

RECYCLING

Blue Bins

Recycling is now mandated by the state, but it is interesting to note that thanks to Mariette Badger and other volunteers, Greenwich recycling has been organized for over twenty-five years. Our recycling program saves the town money and protects the environment. Each week at a designated day and time, the town picks up recyclables and brings them to the Holly Hill Transfer Station. To get your blue bin(s) and recycling details, call 622.0550.

Hazardous Waste

Whenever you wish to dispose of items such as bug spray, engine oil, old paint cans or other items which are not part of the normal recycling program, call 869.6910, 622.7838 or 622.7740 for specific information.

Holly Hill Resource Recovery Facility (aka *The Dump*)
Holly Hill Lane, 622.0550

Greenwich has one of the world's best dumps. You have to see it to believe it. On any given day, you may see BMWs and Mercedes dropping off items. The "in" decal for your car is a dump permit.

Permit applications are available at the Holly Hill entry gate. To get one of these valuable permits, you must show proof of residency, as well as valid vehicle registration and insurance.

Leaf Collection

Town leaf collection is limited to areas zoned one-half acre or less. Most residents with one or more acres compost on their own property. For a schedule of leaf collection, call 622.7718, or watch for the schedule printed by the *Greenwich Time* in the fall.

Refuse Collectors

Garbage collection is done by independent contractors. New residents may call the Greenwich Independent Refuse Collectors Association at 622.0050 to find out which collector services their home.

HOME
SERVICES

Unwelcome Visitors: To rid yourself of furry or feathery visitors see ANIMALS, WILDLIFE & ANIMAL RESCUE.

Home Delivery: for home delivery of groceries, see Whole Foods and Stop & Shop Home Delivery under SHOPPING.

Berman Newspaper Delivery

323.5955

Depending upon where you live, Berman will deliver to your home between 5 and 6 am, where you want it, all of the major papers including: the *New York Times*, *Financial Times* and *USA Today*. The local papers come out too late for this delivery, so unless you want these papers a day late, you should contact them directly: *Greenwich Time*, 625.4400; *Greenwich Post*, 861.9191.

Dark House Service

622.8000

If residents notify the police that they will be away for an extended period of time, Greenwich police will patrol the area with an extra-cautious eye. You can also hire an off-duty police officer to personally check your home each day when you are away.

Deliver Ease of Greenwich

622.3040

For $5 for every 15 minutes of travel time, this reliable service will pamper your every need. They promptly deliver to or pick up from your door just about anything you can imagine: aspirin from your drugstore, poster board for a project, food from your favorite restaurant, forgotten dry cleaning, a late video, or just a cup of Dunkin' Donut's coffee. Why not send a balloon to cheer up someone at the hospital? Hours: every day, 8 am - 10 pm.

Gerhard Feldmann

208 East 70th St. NY,NY 10021

212.717.2907, Cell: 917.686.5946

http://www.bosendorfer-ny.com/

"Star Piano tuner" Specialist for Bösendorfer pianos, but does all makes. Expensive, good choice for professional pianists who tax their instruments through heavy practicing.

HOME
SERVICES

Greenwich Nursery
475 West Putnam Avenue, 622.0182
Call them for your firewood needs.
Hours: weekdays, 8 am - 4 pm.

Honey Doo Services
23 Benedict Place, 861.4202
www.HoneyDoo.com
Call them for emergencies or minor repair / maintenance jobs. They also plan or manage services for large estates.

Horse Ridge Cellars
Somers CT, 860.763.5380
www.HorseRidgeCellars.com
Where serious collectors store their wine. (About a 2 hour drive from Greenwich)

Jason, The Handyman, Inc.
625.0411
If you need a mirror hung, gutters installed or cleaned, walls painted, tile re-grouted, or an electrical outlet installed, call Jason Wahlberg. Reasonably priced and offers senior discounts. If he can't do it, he'll recommend someone who can.

Kennedy Security Services
58 East Elm Street, 661.6814
If you wish extra security while you are away from home, Kennedy Security has been serving Greenwich residents for over 40 years.

Labor Ready
115 N Main Street, Port Chester, 914.934.9167
www.LaborReady.com
English speaking, temporary labor 24-hours a day, 7-days a week at about $15 an hour (4-hour minimum). They pay taxes and handle the administrative headaches.

HOME
SERVICES

Locks and Keys
Charles Stuttig, 158 Greenwich Avenue, 869.6260
A fixture in Greenwich for many years, they provide a wide variety of locks and safes. Whether you have an emergency or just need a key replaced, they can be counted on and trusted.
Hours: weekdays, 7:30 am - 5:30 pm; Saturday, 8 am - 3 pm.

Longo's Rent-a-Tool, Inc
199 Hamilton Avenue, 629-9151
A do-it-yourself's paradise.
Hours: weekdays,

Piano Service
Ken Svec, 359.2231
Ken tunes pianos and is an excellent consultant if you wish or buy or sell a piano.

Protect-a-Child Pool Fencing
www.ProtectAChild.com
The nearest dealer is Art O'Neill, 800.778.8411. The main number is 800.992.2206

David D Tyrrell
44 Holley Street Ext, Danbury, CT 06810-6120, 203.744.3084
A piano tuner with very reasonable prices, good quality work.

TIP: CBYD
Never dig around your home without first calling "Call Before You Dig (CBYD)", 800.922.4455. This clearing house will arrange free-of-charge to locate and mark the underground utilities on your property.

HOME

UTILITIES

Greenwich Telephone System

Greenwich is on the border between Verizon (formerly Bell Atlantic, formerly Nynex) and SNET coverage areas. Old Greenwich exchanges (637 & 698) are covered by SNET. From there you can dial many Connecticut 203 numbers directly. The rest of Greenwich is controlled by Verizon. This means that many numbers outside of Greenwich require you to dial 1-203 first.

Most Stamford numbers do not require the 203 prefix, but information for Stamford requires you to dial 203.555.1212. Greenwich information can be accessed by dialing 411. We have tried to organize the numbers in this guide to make it clear when you have to dial 203 (if you are in the Verizon coverage area) or when you can simply dial the local number.

Verizon: Greenwich, Byram, Cos Cob & Riverside

869.5222 (new service)
661.5444 (repairs), 625.9800 (customer service)
www.bellatlantic.com, www22.verizon.com

SNET: Old Greenwich exchanges 637 & 698

From SNET coverage area, dial 811; from out-of-state, 800.453.SNET (new service); 420.3131 (repairs) or 611
www.snet.com

Aquarion (formerly Connecticut-American Water Company)

869.5200 (office)
661.7200 (emergency), 800.732.9678
869.5350 or 800.292.2928 (customer service), 800-732.9678

Connecticut Natural Gas

869.6900 (customer service)
869.6913 (repair & emergency)

Northeast Utilities/Connecticut Light & Power

800.286.2000 www.nu.com
Your local power company.
For customer service and emergencies, call 800.286.5000.

175

HOME

WHERE TO GET THINGS REPAIRED

For Lock and Key repairs see HOME, SERVICES.

American Typewriter
Route 202, New Milford, CT 860.354.6903
David Morrill repairs typewriters and sells refurbished ones. One of the last places around to do this work.
Hours: weekdays, 10 am - 4:30 pm

Appliance Servicenter of Stamford
15 Cedar Heights Road (off High Ridge Road), Stamford, CT 322.7656
If you can carry it, they can probably repair it. In addition they service stoves, refrigerators, washers and dryers in your home.
Hours: weekdays, 8:30 am - F:30 pm, Saturday, 8:30 am - 1:30 pm.
Directions: Merritt Parkway N to exit 35, R on High Ridge, in about a mile R on Cedar Heights.

Dean's China & Glass Restoration
324 Guineviere Ridge, Cheshire CT, 800.669.1327, 203.271.3659
Their name says it all. Send them a photo of your broken or chipped piece and they will give you an estimate.

Fine Arts Conservation Laboratory
190 Henry Street, Stamford, CT 323.3225
Efrem Capestany is owner and art conservator. His business is geared towards serious art collectors wishing to preserve paintings.

Greenwich Metal Finishing
67 Church Street, 629.8479
If you have an ailing silver piece or chandelier, you may want to visit these metal artisans. They polish, replate, refinish and even fabricate metal items. They will completely refinish and rewire your chandelier.
Hours: Closed Monday; Open Tuesday - Friday, 9 am - 4:30 pm; Saturday, 9:30 am - 2 pm, June only 9 am - 1 pm.

HOME

WHERE TO GET THINGS REPAIRED

Kiev USA

248 Mill Street, Byram, 531.0900

How lucky we are to have an in-town shop which can repair cameras such as Nikon, Zeiss and Leica. They also sell reconditioned cameras.
Hours: weekdays, 9:30 am - 5:30 pm; Saturday, 10 am - 5 pm (closed on Saturday during the summer).

Nimble Thimble

19 Putnam Avenue, Port Chester, NY, 914.934.2934

The resource for home sewing needs. Lots of fabrics, notions, and quilting supplies and sewing machines. This is the place to have your sewing machine repaired.
Hours: Monday - Saturday, 10 am - 5 pm.

Occhicone

42 North Main Street, Port Chester, NY, 914.937.6327

Expert repairs, by Italian craftsmen, for high-quality leather items, such as handbags, briefcases, leather apparel, suitcases and shoes. They can make just about anything look new.
Hours: Monday - Saturday, 8 am - 5:30 pm. Closed Sunday.

Raphael's Furniture Restoration

655 Atlantic Street, Stamford, CT, 348.3079
www.raphaelsfurniture.com

They will repair and restore just about any piece of furniture, but they specialize in the restoration of eighteenth and nineteenth century antiques. Call for an appointment.
Hours: Summer: Tuesday - Thursday, 8 am - 5 pm; Friday, 8 am - 3 pm; Saturday, 8 am - noon.
Hours Labor Day to Memorial Day: Tuesday - Friday,
8 am - 5 pm; Saturday, 8 am - noon.
Directions: I-95 North to Exit 7 (Greenwich Avenue), straight to 4th light, R on Atlantic, 5th building on the R.

HOME

WHERE TO GET THINGS REPAIRED

Tablescraps

Cheshire, CT, 800.801.4084

www.tabletopdesigns.com

If you are missing a piece of china, crystal or silver from your collection, this is a good place to find a replacement. Call, visit their web site or email them at lenox@ntplx.net.

If for some reason Tablescraps can't help you, try these out-of-the-area replacement services:

China Traders, 800.579.1803

Clintsman International, 800.781.8900

Pattern Finders, 516.928.5158

Replacements Ltd, 800.737.5223

Village Clock Shop

1074 Post Road, Darien, CT, 203.655.2100

They sell exquisite clocks, and repair clocks worthy of their service.

Hours: Tuesday - Saturday, 10 am - 5 pm.

Directions: I-95 N to exit 11, L on US 1.

Wood Den

266 Selleck Street, Stamford, CT, 324.6957

Wood and metal furniture stripping. Chair caning and furniture repairs.

Hours: Monday, 8 am - noon; Tuesday, Wednesday & Friday, 9 am - 5 pm; Thursday, 8 am - 8 pm; Saturday, 9 am - 3:30 pm.

Directions: I-95 N to exit 6, straight to 2nd light, R on West to Selleck.

HOTELS & INNS

Cos Cob Inn

50 River Road, Cos Cob 661.5845

www.coscobinn.com

Charmingly redecorated, 1870 Federal bed-and-breakfast. Many of the fourteen rooms have scenic views of the Mianus River; each has its own bath. Continental breakfast, no restaurant.

Rate: $119 - $249 per night, Suites $169 - 249 per night.

Delamar - Greenwich Harbor

500 Steamboat Road, 203.661.9800

www.TheDelamar.com

Greenwich's newest hotel. An 83-room Mediterranean style, luxury hotel with wonderful harbor views, just minutes from the Greenwich train station and Greenwich Avenue. Yachts can safely dock at their 600-foot private dock.

Rates: $295 to $1,200.

Harbor House Inn

165 Shore Road, Old Greenwich, 637.0145   www.hhinn.com

This 100-year-old Victorian mansion has always served as an inn. Guests are corporate clients, people relocating and out-of-town visitors. The twenty-three room bed-and-breakfast is within walking distance of the beach. No restaurant. The atmosphere is very informal. If you need the latest amenities, this may not be your place.

Rates: $129 - $279

Homestead Inn

420 Field Point Road, 869.7500

www.homesteadinn.com

Exceptionally attractive country inn, with twenty-two lovely rooms/suites and superb food. A great choice.

Rates: $250 - $495

HOTELS & INNS

Hyatt Regency

1800 East Putnam Avenue, Old Greenwich, 637.1234
www.Hyatt.com
This 374-room luxury hotel has an elegant interior with excellent food.
Greenwich residents often check into this hotel for a weekend of pampering. The hotel also has a very nice health club.
Rates: $149 - $1,000

Rye Town Hilton

699 Westchester Avenue, Rye Brook, NY, 914.939.6300
www.hilton.com
Situated on 45 acres just next to Greenwich. A large hotel with a pleasant restaurant. It hosts many conventions.
Directions: I-95 S to exit 21, 287 W to exit 10, at second light, R on Westchester Ave.
Rates: $219 - $ $650

Stanton House Inn

76 North Maple Avenue, 869.2110
www.inns.com
Located in Central Greenwich, within walking distance of the shops and restaurants, this turn-of-the-century home, converted into a twenty-four room bed-and-breakfast, is a welcoming first-stop for many new residents.   No restaurant.
Rates: $129 - $239

Stamford Suites

720 Bedford Street, Stamford, CT, 369.7300
www.stamfordsuites.com
An extended-stay hotel with 45 furnished suites for nightly or longer term residence. Each unit contains a bedroom, living room, bathroom and a full-size kitchen. Renovated in 1998.
Directions: I-95 N, exit 8, L on Atlantic (becomes Bedford).
Rates: Daily $99 - $139
              Seven-day rate: $125
              30-day rate: $110

HOTELS & INNS

WORTH A VISIT

Connecticut River Valley Inns

The Connecticut River Valley, www.rotr.com, has outstanding inns in interesting, quaint New England towns, particularly: Chester, Clinton, Deep River, Essex, and Old Lyme. They are loaded with antique shops, art galleries and interesting activities such as the Essex Steam Train (described under Family Outings), the beach in Old Lyme and the Camelot dinner, Long Island or Murder Mystery dinner cruises, Rte.9, exit 7 in Hadden, 860.345.8591. Excellent restaurants also abound in the area. The **Restaurant Du Village** is located in Chester at 59 Main Street, 860.526.2528. This restaurant is one of the best French restaurants in the entire state. You should also try what many consider the best pizza in Connecticut, served at **Alforno**, 1654 Boston Post Road, Brian Alden Shopping Plaza, Old Saybrook, open daily from 4:30 pm - 10 pm, 860.399.4166. Another great place for lunch or Sunday brunch is the **Water's Edge** at 1525 Post Road (I-95 exit 65) in Westbrook, 860.399.5901. Ask for a table on the water. You will also want to try these two Old Lyme Inns for a meal: the **Old Lyme Inn**, 85 Lyme Street, Old Lyme, 800.434.5352, and the **Bee and Thistle Inn**, 100 Lyme Street, (Rte.1, I-95 exit 70), Old Lyme, 860.434.1667. Both inns, particularly the Bee and Thistle, have received many awards for excellent dining. In the area, there is a large shopping mall (Clinton Crossing—see description under Outlets)at I-95 exit 63 and another large mall in Westbrook at exit 65. The state's two casinos, Foxwoods (I-95 exit 92) and Mohegan Sun (I-95 exit 76) are within striking distance (see directions under Gambling).

HOTELS & INNS

WORTH A VISIT

Copper Beach Inn

46 Main Street, Ivoryton, CT
www.CopperBeechInn.com
860.767.0330, 888.809.2056

Gracious inn with 13 guest rooms and excellent food in a charming New England town. High on our list, this inn fits the perfect image of what a New England Inn should be. The inn is best suited for adults unless the children have very nice manners. Rooms range from $125 to $175 per night. January through March, the dining room is closed Tuesday as well as Monday evening.

Directions: I-95 N to Exit 69, Rte 9 N to exit 3, L (west) 1.75 miles.

Inn at Chester

318 West Main Street (Rte. 148), Chester, CT, 860.526.1307
www.InnAtChester.com

The inn is relatively large with 42 rooms. It is open every day for lunch and` dinner and serves very good food in attractive surroundings.

Directions: I-95 N to Exit 69, Rt. 9 North to exit 6 (Chester), L off ramp. The Inn is 3.2 miles on the right.

INFORMATION SOURCES

Community Answers

101 West Putnam Avenue, 622.7979
www.greenwich.lib.ct.us
Funded by the United Way and private donations, this volunteer group is located in the Greenwich Library. Ask them anything about Greenwich—all calls are confidential. You can also find information on their web site.

Community Calendar:

Community Answers provides a Community Calendar of all town events. It comes out every three months. Be sure to call and ask for it.

Useful Article Reprints:

Stop by and pick up articles which might be helpful, such as: *Finding Senior Services in Greenwich; Newcomers Guide to Town Government; Thrift Shops; Childcare and Parenting Services.*
Hours: weekdays, 9 am - 5 pm.

MONEY & BANKING

The Greenwich Bank & Trust Company

115 East Putnam Avenue, 618.8912

1103 East Putnam, Riverside, 698.4030

For as long as we can remember, Greenwich residents have preferred to work with in-town banks. Friendly hellos and loans from bankers who know and work in the community are a much more civilized way to bank than dealing anonymously with a big, inflexible institution. Greenwich is fortunate to have a hometown bank. Drop in and say hello.

Hours: Monday - Thursday, 8:30 am - 4 pm; Friday 8:30 am - 5 pm; Saturday 9 am - 1 pm.

NEWS

MAGAZINES

Connecticut Family

203.625.9825 www.ctfamily.com

A must for anyone with young children. A monthly magazine with good reviews of children's activities in the Connecticut area.

Connecticut Magazine

800.974.2001 x 313 www.connecticutmag.com

This comprehensive magazine always has well-researched articles on the best of Connecticut.

Greenwich Magazine

869.0009

www.greenwichmag.com

Sophisticated articles on topics of interest for everyone. A valuable source of information about Greenwich and Greenwich residents. A subscripton to Greenwich Magazine is essential. The Moffly's also publish the leading magazines for Westport and New Caanan-Darien.

Inside FC/ Greenwich Lifestyles

203.849.3281

A free monthly publication—26,000 are sent out each issue. A good way to keep current on design and style in and around Greenwich.

Westchester Magazine

800.254.2213

www.WestchesterMagazine.com

This magazine focuses on Westchester and Fairfield counties. It often has articles on Greenwich. It is an excellent resource for discovering events and resources you will want to take advantage of in our neighboring towns.

NEWS

NEWSPAPERS

See HOME, SERVICES for newspaper delivery information.

Fairfield County Business Journal
914.694.3600

www.businessjrnls.com

This weekly newspaper tracks trends and developments that impact local businesses. If you are thinking of opening a business or simply want to know the commercial news, this paper is just the ticket.

Greenwich Post
22 West Putnam Avenue, 861.9191

www.GreenwichPost.com

As they say and we agree "Only moonlight covers more homes in the town of Greenwich". This weekly newspaper is devoted exclusively to local Greenwich news. Its interesting articles and editorials have become a must read for anyone living in town.

Greenwich Time
625.4400   www.GreenwichTime.com

If we were entering a national competition for the best daily local newspaper, *Greenwich Time* would win the top award. Joseph Pisani's editorials stimulate thought about important town topics. The *Letters from Readers* section is a good barometer of town concerns.

Guide to Arts and Entertainment in Fairfield CT
324.9799

Published as a separate weekly paper by the *Greenwich Time,* it has movie reviews and a good calendar of weekend shows and special events around the area.

TeenSpeak
42 Greenwich Avenue, 622.0232, Fax: 869.9044

This newspaper by and for teenagers was founded by Greenwich resident Debra Mamorsky. It is operated and published by The Institute for Young Journalists, a nonprofit organization that also brings prominent media people to Greenwich to help educate young journalists. It is published quarterly and is available at Marks Brothers.

NEWS

RADIO & TELEVISION

Bloomberg News - AM 1130
www.bloomberg.com/wbbr
Good national and international news. Best for financial news.

Connecticut Television
www.cpbi.org
Connecticut Public Television has Connecticut-based documentaries as well as sports coverage of Connecticut teams.

Channel 27 is our local community access station. It broadcasts "Greenwich Weekly Video Magazine" Wednesdays at 10:30 pm and Fridays at 9:30 am.

Channel 70 is the Connecticut government access station.

Continuous news, weather and traffic reports.
CBS - AM 880   www.NewsRadio88.com
WINS - AM 1010   www.1010wins.com

Greenwich Radio
1490 Dayton Avenue, 869.1490
www.wgcham.com
Greenwich Radio has been so successful that they had to buy a second station to cover a wider area. Greenwich Radio now broadcasts simultaneously on WGCH - 1490 am & on WVIP - 1310 am. Tune in between 6 am and 10 am for an update on Greenwich happenings, as well as public notices such as school closings and information. Their interviews with Greenwich people making the news are essential to understanding town issues.

Public Radio
Connecticut Public Radio - FM 88.5   www.cpbi.org/radio
National Public Radio - AM 820   www.npr.org
Best in-depth coverage of national and international events.

NUMBERS YOU SHOULD KNOW

Anderson Associates
629.4519
info@Anderson-Real-Estate.com   www.GreenwichSpecialists.com
If you don't know where to turn, call us, your home-town realtor.

Aquarion (formerly The Connecticut-American Water Company)
www.aquarion.com
869.5200 (office)
661.7200 (emergency) 800.732.9678
800.292.2928 (customer service) 800.732.9678

Cablevision of Connecticut
348.9211, 203.846.4700

Connecticut Natural Gas
869.6900 (customer service)
869.6913 (repair & emergency)

Connecticut Vacation Planning Guide
800.282.6863 www.ctbound.org
You might also try Coastal Fairfield County Tourist Information
at 800.866.7925 or 203.854.7825.

Federal Express
800.238.5355, 800.GO.FEDEX, www.fedex.com

Greenwich Fire Department
911 Emergency
622.3950 (non-emergency)

Greenwich Hospital
863.3000

Greenwich Police
911 Emergency
622.8000 (complaints and information)
www.GreenwichPolice.com

NUMBERS YOU SHOULD KNOW

Greenwich Police/Ambulance
911 Emergency
622.8000 (non-emergency)

Greenwich Public Schools
625.7400, www.greenwich.k12.ct.us

Northeast Utilities/Connecticut Light & Power
www.nu.com
800.286.2000, 800.286.5000

Poison Control Center
800.343.2722 (Connecticut)
800.222.1222 (national)

SNET
811 (from SNET coverage area)
800.453.SNET (from outside SNET coverage area)
420-3131 (repairs) or 611

Telemarketing "NO CALL" List
Ct Department of Consumer Protection
800.842.2649
www.state.ct.us/dcp/nocall.htm

Town Hall
622.7700 (all departments)

USE - Senior Center Job Placement Service
629.8031
Utilize Senior Energy, a volunteer activity is open weekdays, 9:30 am - 12:30 pm. It is a good resource for everything from painters to babysitters.

Verizon
www22.verizon.com
869.5222 (new service)
661.5444 (repairs)
625.9800 (customer service)

PARKS & RECREATION

BEACHES

Greenwich beaches are open to residents and non-residents. You must have a beach pass before entering the beach. Passes are strictly enforced. Apply early and be sure to have it when you enter.

Beach Card Office
622.7817
Call for information about beach passes.
You will need a utility bill as proof of residency
and a photo ID.

Byram Beach
531.8938
This beach on Byram Shore Road has a swimming pool, three tennis courts, picnic area and playground.

Ferry Information
661.5957
The ferry service from the Arch Street dock to Great Captain Island or Island Beach varies according to the tides. Service begins in the middle of June and lasts until September.

Great Captain's Island
622.7814
Take a ferry from the Arch Street dock to this 17-acre island with beach and picnic area. There is only one ferry in the morning and one in the afternoon. Captain's Island is rustic with no concession stand, so bring a picnic lunch. Camp sites available with permits. For camping reservations, call 622.7824.

Greenwich Point (Tod's Point)
Entrance at the south end of Shore Road in Old Greenwich. This 147-acre beach, with concession stand, has jogging, hiking and biking trails, lots of picnic facilities and wind surfing.

Island Beach (Little Captain's Island)
661.5957
Take a ferry from the Arch Street dock to this 4-acre island with beaches, picnic area and concession stand.

PARKS & RECREATION

CIVIC CENTERS

The Civic centers are the sites for many sporting events and public events such as antique shows. Call for their latest catalog of events.

Eastern Greenwich Civic Center
90 Harding Road, Old Greenwich, 637.4583
Also called: Greenwich Civic Center or Old Greenwich-Riverside Civic Center.

Western Greenwich Civic Center
449 Pemberwick Road, Glenville, 622.7830
www.greenwichct.org
Call for a program guide. Many activities available such as swing dance lessons, piano lessons and peewee soccer.

TIP: THE ENCHANTED FOREST
Each year in early November at the Old Greenwich Civic Center, the Junior League organizes a magical display of beautifully decorated Christmas trees and ginger bread houses - all donations from Greenwich organizations and individuals. The auction of these items helps support the good works of the Junior League. This is fun event for the whole family.
Call 869-1979 for details.

PARKS & RECREATION

PARKS & NATURE PRESERVES

Greenwich, in addition to its beaches and 32 miles of coastline, has 8,000 acres of protected land, with over 1,000 acres of town parks. The parks and nature preserves listed below are some of the more popular of the twenty parks in Greenwich. Call Greenwich Department of Parks & Recreation (622.7830) for a complete list and directions.

Audubon Center
613 Riversville Road, 869.5272
www.audibon.org
686 acres with well-kept trails, a great place to walk.

Babcock Preserve
North Street, 622.7824
297 acres located two miles north of the Merritt Parkway. Well-marked running, hiking, and cross-country ski trails.

Binney Park
Sound Beach Avenue, Old Greenwich
Four tennis courts, playground, fields, pond skating. A favorite place for wedding photos.

Bruce Park
Bruce Park Drive and Indian Field Road
Athletic fields, bowling green, fitness trail, picnic area, tennis courts and playground.

Mianus River Park
Cognewaugh Road, 622.7814
215 acres owned by Greenwich and Stamford. Trout fishing. Wooded hills and steep cliffs with miles of hiking trails. Take Valley Road to Cognewaugh, the entrance is on Cognewaugh Road about three miles on the right (there is no sign).

PARKS & RECREATION

PARKS & NATURE PRESERVES

Greenwich Land Trust

629.2151

Greenwich and its residents are committed to expanding the town's large amount of green space. Funding comes from a variety of sources, including the town, the state, the Federal Government (www.TPL.org), the Greenwich Land Trust (www.GLTrust.org) and private donations. Some of the most recent acquisitions are:

Treetops

In 2002 the town of Greenwich and 3 land trusts raised $11.5 million dollars to purchase 110-acres bordering the Mianus River, this tract forms the southern boundary of the 220-acre Mianus River Park. Inspired by David Ogilvy, residents from town officials to school children united to make this possible.

Sabine Farm Field

A field along Round Hill Road was purchased in 2001 for $2.9 million by the Greenwich Land Trust. However, all of the money came from private donations, raised primarily through the efforts of a local resident, Edward Bragg.

Calves Island

This 28-acre island off Byram Shore is likely to be purchased in 2002 for $6 million. The money will be coming from the Greenwich Land Trust and the Federal Government.

Pomerance-Tuchman Preserve

This 118-acre tract adjacent to the Montgomery Pinetum lies between Orchard and Bible Streets in Cos Cob. The Town has undertaken to purchase the property for $35 million. Along with the Pinetum and Bible Street playing fields, this tract gives the Town a corridor of 227-acres of pristine woodlands.

PHOTOGRAPHY

PHOTOGRAPHERS

Bob Capazzo

358.3402

Bob is the senior photographer for Greenwich Magazine. He likes to photograph people and events and he has a wonderful way of making people relax and look their best.

Kathleen DiGiovanna

661 Steamboat Road, 869.5432

A freelance photographer specializing in weddings and special events. You can depend on her to capture the spirit of the occasion.

Jeffery Shaw Portrait Photography

39 Lewis Street, 622.4838

His photographs capture your family in a way you will treasure for ever.

Hours: Tuesday-Friday, 10 am - 5 pm.

POST OFFICES & ZIP CODES

There are six post offices and five zip codes in town. The window service hours are different for each office. Mail for Greenwich zip codes is usually sent to Stamford to be sorted. The only post office with bins for all Greenwich zip codes is in Old Greenwich.

Greenwich Avenue Post Office [Zip: 06830]
310 Greenwich Avenue, 869.3737
Hours: weekdays, 8:30 am - 5 pm;
Saturday, 8:30 am - 2 pm.

Greenwich Post Office [Zip: 06831]
29 Valley Drive, 625.3168
Hours: weekdays, 8:30 am - 5 pm;
Saturday, 8:30 am - 2 pm.

Glenville Post Office [Zip: 06831]
25 Glen Ridge Plaza, 531.8744
Hours: weekdays, 8:30 am - 4:30 pm;
Saturday, 8:30 am - noon.

Cos Cob Post Office [Zip: 06807]
152 East Putnam Avenue, 869.1470
Hours: weekdays, 8:30 am - 4:30 pm;
Saturday, 8:30 am - 12:30 pm.

Riverside Post Office [Zip: 06878]
1273 East Putnam Avenue, 637.9332
Hours: weekdays, 7:30 am - 5 pm;
Saturday, 8 am - 1 pm.

Old Greenwich Post Office [Zip: 06870]
36 Arcadia Road, 637.1405
Hours: weekdays, 8 am - 5 pm;
Saturday, 9 am - 1 pm.

REAL ESTATE

Buyer Agency

On June 1, 1997, Connecticut mandated that realtors represent either the buyer or the seller, but not both (unless dual or designated agency is disclosed and agreed to by both parties) in the same transaction.

Buyers like being represented by their own realtor because their realtor can now tell them what they think a house is worth and provide excellent guidance through the real estate process. This extra protection costs the buyer nothing because the buyer's realtor is still paid by the seller. In the first meeting, the buyer signs a representation agreement with their realtor much the way a seller signs a listing agreement with their realtor.

Greenwich Multiple Listing Service

Greenwich has an outstanding organization devoted to local real estate. This service is funded by the realtors in town and is extremely helpful to homeowners, buyers and realtors. Member Realtors follow a strict code of ethics. Greenwich properties are valuable and unique. It is important to understand how Greenwich real estate works.

When many other towns gave up their local boards, Greenwich did not. In Greenwich all properties - with rare exceptions - are multiple-listed with the Greenwich "MLS". To buy property in Greenwich, you need to select a realtor you like and trust—and you will have access through your realtor to the entire market.

TIP: TOUR GREENWICH HOMES
Each year in December, the Historical Society organizes a fabulous tour of some of Greenwich's most beautiful homes. The annual fund raiser costs $100. You can also ticket for lunch.
Call Melinda at 869.6899 ext 15 for details.

REAL ESTATE

Anderson Associates

164 Mason Street, 629.4519, 800.223.4519; fax: 629.4786
www.GreenwichSpecialists.com

Anderson Associates are Greenwich real estate specialists.
We all live, as well as work, in Greenwich. We spend our full time on Greenwich real estate. You can depend on us to represent your best interests. Our knowledge of Greenwich and our real estate expertise will make your real estate transaction rewarding and stress-free. As you can see from the introduction, we originally wrote the book you are reading to help our buyers feel immediately at home in this wonderful community.

> *"Whether you are buying or selling, you will love working with Anderson Associates. Their website is second to none—just what you'd expect from a company as customer driven as they are. I found information on renovating my house, my children found statistics for school projects, and there are pictures of lots of Greenwich houses for sale. Highly recommended."*
> Melanie Kuperberg

> *"With special thanks for all you do;*
> *- for knowing what we wanted better than we did;*
> *- for giving us that extra push when we needed it, but never pushing us hard;*
> *- for your expertise;*
> *- for much more, but especially for just being you."*
> Naomi & Steve Myers

> *"Thank you all for your creative marketing and constant support during the selling of my home. You have been the guiding light throughout the process. I am recommending Anderson Associates to all of my friends."*
> Catherine "Kay" Spiers

REAL ESTATE

Strategy Mortgage Corp.
15 Neil Lane, Riverside, 637.3333. 800.707.0000; Fax: 698.2222
Call Lucy Krasnor, Vice President Loan Origination.
Strategy is located in Greenwich. They started in 1994 and originated over $42 million in their first year. Strategy now represents fifty-eight of the most aggressive national and regional lenders and generates over $400 million a year in mortgage loans. They work hard to find the best loans for their clients, and best of all, they are available from 8 am - 10 pm every day.

TIP: HOW TO PRICE YOUR GREENWICH HOME
How much your home is worth is determined not by Realtors, but by supply and demand at the time you list. Buyers are comparison shoppers. They look at what has sold and what is for sale. Then they decide value. It is the job of your Realtor to educate you about the local real estate market and how your home fits into it. It is your job to set an informed price for your home.
When you list your home it will be competing with similar homes on the market—as well as those that have recently sold. Your Realtor should provide you with a complete analysis of the real estate market, the sales in your neighborhood and comparable homes presently for sale. You should consider driving by these homes and let your Realtor explain how they compare, and why they sold or were priced the way they were. Don't confuse pricing your property with choosing your Realtor. *Choose the Realtor you like and trust first. Then work with them to price your home.*

RELIGION
HOUSES OF WORSHIP

Each week the *Greenwich Time* publishes Sabbath services in the Thursday issue and church services in the Saturday issue. This is the best place to find updated information and times of services.

Albertson Memorial Church
293 Sound Beach Avenue, Old Greenwich, 637.4615

Anglican Church of the Advent
606 Riversville Road, 329.9885 or 861.2432
At North Greenwich Congregational Church or 16 Lexington Avenue.

Annunciation Greek Orthodox Church
1230 Newfield Avenue, Stamford, CT, 322.2093

Bethel African Methodist Episcopal Church
44 Lake Avenue, 661.3099

Bethel Tabernacle
United Pentecostal Church
Meets at Greenwich YMCA, 50 East Putnam Avenue, 357.8249

Chabad Center for Living Judaism
75 Mason Street , 629. 9059

Chavurat Deevray Torah
Reform/Conservative Jewish Study Group, 661.0949

Christ Church of Greenwich
254 East Putnam Avenue, 869.6600
www.christchurchgreenwich.com

Church of Jesus Christ of Latter-Day Saints
800 Stillwater Road, Stamford, 622.0867

Church of the New Covenant
289 Delavan Avenue, 324.5797
Services held at Byram Archibald Neighborhood Center.

RELIGION

HOUSES OF WORSHIP

Diamond Hill United Methodist Church
521 East Putnam Avenue, 869.2395

Dingletown Community Church
Stanwich Road and Barnstable Lane, 629.5923

First Baptist Church
10 Northfield Street, 869.7988

First Church of Christ, Scientist
11 Park Place, 869.1555
Reading Room, 333 Greenwich Avenue, 869.2503

First Church of Round Hill
464 Round Hill Road, 629.3876

First Congregational Church
108 Sound Beach Avenue, Old Greenwich, 637.1791
www.fccog.org

First Lutheran Church
38 Field Point Road, 869.0032

First Presbyterian Church
One West Putnam Avenue, 869.8686

First United Methodist Church
59 East Putnam Avenue, 629.9584

Grace Church of Greenwich
PO Box 1673, Greenwich, CT 06836, 861.7555
Meets at Women's Club of Greenwich, 89 Maple Avenue.

Greek Orthodox Church of the Archangels
1527 Bedford Street, Stamford, CT, 348.4216

Greenwich Baptist Church
10 Indian Rock Lane, 869.2437

RELIGION

HOUSES OF WORSHIP

Greenwich Congregation of Jehovah's Witnesses
471 Stanwich Road, 661.1244

Greenwich Reform Synagogue
257 Stanwich Road, 629.0018

Harvest Time Assembly of God
449 Pemberwick Road
Western Civic Center, Glenville, 531.7778

Japanese Gospel Church
St. Paul Evangelical Lutheran Church
286 Delavan Avenue, 531.6450

North Greenwich Congregational Church
606 Riversville Road, 869.7763

Presbyterian Church of Old Greenwich
38 West End Avenue, Old Greenwich, 637.3669

Religion in American Life
2001 West Main Street, Suite.120,Stamford CT, 355.1220
www.inviteAFriend.org

Round Hill Community Church
395 Round Hill Road, 869.1091

Russian Orthodox St Mary's Holy Assumption
141 Den Road, Stamford, 329.9933

Sacred Heart Roman Catholic Church
95 Henry Street, Byram, 531.8730

St. Agnes Roman Catholic Church
247 Stanwich Road, 869.5396

RELIGION

HOUSES OF WORSHIP

St. Barnabas Episcopal Church
954 Lake Avenue, 661.5526

St. Catherine of Siena Roman Catholic Church
4 Riverside Avenue, 637.3661

St. Mary Roman Catholic Church
178 Greenwich Avenue, 869.9393

St. Michael's Roman Catholic Church
469 North Street, 869.5421

St. Paul Evangelical Lutheran Church
286 Delavan Avenue, 531.8466

St. Paul Roman Catholic Church
84 Sherwood Avenue and King Street, 531.8741

St. Paul's Episcopal Church
200 Riverside Avenue, 637.2447

St. Roch Roman Catholic Church
10 St. Roch Avenue, 869.4176

St. Saviour's Episcopal Church
350 Sound Beach Avenue, Old Greenwich, 637.2262

St. Timothy Church
1034 North Street, Banksville, NY, 661.5196

Second Congregational Church
139 East Putnam Avenue, 869.9311

Stanwich Congregational Church
237 Taconic Road, 661.4420

RELIGION

HOUSES OF WORSHIP

Stamford-Greenwich Religious Society of Friends
572 Roxbury Road, Stamford, CT, 869.0445

Temple Shalom
300 East Putnam Avenue, 869.7191

Trinity Church
15 Sherwood Place, 618.0808
www.TrinityChurchOnLine.org

Unitarian Universalist Society
Bedford Street, Stamford, 348.0708

TIP: BEACH SERVICES

Two churches in Greenwich conduct Sunday services on the beach at Tod's Point during the summer months; the First Congregational Church of Old Greenwich at 8:00 am and Christ Church at 10 am. Both groups welcome visitors. A beach pass is not required for these services. The Saturday Greenwich Time lists all of the religious services in the area.

RELIGION

ORGANIZATIONS

Church Women United of Greenwich
28 Wiffle Tree Lane, Riverside
Pat Brandt, President - 637.4870
Contact: Kate Bryner, Publicity - 869.6261

Council of Churches and Synagogues
461 Glenbrook Road, Stamford, CT, 348.2800
Rev. James Carter, Executive Director

Hadassah, Greenwich Chapter
Temple Sholom, 300 East Putnam Avenue
Fran Blaustein, Co-President - 622.0225
Felice Robinou, Co-President - 625.9666

UJA Federation of Greenwich
One Holly Hill Lane, Greenwich 06830-6080, 622.1434
Pamela Zur, President

RESTAURANTS

ABOUT RESTAURANTS

How Restaurants are Selected

We do not accept advertisements; restaurants are included strictly on merit. Restaurants are visited anonymously several times a year. If we have more than one bad meal, we don't include that restaurant. Our reviews are intended to give you our impression of the restaurant's ambiance, service and food. If a negative note is included, it is because we believe the restaurant has potential. If you have positive or negative comments about a restaurant or our review, please call, write or send us an e-mail to: restaurants@greenwichspecialists.com

How the Restaurant Section is organized

We begin with an index which provides categories (by type of food and by specialty) to help you make your restaurant selection. Restaurant reviews are in alphabetical order.

Reservations

In most restaurants, reservations are a must. This is especially true if you are going out on Friday or Saturday evening.

Restaurants Outside of Greenwich

We include restaurants outside of Greenwich when they are worth the trip. Close to Greenwich are two restaurant areas that draw large Greenwich crowds: Port Chester, NY and SONO (South Norwalk) just off exit 14 of I-95. Very much like SOHO (South of Houston) in Manhattan, SONO contains a mixture of art shops and trendy restaurants.

Restaurant Design

Although a few restaurants such as Jean Louis and Le Figaro are exceptions, many restaurants are moving towards Minimalist Modern. Unfortunately, these trendy restaurants accentuate a problem common to many restaurants—overpowering noise that drowns out conversation. Restaurants should be a place for relaxation, good food, and good company. In some restaurants, the noise level is so high that you can't enjoy your company.

Hours

Establishments change their hours as business dictates. Many change their hours for winter and summer, and during holidays. Some chefs even take vacations. Please don't consider our listings definitive.

RESTAURANTS
BY CUISINE

* Our favorite in the category

Asian / Pacific Rim (Indian, Chinese & Japanese are listed separately)
Asiana Café
* Baang
Penang Grill
Splash
Tamarind

Brew Pubs
* Brewhouse
Bank Street Brewing
   Company

Casual American
Augie's
Cobble Stone
Collyer Café
Cos Cob Grill
Gates
Horseneck Tavern
Hubba-Hubba
I-Hop
Katzenberg's Gourmet
   Deli
Landmark Diner
MacKenzie's Grill
Putnam Restaurant
Skylight Café
Smokey Joe's
* Sundown Saloon
Thataway Café

Chinese
Green Symphony
Hunan Café
Hunan Gourmet
* Panda Pavilion

Coffee Shops
Arcadia Coffee Co.
Coffee Tree
Dunkin' Donuts
Ground Zero
* Moonstruck
Starbucks

Contemporary American
Beacon
Boxing Cat Grill
Bleu
Cobble Creek Café
Dome
Equus
Inn at Pound Ridge
Match
Mediterraneo
* Rebeccas
River Cat Grill
Roger Sherman Inn
Silvermine Tavern
Sky Top Restaurant
Vuli
Winfields at the Hyatt
Xaviars
Zanghi

Cuban
Habana

Delicatessens and Take-Out
Alpen Pantry
Apache Place
Arcuris
Aux Délices
* Bruckner's
Garden Caterers
Garelick and Herbs
Hay Day
Katzenberg's Express
Kneaded Bread
Paesano's Deli
Upper Crust Bagel Co.
Whole Foods

Diners
City Limits
Glory Days
* Landmark Diner

Fast Food
Boston Market
Hubba Hubba
* Jimmy's Grill
McDonald's
Subway Sandwich
Wendy's

RESTAURANTS
BY CUISINE

French
Aux Délices
(Le) Chateau
(La) Cremaillere
Equus
(Le) Figaro
Thomas Henkelmann
* Jean Louis
Meli-Melo
Mirage Café
(La) Panetiere
Stonehenge Inn
Versailles

German
Brew House

Greek
Famous Pizza &
    Souvlaki
* Viscardi's Colonial
    Inn

Ice Cream
Capriccio
Carvel
Häagen-Dazs
Longford's
* Meli-Melo

Indian
Chola
Dawat
* Tandoori

Italian
Applausi Osteria
Bella Nonna
Benny's Restaurant
Centro
Da Vinci's
Fontanella
Giorgio's
Hostaria Mazzei
Pasquale
Pasta Nostra
Pasta Vera
Piero's
Polpo
Quattro Pazzi
That Little Italian
    Restaurant
Terra
* Valbella

Japanese
Abis
Kagetsu
Kazu
* Maya of Japan

Latin American
Café Rue (Argentine)
Pantanal (Brazilian)
* Sonora

Mexican
Fonda La Paloma
* Olé Mole

Pizza
Arcuris
Bella Nonna
Famous Pizza &
    Souvlaki
Match
Pizza Express
Pizza Factory
* Pizza Glenville
Pizza Hut
Pizza Post
Planet Pizza

Seafood
Alta
Elm Street Oyster
Crabshell
* Ocean 211
Ocean Drive
Paradise Bar & Grill
Rowayton Seafood
Sono Seaport Seafood

Southwestern
* Boxcar Cantina
Smokey Joe's Bar-B-Q
Sundown Saloon
Telluride

RESTAURANTS
BY CUISINE

Spanish
* Barcelona
Mecca
Meigas

Steak
Manero's
Maya of Japan
* Morton's of Chicago
Porterhouse
Smokey Joe's Bar-B-Q
Willett House

Swiss
Roger Sherman Inn

Thai
Mhai Thai

Vegetarian
Bruckner's
Chola
* Green Symphony

RESTAURANTS
BY SPECIALTY

10 Best
1. Jean Louis
2. Rebeccas
3. Xaviars
4. Thomas Henkelmann
5. Zanghi
6. Beacon
7. Valbella
8. (La) Panetiere
9. Roger Sherman Inn
10. Cobble Creek Café

Breakfast
Aux Delices
City Limits
* Glory Days
I-Hop
Katzenberg's Gourmet Deli
Landmark Diner
Meli-Melo
Putnam Restaurant
Thomas Henkelmann
Versailles
Winfields at the Hyatt

Brunch on Sunday
Beacon
Boxing Cat Grill
(Le) Chateau
Dome
Figaro
Hunan Café
Inn at Pound Ridge
Rebecca's
Roger Sherman Inn
Silvermine Tavern
* Winfields at the Hyatt

Dinner, Late Night
Barcelona
Bleu
* Mirage Café
City Limits
Cobble Stone
Glory Days
Hubba-Hubba
MacKenzie's Grill
Thataway Café

Less Expensive
Asiana Café
Augie's
Bella Nonna
Benny's Restaurant
Boxcar Cantina
Brew House
Café Rue
Centro
Cobble Stone
Famous Pizza & Souvlaki
Glory Days
Horseneck Tavern
Hubba-Hubba
Hunan Café
Hunan Gourmet
I-Hop
Katzenberg's Gourmet Deli
Landmark Diner
MacKenzie's Grill
* Meli-Melo
Olé Mole
Panda Pavilion
Pasquale
Pasta Vera
Putnam Restaurant
Quattro Pazzi
SoNo Seaport Seafood
Smokey Joe's Bar-B-Q
Sundown Saloon
Tandoori
That Little Italian
Viscardi's Colonial

RESTAURANTS
BY SPECIALTY

Family Restaurants

Abis
Bella Nonna
Boxcar Cantina
Centro
Cobble Stone
Collyer Café
Cos Cob Grill
Glory Days
Hunan Gourmet
Hunan Café
I-Hop
Katzenberg's Gourmet
  Deli
Landmark Diner
* Maneros
Maya of Japan
Panda Pavilion
Paradise Bar & Grill
Pasquale
Putnam Restaurant
Quattro Pazzi
Rowayton Seafood
Silvermine Tavern
Smokey Joe's Bar-B-Q
SoNo Seaport Seafood
Sundown Saloon
Thataway Café
That Little Italian
Viscardi's Colonial

Hot Spots

Bank Street Brewing
Barcelona
Bleu
Boxing Cat Grill
Crabshell
Dome
MacKenzie's Grill
Splash

Lunch, For Ladies Who...

Da Vinci's
* Figaro
Jean-Louis
Mediterraneo
Rebecca's
Terra
Versailles

Lunch, Late

Asiana
Brew House
Café Rue
City Limits
Cobble Stone
* Da Vinci's
Dome
Elm Street Oyster
Horseneck Tavern
Hunan Café
Katzenberg's Gourmet
  Deli
Landmark Diner
MacKenzie's Grill
Pasta Vera
Versailles

Open on Many Major Holidays

Abis
Café Rue
Cobble Creek Café
Cobble Stone
Glory Days
Hunan Café
Hunan Gourmet
MacKenzie's Grill
Mhai Thai
Pasta Vera
Sundown

Romantic

(Le) Chateau
Cobble Creek Café
(La) Cremaillere
Equus
Giorgio's
Rober Sherman Inn
Stonehenge
Thomas Henkelman
Xaviers

RESTAURANTS

BY NEIGHBORHOOD

Banksville, NY
(La) Cremaillere

Byram
Famous Pizza &
  Souvlaki
Garden Caterers
That Little Italian

Cos Cob
Augie's
Bella Nonna
Cos Cob Grill
Dunkin' Donuts
Fonda La Paloma
Garden Caterers
Landmark Diner
Pizza Post

Glenville
Centro Ristorante
Pizza Glenville
Pizza Hut
Rebecca's

**Central
Greenwich**
Abis
Alta
Asiana Café
Aux Délices
Boxcar Cantina
Barcelona
Benny's Restaurant
Bleu
Bruckner's
Café Rue
Coffee Tree

Chola
Da Vinci's
Dome
Dunkin' Donuts
Elm Street Oyster
Figaro
Garelick & Herbs
Glory Days
Häagen-Dazs
Horseneck Tavern
Hunan Gourmet
Jean-Louis
Jimmy's Grill
Kagetsu
Katzenberg's
McDonalds
Manero's
Maya of Japan
Mediterraneo
Meli-Melo
Mhai Thai
Moonstruck
Paesano's Deli
Panda Pavilion
Pasta Vera
Penang Grill
Pizza Express
Pizza Factory
Planet Pizza
Polpo
Putnam Restaurant
Skylight Café (YWCA)
Starbucks
Subway Sandwich
Sundown Saloon
Terra
Thataway Café
Thomas Henkelmann

Versailles
Wendy's
Whole Foods

New Canaan, CT
Roger Sherman Inn
Gates

Norwalk, CT
Barcelona
Brewhouse
Ground Zero
Habana
Kazu
Meigas
Match
Mecca
Ocean Drive
Pasta Nostra
Porter House
Silvermine Tavern
SoNo Seaport Seafood

Old Greenwich
Alpen Pantry
Arcadia Coffee Co
Applausi Osteria
Arcuris
Boston Market
Boxing Cat Grill
Garden Caterers
Hunan Café
MacKenzie's Grill
Upper Crust Bagel Co
Viscardi's Colonial
Winfields

RESTAURANTS
BY NEIGHBORHOOD

Port Chester, NY
Carvel
Giorgio's
Green Symphony
Hostaria Mazzei
Mirage Café
Pantanal
Pasquale
Piero's
Sonora
Tamarind
Tandoori
Willett House

Purchase, NY
Cobble Creek Café
Cobble Stone

Riverside
Apache Place
Aux Délices
Baang
Hay Day
McDonald's
Valbella

Rowayton, CT
River Cat Grill
Rowayton Seafood

Rye, NY
Longford's Ice Cream
(La) Panetiere

Stamford, CT
Bank Street Brewing
    Company
Beacon
Capriccio
City Limits
Crab Shell
Collyer Café
(La) Fontanella
Hubba-Hubba
I-Hop
Morton's of Chicago
Ocean 211
Olé Mole
Paradise Bar/Grill
Quattro Pazzi
Smokey Joe's Bar-B-Q
Telluride
Vuli
Zanghi

White Plains, NY
Dawat
Sky Top Restaurant

Westport, CT
Splash

Worth the Trip but more than 30 Minutes away
(See also Inns Worth a Trip)
(Le) Chateau,
    Salem, NY
Equus,
    Tareytown, NY
Inn at Pound Ridge,
    Pound Ridge, NY
Stonehenge Inn,
    Ridgefield, CT
Xaviars
    Piermont, NY

Abis

381 Greenwich Avenue, 862.9100

A full menu with lots of choices, including a sushi bar. We are fans of their Japanese noodle dishes such as udon or soba. If you have a large party, consider ordering Shabu-Shabu. One side of the restaurant is traditional Japanese cuisine, the other side serves hibachi. Youngsters have a wonderful time watching their hibachi meals being prepared.

Hours: Lunch, weekdays, 11:30 am - 2:30 pm, Saturday, noon - 2:30 pm; Sunday, 11:30 am - 2:30 pm; Dinner, weekdays, 5:30 pm - 9:30 pm (Friday until 10:30 pm); Saturday, 5 pm - 10:30 pm; Sunday, 5 pm - 9:30 pm. Open most holidays, including Christmas and New Year's.

Main course price range: Traditional Japanese: Lunch, $8 - $25; Dinner, $10 - $33 (Shabu-Shabu for two). Hibachi: Lunch, $11 - $32; Dinner, $12 - $38.

Alpen Pantry

23 Arcadia Road, Old Greenwich, 637.3818

Nice take-out sandwich selection. Order a cheese ball or cheese dip for a party. Hours: Monday - Saturday, 9 am - 5 pm.

Alta

363 Greenwich Avenue, 622.5138

Chef Larsson named his restaurant, Alta, after a Norwegian town known for salmon. The refined simplicity of the decor and the attentive service combined with stunning seafood dishes make this restaurant a winner.

Hours: Lunch: weekdays, noon - 2:30 pm; Dinner; Tuesday - Sunday, 5:30 pm - 10:30 pm.

Dinner main course price range: $26 - $34; For lunch they have two price fixed menus: one at $19 and the other at $24.

RESTAURANTS

DINING OUT

Apache Place

7 Apache Place, Riverside, 637.3232

www.apacheplace.com

Where is Apache Place you say? This well-liked, but off the beaten path, delicatessen is just one street in from the intersection of Sheephill Road and the Post Road and well worth finding. The Chef-Owner is Dale Ritchey, a graduate of the Culinary Institute of America. He makes an assortment of interesting and well-priced items not normally found in a deli. Take-out only.

Hours: Monday - Thursday, 6 am - 6 pm; Friday, 6 am - 3 pm; Saturday, 7 am - 3 pm. Closed many Sundays.

Applausi Osteria

199 Sound Beach Avenue, Old Greenwich, 637.4447

Since its opening in 1993, Applausi has continued to be a favorite in Old Greenwich. Its refined atmosphere, good Italian dishes, such as Osso Bucco and homemade pastas, explain its popularity.

Hours: Closed Sunday. Lunch, weekdays, noon - 2:30 pm; Dinner, weekdays, 5 pm - 10 pm; (Saturday until 10:30 pm). Main course price range: $16 -$27.

Arcadia Coffee Co.

20 Arcadia Road, Old Greenwich, 637.8766

www.ArcadiaCoffee.com

This is a fun place where you can take your newspaper and relax with a good cup of coffee and a sandwich. The walls are decorated with works for sale by local artists.

Hours: weekdays, 6:30 am - 5 pm; weekends: 7 am - 5 pm (during the summer they close on Sundays at 1 pm).

Arcuri's

178 Sound Beach Avenue, Old Greenwich, 637.1085

226 East Putnam Avenue, Cos Cob, 869.6999

Extensive selection of specialty pizzas. They are well known for their delicious salads.

Hours: Open 7 days, Lunch, 11 am - 4 pm; Dinner, 4 pm - 10 pm, Friday until 10:30.

RESTAURANTS

DINING OUT

Asiana Café

130 East Putnam Avenue, 622.6833

Ready for a savory twist on pan-Asian food? Try this restaurant, newly opened by the owners of the Penang Grill. Don't expect their dishes (Vietnamese, Chinese, Thai and Japanese) to be like you have had in other restaurants. My Szechuan Spicy Beef came mixed with shredded jicama and was oh-so-good. The helpings are generous and the service attentive. The atmosphere is rather modern and severe.

Hours: Monday-Thursday, 11 am - 10 pm; Friday & Saturday, 11 am - 11 pm; Sunday, noon - 10 pm.

Main Course Prices: $11 - $20

Augie's (formerly Mianus River Tavern)

136 River Road Extension, Cos Cob, 862.0640

On a small street just off the Post Road, Augie's has been redecorated and turned into a charming restaurant. Although there are a number of entrees, we would suggest you stick with the tavern fare portion of the menu.

Hours: Sunday - Thursday, 11 am - 10 pm;
Friday and Saturday, 11 am - 11 pm.

The bar is open until 1am during the week and until 2 am on weekends.

Main course price range: $8 - $24, tavern fare $8 - $10.

Aux Délices

1075 East Putnam Avenue, Riverside, 698.1066

3 West Elm, Greenwich, 622.6644

www.AuxDelicesFoods.com

Provencal style food with an American twist prepared under the direction of well known Chef Debra Ponzek. Top quality gourmet take-away food. Both locations have a few tables, excellent for a quick breakfast or late lunch. They have a weekday home delivery service and will deliver your order even when you are not home, packaged to keep the food at the proper temperature.

Greenwich Hours: weekdays, 7 am - 6:30 pm: Saturday, 8 am - 6:30 pm; Sunday, 9 am - 4 pm. Riverside Hours: Monday - Saturday, 7:30 am - 6:30 pm; Sunday, 7:30 am - 2:30 pm.

Main Course Prices: Lunch, $5.50 - $12; Dinner, $9.50 - $30.

RESTAURANTS

DINING OUT

Baang Café

1191 East Putnam Avenue, Riverside, 637.2114

www.DecaroRestaurantGroup.com

Since 1995, this lively, very noisy restaurant has continued to delight its diners with interesting drinks (Margarita made with red oranges) and innovative, delicious Pan Asian cuisine. Try the charred, rare tuna or Szechuan beef. Outdoor dining in the summer.

Hours: Lunch, Friday, noon - 2:30 pm; Dinner, Monday - Thursday, 6 pm - 10 pm; Friday & Saturday, 6 pm - 11 pm; Sunday 6 pm - 9 pm.

Reservations are only accepted for parties of six or more, so arrive early, especially on Friday and Saturday nights.

Main course price range: Dinner, $21 - $32.

Bank Street Brewing Company

65 Bank Street, Stamford, CT, 325.2739

Fun atmosphere and good bar food such as quesidillas and chicken fingers. If beer is not your thing, it's ok. They have a full bar which is open late.

Hours: Open everyday, 5:30 pm - 10 pm (weekends open until 11 pm).

Directions: I-95 N to exit 8, L on Atlantic (park on Bell or Main Street).

Barcelona

63 North Main Street, South Norwalk, CT, 203.899.0088

18 West Putnam Avenue, 983.6400

www.BarcelonaWineBar.com

We first enjoyed this authentic tapas restaurant near SoNo theaters in Norwalk. Now there is one in Greenwich. The bar is loud and lively and there is an excellent wine list. For a quieter spot, dine on the patio in Norwalk. We love all of the tapas. The chocolate indulgence with coconut ice cream is scrumptious. On Friday and Saturday nights reservations are only accepted for dining before 7 pm.

Greenwich Hours: Lunch, weekdays, noon - 3 pm; Dinner every night, 5 pm - 1 am (Friday & Saturday until 2 am).

Norwalk Hours: Dinner, Thursday - Sunday, 5 pm - Midnight, (Friday and Saturday until 2 am).

Main course price range: Lunch, $9 - $12; Dinner, $16 - $25; Tapas, $3.50 - $8.

Directions to SoNo location: I-95 North, Exit 14, R at stop sign, L at 2nd traffic light into SoNo Plaza.

RESTAURANTS

DINING OUT

Beacon Restaurant
183 Harbor Drive (Shippan Point), Stamford, 327.4600
www.beaconNYC.com
Definitely worth the trip. It is located on the waterfront and their new American cuisine is simply brilliant. Be sure to try their wood roasted oysters, rib eye steak or swordfish, and chocolate chip souffle. The Sunday Brunch buffet is bountiful and irresistible.
Hours: Closed Mondays, January - March. Sunday Brunch, noon - 2:30 pm; Lunch, Fridays, noon - 2:30 pm; Dinner, Tuesday - Saturday, 5:30 pm - 10 pm (Friday & Saturday until 11 pm), Sunday 5 pm - 9 pm.
Main course price range: Lunch, $12 - $17; Dinner, $19 - $28.
Directions: I-95 to exit 8, second Light R on canal, L on Jefferson, R on McGee, R on Harbor.

Bella Nonna
371 East Putnam Avenue, Cos Cob, 869.4445
A family-oriented restaurant, serving pizzas and traditional Italian cuisine.
Hours: Breakfast, Saturday & Sunday, 7 am - 11:30 am; Lunch, Monday - Sunday, 11:30 am - 3 pm; Dinner, Monday -Sunday, 3 pm - 11 pm. Reservations for 6 or more.
Prices for Dinner: Pizzas $8 - $16; Pastas & Entrees, $10 - $16.

Benny's Restaurant
355 Greenwich Avenue, 661.6108
This small Italian restaurant is straight out of the 1950's. They even have a Wednesday night all-you-can-eat spaghetti day for $6. The service is quite friendly and the food is plentiful. We especially like the Fettuccini Alfredo.
Main course prices: Lunch, $4 - $11; Dinner, $11 - $20.
Hours: Lunch every day except Sunday, 11:30 am - 3 pm; Dinner every day 5 pm - 10:30 pm, Sunday until 9 pm.

RESTAURANTS

DINING OUT

Bleu

339 Greenwich Avenue, 661.9377

www.Bleu-Café.com

If you think everybody in Greenwich is tucked in by 10, check out this lively, noisy, trendy hot spot on the Avenue. In the summer, the windows are out and crowds of young adults overflow onto the sidewalk. This is one of those restaurants where people gather to be seen, occasionally heard and the food is incidental to the fun. The see-through bathroom can be a surprise until you lock the door and the window fogs. When ordering, try the Salade Bleu, the steak frites or salmon.

Hours: Sunday Brunch, 11:30 am - 3:30 pm: Lunch, weekdays, 11:30 am - 2:30 pm: Dinner, Monday - Sunday 5:30 pm - 11:30 pm (Friday & Saturday until midnight). Reservations accepted for parties of 6 or more.

Main course price range: Lunch, $8 - $21; Dinner, $19 - $32.

Boston Market

1345 East Putnam Avenue, Old Greenwich, 637.4088

www.BostonMarket.com

Home-style cooking in a fast food setting.

Hours: Open everyday, 11 am - 9 pm.

Boxcar Cantina

44 Old Field Point Road, 661.4774

Popular, informal, and child-friendly, this restaurant is an incredible hit in town. It is conceived as a homage to all of the Route 66 Cantinas of the Southwest, serving a mix of high quality, ultra-fresh Mexican and Southwestern food. We are hooked on their posole soup, Mexican pizza and salmon burritos. Choose from an original menu of home-made margaritas.

Hours: Lunch, weekdays, 11 am - 3 pm; Dinner, Monday -Thursday, 5:30 pm - 9 pm; Friday & Saturday, 5 pm - 10:30 pm; Sunday, 5 pm - 9 pm. Reservations are accepted only for large parties. On Friday and Saturday nights, be sure to arrive early.

Main course price range: Lunch, $8 - $12; Dinner, $12 - $18.

DINING OUT

Boxing Cat Grill

1392 East Putnam Avenue, Old Greenwich, 698.1995

Its creative American food has kept this restaurant popular for over ten years. The varied menu makes this a perfect choice when you have guests with unpredictable tastes. It is an evening hot spot with live music Thursday and Friday nights.

Hours: Sunday, Brunch, 11:30 am - 3 pm;

Lunch, weekdays, 11:30 am - 3 pm;

Dinner, Monday - Saturday, 5:30 pm - 10 pm, Sunday, 5 pm - 9 pm.

Main course price range: $10 - $29.

Brewhouse (New England Brewing)

13 Marshall street, South Norwalk, CT , 203.853.9110

When you feel like a casual evening in a friendly, informal restaurant, this is the place. In some ways reminiscent of an upscale German beer hall, this large, comfortable restaurant attracts the young at heart. There is a nice selection of German foods on the menu, and of course, a large selection of beers. Try the beer burger or wiener schnitzel. The seafood chowder is a real winner as is the apple strudel. Be sure to order the strudel in advance, it takes 20 minutes to prepare.

Hours: Lunch, Monday - Sunday, 11:30 am - 5 pm: Dinner, Monday - Thursday, 5 pm - 10 pm; Friday & Saturday, 5 pm - 11 pm; Sunday, 4 pm - 10 pm.

Main course price range: Lunch, $8 - $13; Dinner, $10 - $20.

Directions: I-95 N to exit 14, go straight on Reed, R on West (which becomes N Main), L on Marshall.

Bruckner's

1 Grigg Street, 422.6300

www.bruckners.com

Just off the Avenue, this friendly, small restaurant has quick service and tasty, healthy wraps and soups. It is the "in" place for a good take-out lunch. A few tables are also available. The owner-chef Richard Fertig, has an impressive ability to spice his food just right. They have excellent vegetarian food as well as smoothie power drinks.

Hours: weekdays, 7 am - 4:30 pm; Saturday, 8 am - 4 pm.

Main course price range: $6 - $8.

DINING OUT

Café Rue

95 Railroad Avenue, 629.1056

The fare in this charming little restaurant resembles food from a Buenos Aires bistro. It is a convenient place for a light meal before or after a movie. If you call in advance, they will even buy theater tickets for you. When in doubt, try their lomito sandwich, lobster ravioli or spinach crepe.

Hours: Lunch, every day, 11 am - 5 pm; Dinner everyday, 5 pm 10 pm. Open Christmas and New Year's. Only closed on Thanksgiving.

Main course price range: Lunch, $5 - $15, Dinner $12 - $20.

Capriccio

189 Bedford Street, Stamford, 356.9819

Gelato to die for, tucked inside a small pizza Café. Our favorite is the hazelnut.

Hours: Monday-Saturday, 11 am - 11 pm, (Saturday until Midnight), Sunday, 11 am - 10 pm. Directions: I-95 N to exit 8, L on Atlantic, continue on Atlantic which become Bedford as it crosses Main.

Carvel

604 North Main Street, Port Chester, NY, 914.939.1487

Located just on the border of Greenwich and Port Chester on US 1, this standby is open seven days a week. If you like hot fudge sundaes the way we do, Wednesday is your day. You can get two for the price of one.

Hours: Sunday - Thursday, 10 am - 10 pm;
Friday & Saturday, 10 am - 11 pm.

RESTAURANTS

DINING OUT

Centro Ristorante

328 Pemberwick Road, Glenville, 531.5514

www.menusite.com/centro.html

Relaxed atmosphere —just right when you hunger for homemade pastas and a good glass of wine from their extensive list. Try the outdoor patio overlooking the waterfall and order one of their raviolis. Some of our friends go just for the desserts. Child friendly with crayons.

Hours: Lunch, Monday - Saturday, 11:30 am - 3 pm;

pizzas & light fare, Monday - Saturday, 3 pm - 5:30 pm;

Dinner, Monday - Thursday, 5:30 pm - 10 pm, Friday & Saturday, 5:30 pm - 11 pm, Sunday 5 pm - 9:30 pm.

Main course price range: Lunch, $8 - $14, Dinner, $8 - $17.

(Le) Chateau

Junction of Routes 35 and 123, Salem, NY, 914.533.6631

www.LeChateauNY.com

About thirty minutes from Greenwich, on the grounds of the 1907 J.P. Morgan estate. It is a spacious, romantic and rather elaborate background for a large party or just a night out with friends. The food is classic French. Their new chef, Andre Molle, started in April 2002. Be sure to order the rack of lamb and chocolate souffle. Make a reservation in advance.

Hours: Sunday Brunch, 11:30 - 3 pm; Dinner, Tuesday - Saturday, 6 pm - 9 pm, Sunday, 3 pm - 9 pm. Closed Monday.

Main course price range: $20 - $35.

Directions: Merritt Parkway N to exit 38, 123 N, R on Rte 35.

Chola

107-109 Greenwich Avenue, 869.0700

www.FineIndianDining.com

This restaurant, hidden away upstairs next to the back of CVS, has good food and a staff eager to please. There are entrees from many Indian regions, including a large selection of vegetarian dishes. We particularly liked the Baingan Bhartha and Aloo Gobi Palak.

Hours: Lunch, every day, noon - 2:30 pm;

Dinner, every day, 5 pm - 10 pm (Friday & Saturday, until 11 pm).

Main course price range: Lunch boxes to go, $7 - $9,

main courses $8 - $10; Dinner, $12 - $20.

RESTAURANTS

DINING OUT

City Limits

135 Harvard Avenue, Stamford, CT 348.7000

A very large, upscale diner with upscale pricing. The food and service are uneven, however if you are looking for a good early morning breakfast (orange-lemon waffle at $7.95) or a late night meal give them a try. They had just opened when this review went to press.

Hours: Monday - Thursday, 7 am - 12 am; Friday & Saturday, 7 am - 1 am; Sunday, 7 am - 11 pm. Lunch menu from 11 am - 4 pm.

Dinner price range: Entrees from $13 - $26; wraps, sandwiches and burgers, $7 - $12.

Directions: I-95 N to exit 6, R on Harvard.

Coffee Tree

22 Railroad Avenue, 861.7800

This is where commuters get their morning caffeine. Indulge in a treat along with your gourmet coffee.

Hours: weekdays, 6 am - 6 pm (Friday, until 7 pm); Saturday, 7 am - 7 pm; Sunday, 8 am - 4 pm.

Cobble Creek Café

586 Anderson Hill Road, Purchase, NY, 914.761.0050

A charming, romantic setting with excellent contemporary American food and a very good wine list. Try the sauteed foie gras, sweet potato ravioli, striped bass or tuna. Indulge in profiteroles for dessert. This out-of-the-way restaurant is high on our list!

Hours: Lunch, weekdays, 11:30 am - 3 pm; Dinner, Sunday - Thursday, 5:30 pm - 9 pm, Friday & Saturday, 5:30 pm - 11 pm. Open most major holidays. Reservations are recommended.

Main course price range: Lunch, $8 - $17; Dinner, $14 - $25.

Directions: King Street to Anderson Hill Road, on the left, just past SUNY Purchase.

RESTAURANTS

DINING OUT

Cobble Stone

Anderson Hill Road, Purchase, NY, 914.253.9678

Open since 1933, this informal, pub-style restaurant welcomes people of all ages. There is always a children's menu. Try the onion soup, Maryland crab cakes, chili & beans, or one of their many hamburgers. For dessert, have their Oreo cookie madness.

Hours: Sunday brunch, 11:30 am - 3 pm; Lunch, every day, 11:30 am - 5 pm; Dinner, every day, 5 pm - 10 pm. Late-night drinks and light meals, 10 am - midnight.

Main course price range: Brunch, $4 - $11; Lunch, $4 - $11; Dinner, $5 - $17; Late night, $4 - $12.

Directions: King Street to Anderson Hill Road, just past SUNY Purchase on the left.

Collyer Café

49 Brown House Road (in the SportsPlex), Stamford, CT, 353-4315

A casual, child friendly spot to have a tasty wrap, sandwich or omelet made by Collyer Catering. The food they provide for children's parties pleases mothers and children alike.

Hours: Monday - Saturday, 8 am - 6 pm, longer hours from September through June.

Prices: $4 - $12.

Cos Cob Grill

203 East Putnam Avenue (Mill Pond Shopping Center), Cos Cob, 629.9029

One of our favorite chefs is in this kitchen, making an eclectic mix of mouth-watering dishes. Start out by trying their BBQ pulled pork sandwich and fries. This is a very child friendly place, with crayons on the table and a kid's menu.

Hours: Lunch every day, 11:30 am - 3 pm; Dinner, Sunday & Monday, 5 pm - 9 pm, Tuesday & Wednesday, 5 pm - 9:30 pm; Thursday, Friday & Saturday, 5 pm - 10 pm.

Main course prices: Lunch, $7 - $16; Dinner, $8 - $27.

RESTAURANTS

DINING OUT

Crabshell

46 Southfield Avenue, Stamford, CT, 967.7229

www.CrabShell.com

At Stamford Landing, near Dolphin Cove. A seafood restaurant that is primarily a meeting ground for 30 - 50 year-olds. During the summer the restaurant expands onto a huge outdoor deck which can accommodate over 200.

Hours: Open every day; Summer hours: Lunch, 11 am - 3 pm; Dinner, 5 pm - 11 pm; Bar open to 1:30 am or later. The kitchen often stays open until they run out of food.

Directions: I-95 N to exit 7, R on Southfield.

(La) Cremaillere

46 Bedford/Banksville Road, Banksville, NY, 914.234.9647

www.cremaillere.com

Fine wines with traditional French food in a dressy, romantic setting with formal service. Jackets and ties are recommended. Open since 1947, there is a lot of tradition here. Many Greenwich couples have become engaged in this restaurant. They are known for their extensive wine list as well as their home made sorbets and ice cream.

Hours: Lunch, Thursday - Saturday, noon - 2:30 pm ; Dinner, Tuesday -Saturday, 6 pm - 9:30 pm; Sunday, 1 pm - 8 pm.

Main course price range: Lunch is prix-fixed at $33; Dinner, $20 - $36.

Directions: Four miles N of the Merritt on North Street.

Da Vinci's

235 Greenwich Avenue, 661.5831

There have been lots of changes on the Avenue, but Lisa Vitiello's landmark Italian is one you can count on. Always popular for its gourmet pizzas and its regional Italian dishes, it is a favorite for ladies' luncheons. Once a month diners are treated to a special evening of opera.

Hours: Tuesday - Friday, 11:30 am - 9:30 (Friday until 10:30 pm); Saturday, 1 pm - 10:30 pm; Sunday, 1 pm - 9:30 pm.

Main course price range: Lunch, $8 - $19; Dinner, $8 - $28.

RESTAURANTS

DINING OUT

Dawat

230 East Post Road, White Plains, NY, 914.428.4411

This is the sister to the famed Manhattan top-rated Indian restaurant. Order the assorted appetizers to begin and follow it with the gosht chennai as your entree. Don't forget to order sweet lassi to drink.

Hours: Lunch, noon - 2:45 pm every day; Dinner, Monday - Thursday, 5:30 pm - 10:15 pm; Friday & Saturday, 5:30 pm - 10:45 pm; Sunday, 5 pm - 9:45 pm.

Main course price range: Lunch, $10; Dinner, $8 - $22.

Directions: 287 West, exit 6, left at first light; left onto 22 South, 1 mile (sign for South Broadway and E. Post Road), bear right onto E. Post Road.

Dome

253 Greenwich Avenue, 661.3443

www.DomeRestaurant.com

Always lively, often crowded, Dome's menu is contemporary American eclectic and inviting. We have a good time here and leave with spirits heightened. The restaurant—with its high, vaulted ceiling—was originally built for a bank. The atmosphere is relaxed, and somewhat noisy, but quieter seating is available upstairs. It is a weekend evening hot spot. Try the shrimp á la plancha or chicken scarpiello.

Hours: Lunch, every day, 11:30 am - 3:30 pm (brunch is served on Saturday & Sunday); Light Lunch is served daily from 3:30 pm - 5:30 pm; Dinner, Monday - Thursday, 5:30 pm - 10 pm, Friday & Saturday, 5:30 pm - 11 pm. Make reservations in advance.

Main course price range: Brunch, $7 - $13; Lunch, $7 - $17; Dinner, $10 - $24.

Dunkin' Donuts

375 East Putnam

271 West Putnam Avenue

We are addicted to their coffee.

Hours: Open every day, 5:30 am - 10 pm.

RESTAURANTS

DINING OUT

Elm Street Oyster House

11 West Elm Street, 629.5795

www.ElmStreetOysterHouse.com

Their raw bar and chowders are hard to beat. Our friends agree it is the best seafood in Greenwich and we have yet to be disappointed. You will like the creative recipes and yummy desserts. Try their seared tuna and oriental vegetable salad. The pan-fried oysters are top-rate for an appetizer. A great place to meet after work and to stay for dinner.

Hours: Monday - Thursday, 11:30 am - 10 pm; Friday & Saturday, 11:30 am - 11 pm; Sunday, 5 pm - 9 pm. No reservations, so for dinner arrive before 7 pm or after 9 pm for your best chance to get quick seating.

Main course price range: $20 - $30.

Equus

The Castle at Tarrytown

400 Benedict Avenue, Tarrytown, NY 914.631.1980

www.CastleAtTarrytown.com

The continental food at this elegant restaurant with its romantic European castle ambiance is sure to please the most discriminating tastes. The perfect place to propose or have a great weekend in one of the Relais' 31 rooms.

Hours: Open 7-days a week and most holidays, Lunch, noon - 1:30 pm, Dinner, 6 pm - 9pm. Be sure to reserve in advance.

Price: Dinner is price fixed at $59 each for a three course meal.

Directions: I-287 West to Exit 1 (Tarrytown). R off the access road on 119 West. At first light, right on Benedict. The Castle is on the left at the 2nd light across from the Hackley school. About 25 minutes from Greenwich.

TIP: TOUR GREENWICH KITCHENS

For the last three years in June, the Old Greenwich-Riverside Community Center (OGRCC), has been organizing a tour of the ultimate kitchens in Old Greenwich and Riverside. The tour is $60 per person. Luncheon in a private home can be ticketed separately. For more information contact the OGRCC office at 637-3659.

RESTAURANTS

DINING OUT

Famous Pizza & Souvlaki Restaurant
10 North Water Street, Byram, 531.6887

A friendly, owner-run restaurant. Delicious Greek sandwiches and thin-crust pizza are the hallmark of this Byram restaurant. Don't miss the gyro sandwich, chicken souvlaki or the baklava. A perfect lunch or late-night snack for the casual diner.

Hours: Open every day: Breakfast, weekdays, 9 am - noon, Saturday & Sunday, 7 am - noon; Lunch, noon - 3 pm; Dinner, 5 pm - 10 pm.

Main course price range: Breakfast, $4 - $6; Lunch $7 - $10; Dinner, $10 - $14.

(Le) Figaro
327 Greenwich Avenue, 622.0018

Le Figaro calls itself a Paris bistro and nothing could be more descriptive. From the moment you enter you feel like you are in France, albeit in a rather elegant bistro. The service is very friendly and at the pace you would expect in France. We particularly enjoy the Mediterranean salad with sesame tuna or their grilled salmon. Be sure to try the warm dark chocolate cake.

Hours: Sunday Brunch, 11 am - 3 pm; Lunch, Monday - Saturday, noon - 2:30 pm; Dinner, Monday - Sunday, 5:30 pm - 9:30 pm; (Friday & Saturday until 10:30 pm).

Main course price range: Lunch, $ 9 - $17; Dinner, $17 - $28.

Fonda La Paloma
531 Post Road, Cos Cob, 661.9395

For years this has been our town's traditional Mexican (not "Tex-Mex") restaurant, complete with strolling mariachi band on Friday and Saturday evenings. They are well known for their Mole Poblano and Mole Verde. We are not sure why, but it still has a loyal following despite its dated decor and indifferent service.

Hours: Lunch, weekdays, 11:30 am - 3 pm; Dinner, Monday -Thursday, 5 pm - 10 pm; Friday, 5 pm - 11 pm; Sunday, 4:30 pm - 9 pm. Be sure to verify the hours.

Main course price range: Lunch, $5 - $13; Dinner, $11 - $23.

RESTAURANTS

DINING OUT

(La) Fontanella

844 High Ridge Road, Stamford, 322.3003

Good friends with good taste invited us to join them at this excellent Italian restaurant. We agree that the attentive service and classic food make it well worth the trip. The exterior, a shopping center store front, belies the refined interior.

Hours: Lunch, weekdays, 11:30 am - 2:30 pm; Dinner, Monday - Saturday, 5 pm - 10 pm (Friday & Saturday until 11 pm).

Main course prices: Lunch, $12 - $16, Dinner, $16 - $26.

Directions: Merritt Parkway N to exit 35, R on High Ridge. Restaurant is on the R in a shopping center.

Garden Caterers

235 East Putnam Avenue, Cos Cob, 861.0099

185 ½ Sound Beach Avenue, Old Greenwich, 698.2900

177 Hamilton Avenue, Byram, 422.2555

If you like fried chicken, don't miss this take-out.

Hours: Old Greenwich, weekdays, 6 am - 6:30 pm;
Saturday, 6 am - 4:30 pm.
Cos Cob: weekdays, 4 am - 8 pm; Saturday, 6 am - 8 pm;
Sunday, 7 am - 6 pm
Byram: weekdays, 6 am - 6:30 pm; Saturday, 7 am - 7 pm;
Sunday, 7 am - 3pm.

Garelick & Herbs

48 West Putnam Avenue, 661.7373

A sophisticated deli with a second location in Westport. It has a wide selection of first-rate ready-to-serve dishes. They also have special take-out menus for major holidays. Primarily a take-out store, although there are places to sit for the lucky few who get there first.

Hours: weekdays, 7 am - 8 pm; Saturday, 8 am - 7 pm;
Sunday, 9 am - 5 pm.

RESTAURANTS

DINING OUT

Gates

10 Forest Street, New Canaan, CT, 203.966.8666
http://www.menusite.com/gates.html
An informal standby for almost 20 years. On a back street, this large, gaily decorated, cheerful restaurant, is a popular place to have lunch if you are shopping in New Canaan. Service is good humored and youthful. The menu is strong on burgers, salads and wraps as well as some more sophisticated entrees. Live music on Friday and Saturday nights. Main course prices: Lunch, $6 - $11; Dinner, $7 - $20.
Hours: Lunch, every day 11:30 am - 3:30 pm;
Dinner, Monday - Thursday, 5:30 pm - 10 pm;
Friday & Saturday, - 11 pm; Sunday, 4:30 pm - 9:30 pm.
Directions: Merritt Parkway N to exit 36, L on CT -106 (which become Main Street), R on East , L on Forest.

Giorgio's

64 Merritt Street, Port Chester, NY 914.937.4906 or 1096
Good service and good Italian food in a romantic, rather out-of-the way location. It is the favorite restaurant of one of our friends. Quiet enough that you can actually have a conversation. Small enough that you should be sure to make a reservation.
Hours: Lunch, weekdays, noon - 3 pm;
Dinner, every day, 5 pm - 10 pm (Friday & Saturday to 11 pm).
Main course prices: Lunch, $15 - $20; Dinner, $18 - $28.
Directions: Post Road to Main Street in Port Chester, R on Westchester Avenue, L on South Regent Street, R on Ellendale (just past Piero's restaurant).

TIP: CHOWDER COOKOFF
Want to find the best bowl of New England clam chowder? Every year, in early June, chefs in Norwalk, CT compete in the annual "Splash! Clam Chowder Cook-Off". Check their website (http://norwalk.ws/splashfestival/chowder1.htm)for the annual winner and their recipe. Better yet, for a $5 donation you can attend the festival, taste the soups and place a vote for the best. Call 203.838.9444 for details.

DINING OUT

Glory Days Diner

Previously know as the Colonial Diner, a.k.a. Greenwich Diner

69 East Putnam Avenue, 661.9067

A welcoming landmark diner that has been open since 1923. It was completely rebuilt in 2002 with a sleek new look. Nick, the friendly owner, has operated the restaurant for 15 years. He keeps prices low and serves hearty portions. This is what a diner is supposed to be. Everyone has their favorites here; we particularly like their Greek salad and Baklava. It is a popular late-night meeting place for students.

Hours: Open 24 hours a day, every day, even holidays. They will deliver. No reservations.

Main course price range: Breakfast, $2 - $5; Lunch, $4 - $7; Dinner, $8 - $15.

Green Symphony

427 Boston Post Road (Kohl Shopping Center), Port Chester, NY, 914.937.6537

Vegetarian food based on Buddhist culinary tradition. Even if you are not a committed vegetarian, this is a fun place to dine. You will be amazed at the attractive presentations and favorable dishes. Be sure to order their Orange Sensation and a Kiwi drink.

Hours: Sunday - Thursday, 11:30 am - 10 pm; Friday & Saturday, 11:30 am - 11 pm.

Main Course Prices: $11 - $15

Directions: Follow US 1 through the main part of Port Chester, restaurant is in the shopping center to the left of Kohl's department store.

DINING OUT

Ground Zero
79 Washington Street, Norwalk, CT, 203.853.9376
An inviting, laid back coffee and pastry café in the heart of historic South Norwalk. They also have great wraps. They display the works of the artist of the month, hold chess tournaments and poetry readings.
Hours: Breakfast, weekdays, 7 am - 10 am;
Lunch, Monday - Sunday, 11 am - 4 pm;
Dinner, Thursday, Friday & Saturday, until midnight or 2 am, depending upon the time of the year.
Directions: I-95 N to exit 14, West Avenue to North Main, L at railroad trestle onto Washington.

Häagen-Dazs
374 Greenwich Avenue, 629.8000
It's a toss-up between a hot fudge sundae or a chocolate-laced cone filled with creamy dulce de leche.
Hours: Every day, 11 am - 10 pm.

Habana
70 North Main Street, South Norwalk, CT, 203.852.9790
Enjoy the tropical atmosphere and music, while dining on excellent contemporary Cuban cuisine. Be sure to try the spring rolls, tuna citrones or plantain-coated sea bass. Don't forget to have some red sangria or Chilean merlot to go with your meal.
Hours: Dinner, every night, 5 pm - 10 pm (Friday & Saturday until 11 pm). Reservations are a good idea.
Main course price range: $19 - $24.
Directions: I-95 North, Exit 14, R at stop sign, L at 2nd traffic light into SoNo Plaza.

Hayday
1050 East Putnam Avenue, Riverside, 637.7600
A sophisticated gourmet deli and country shop for fruits, vegetables and treats. Hayday carries hundreds of imported and American cheeses. A good place to order your holiday pies. Don't go in hungry.
Hours: Monday - Saturday, 8 am - 8 pm; Sunday, 8 am - 7 pm.

RESTAURANTS

DINING OUT

Horseneck Tavern

338 West Putnam Avenue, 661.8448

The motto of this restaurant is "good food and good times!" Step inside this attractive, old-fashioned restaurant and bar and you will know why residents have been going there for generations. This is the place to have a superb burger, served by a friendly staff.

Hours: Monday - Thursday, 11 am - 10 pm; Friday & Saturday, 11 am - 11 pm; Sunday, 11 am - 9 pm.

Main course price range: $6 - $14

Hostaria Mazzei

25 South Regent Street, Port Chester, NY 914.939.2727

This is a large, attractive restaurant with friendly service and authentic southern Italian cuisine. They specialize in seasonal fish entrees.

Hours: Lunch, weekdays, noon - 2:30; Dinner, 7 days a week, 5 pm - 11 pm (Sunday, 4 pm - 9 pm).

Main course prices: Lunch, $6 - $17, Dinner, $7- $29. Specials may be more.

Directions: Follow Post Road to Main street in Port Chester. At 3rd light, R on Westchester, at 4th light, L on South Regent.

Hubba-Hubba

189 Bedford Street, Stamford, CT, 359.1718

This is fast food as served in the 1950's. If you have lived in Greenwich a long time, you will remember their hot chili. No longer in Greenwich, they are now in Stamford. If you are shopping or going to the movies in Stamford and you want a quick snack, this is the place. Try their burgers, steak wedge with hot chili or chili cheese fries. After your wedge, stop in next door at Capricio. The have the most wonderful gelato.

Hours: Sunday - Thursday, 10 am - 1 am;

Friday & Saturday, 10 am - 3 am.

Prices: $2 - $6.

RESTAURANTS

DINING OUT

Hunan Café

1233 East Putnam Avenue, Old Greenwich, 637.4341
Well prepared, authentic Chinese cuisine. On Sundays, they have a habit-forming Dim Sum brunch, which we highly recommend.
Hours: weekdays, 11:30 am - 9:30, Weekends until 10 pm.
Main course price range: Lunch, $5 - $7; Dinner, $8 - $18.

Hunan Gourmet

68 East Putnam Avenue, 869.1940
A Chinese restaurant with white tablecloths and an elegant flair. Count on good food served without much spice. The staff is especially nice to children, making it a popular family place. Free delivery with a minimum purchase of $20.
Hours: weekdays, 11:30 am - 9:45 pm; Saturday, noon - 10:45 pm; Sunday, noon - 9:45 pm. (Lunch is served every day until 3 pm.)
Main course price range: Lunch, $7 - $8; Dinner, $8 - $28.

I-Hop (a.k.a. International House of Pancakes)

2410 Summer Street, Stamford, CT 324.9819
www.IHop.com
As you probably know, this is the place for chocolate pancakes.
Hours: Open every day from 7 am - 10 pm.
Directions: Merritt Parkway N to exit 34, R on Long Ridge which becomes Summer.

Inn at Pound Ridge

258 Westchester Avenue/Route 137, Pound Ridge, NY, 914.764.5779
This historic inn, with its lovely, quiet, country setting, serves elegant, international food. It is perfect for Sunday brunch or celebrations. Although the inn does not have rooms for overnight guests, it has a private dressing/bath suite for brides, hosts and hostesses.
Hours: Closed Monday; Sunday brunch, noon - 2:30 pm; Lunch, Tuesday - Saturday, noon - 2:30 pm; Dinner, Tuesday - Saturday, 6 pm - 9 pm, Sunday, 5 pm - 8:30 pm.
Main course price range: Lunch, $8 - $24; Dinner, $18 - $30; Saturday price fixed at $47.
Directions: Merritt Parkway N to exit 35, L on Rte. 137 N (High Ridge), N for 7.5 miles past Rte. 172 on the left.

RESTAURANTS

DINING OUT

Jean-Louis

61 Lewis Street, 622.8450

www.RestaurantJeanLouis.com

Still our very favorite place, this intimate and refined French restaurant has service intended to make you feel special and comfortable. One of the best in Connecticut. You will be delighted with Jean Louis Gerin's new French cuisine. The menu degustation is always a great choice.

Hours: Lunch, weekdays, noon - 2 pm; Dinner, Monday - Saturday, seating starts at 5:45 pm.

No lunch in June, July & August. Be sure to make reservations.

Prices: Lunch a la Parisienne, $30; Dinner, Menu Degustation, $69.

Jimmy's Grill

101 Field Point Road, Parking Lot of Greenwich Town Hall

An outdoor stand (mobile van). They have yummy chili dogs, chicken souvlaki and Philly cheese steaks, all for very reasonable prices. When you are in a hurry for lunch, it's a great place to go. They even serve breakfast for people on-the-go.

Hours: weekdays, 8 am - 2 pm, though these hours seem flexible.

Kagetsu

28 West Putnam Avenue, 622.9264

A favorite of many Japanese residents, we think they make the best sushi in town. We are hooked on their Futomaki. The atmosphere is slightly dated; we often go there because its quiet enough for a conversation.

Hours: Closed Monday. Lunch, Tuesday, Wednesday, Friday & Saturday, noon - 2:30 pm; Dinner, Tuesday - Thursday, 5 pm - 9:30 pm; Friday & Saturday, 5 pm - 10 pm; Sunday, 5 pm - 9:30 pm.

Main course price range: $11 - $22.

Katzenberg's Express

342 Greenwich Avenue, 625.0103

A New York style deli with a wide selection of sandwiches. Primarily take-out, but there are a few places to sit. Not only is this a kid-friendly place, it's baby-friendly too. Ask for the Katzy's Babies Menu; it features applesauce and mashed potatoes.

Hours: Monday - Sunday, 8 am - 5 pm (closed on Sunday during the Winter).

Katzenberg's Gourmet Deli
33 Lewis Street, 629.8889
A full service New York-style gourmet deli restaurant and bakery. They have a large menu and seating for 100. I love their stuffed cabbage and pastrami sandwiches. If you decide to take out, be sure to choose some of their delicious homemade bakery treats.
Hours: Monday - Saturday, 8 am - 4 pm; Sunday, 9 am - 3 pm.
Main course price range: $5 - $15.

Kazu
64 North Main Street, South Norwalk, CT, 203.866.7492
Very near the Norwalk movies. Order the movie box, it has a tasty sampling of their Japanese specialties. You will also find their sushi or teriyaki good choices.
Hours: Lunch, Monday-Friday, noon - 2 pm; Dinner, weekdays, 5:30 pm - 10:30 pm; Friday & Saturday, 5:30 pm - 11 pm; Sunday, 5 pm - 10 pm.
Main course price range: Lunch, $12 - $16; Dinner, $15 - $28.
Directions: I-95 North, Exit 14, R at stop sign, L at 2nd traffic light into Sono Plaza.

(The) Kneaded Bread
181 North Main Street, Port Chester, NY, 914.937.9489
A first rate bread bakery. Every day they bake over 17 varieties of crusty, European style breads. They also have croissants, danish, and sandwiches. There are a few seats, so stop in for a good coffee and sandwich. Be sure to order holiday breads in advance. They only accept cash or local checks.
Hours: Tuesday - Friday, 7 am - 5 pm; Saturday, 8 am - 4 pm; Sunday, 8 am - 1 pm.

Landmark Diner
31 East Putnam Avenue, Cos Cob, 869.0954
Lucky Greenwich to have two good diners. Landmark—formerly the Country Squire, then Cassi's, now has the same owners as Glory Days. It serves a wide variety of hearty breakfast and dinner dishes and has the great prices, large servings and friendly service you expect.
Hours: Open everyday, 6 am - 11 pm. No reservations.
Main course price range: Breakfast, $3 - $8; Lunch & Dinner, $3 - $16.

DINING OUT

Longford's Ice Cream

4 Elm Place, Rye, NY, 914. 967.3797

Longford's ice cream factory is on Wilkins Street in Port Chester. Many clubs and quality restaurants in and around Greenwich are supplied by Longford's. Fortunately, Longford has one ice cream parlor just a short distance away in downtown Rye. Fill your freezer with ice cream, ice cream pies and sorbets. We haven't tasted a flavor we didn't like.

Hours: Every day, noon - 9:30 pm (Friday & Saturday until 10 pm)

Directions: US-1 South (Boston Post Road West) through Port Chester. Just past the intersections of I-287 and I-95, R on Purdy, L on Purchase, L on Locust, R on Theodore Fremd, R on Elm.

MacKenzie's Grill Room

148 Sound Beach Avenue, Old Greenwich, 698.0223

One of the few places that serves food all day. Casual, friendly restaurant and bar. The perfect place to watch a game. Sit at a bar table and try the nachos, skins or wings. For a meal, try their filet au poivre and Mac's mud pie. On weekends, MacKenzie's is a "hot spot" and tends to get crowded and noisy.

Hours: Open every day, Sunday - Thursday, 11:30 am - midnight (Friday & Saturday, until 1 am).

Main course price range: $8.95 - $20.95. Reservations accepted for 6 or more.

McDonald's

268 West Putnam Avenue, Greenwich, 629.9068;

Hours, open every day, 6 am - 11 pm (Friday & Saturday until 12 pm).

1207 East Putnam Avenue, Riverside, 637.8598;

Hours: Open every day, 6 am - 12 pm.

RESTAURANTS

DINING OUT

Manero's

559 Steamboat Road, 869.0049

www.maneros-greenwichct.com

A Greenwich institution, known for their kindness to children. The restaurant seats 600 and the decor is hopelessly hokey. The waiters sing "Happy Birthday" with gusto. To grow up never having Manero's steak, gorgonzola salad and garlic bread would be too sad. When you are looking for a quick snack, their first rate butcher shop makes wonderful steak sandwiches to go.

Hours: Monday - Thursday, noon - 9:30 pm; Friday, noon - 10 pm; Saturday, noon - 10:30 pm; Sunday, noon - 9 pm. It's best to call for reservations, especially in the evening.

Main course price range: Lunch, $7 - $11; Dinner, $13 - $34.

Match

98 Washington Street, South Norwalk, CT 203.852.1088

Match has a refined atmosphere with helpful, efficient service. Its reputation was built on its top-notch pizzas cooked in a wood-burning oven. However, this is much more than a trendy pizza restaurant now that Chef Matthew Storch has arrived and is creating flavorful entrees. We especially like the orange-glazed swordfish. Our favorite pizza is the "forest" made with spinach and goat cheese.

Hours: Open every day for dinner, Sunday - Thursday, 5 pm - 10 pm; Friday & Saturday, 5 pm - 11 pm.

Price Range: Dinner, pizzas $10 - 15, entrees $17 - 27.

Directions: I-95 N, exit 14, R on West Avenue, left at fork onto Main Street, L onto Washington.

Maya of Japan

4 Lewis Court, 869.4322

Traditional Japanese steak house. Sit around cooktop tables and watch the chef perform. For years this has been a favorite of ours. They also have a good sushi bar.

Hours: Lunch, Tuesday - Friday, noon - 2 pm;

Dinner, Tuesday - Thursday, 5 pm - 9:30 pm,

Friday & Saturday, 5 pm - 10:30 pm; Sunday, 5 pm - 9:30 pm;

Main course price range: Lunch, $13 - $16; Dinner, $17 - $20.

RESTAURANTS

DINING OUT

Mecca

44 Main street, Norwalk, CT 203.831.8636

A spin-off from the popular Meson Galicia, this small, authentic Spanish restaurant will delight you. Located on a drab street in Norwalk, the atmosphere is cozy and bright. There is nothing on their compact menu we did not like. First-timers should try the Paella Valenciana and Arroz a la Vasca.

Hours: Lunch, Tuesday - Friday, 11:30 am - 3 pm;
Dinner, Tuesday - Sunday, 5:30 pm - 10 pm.
Main course prices: Lunch, $8 - $15; Dinner, $15 - $22.
Directions: I-95 N to exit 16, L on East, L on East Wall, R on Main.

Mediterraneo Restaurant

366 Greenwich Avenue, 629.4747

Atmosphere and good Mediterranean food. This is still a happening scene. The terrace provides an interesting perspective on life along Greenwich Avenue and also allows you to have a conversation. We like their pasta dishes, wood-roasted mahi-mahi and nice wine selection. The same group owns another good Greenwich restaurant, Terra Ristorante Italiano.

Hours: Closed Sunday. Lunch, Monday - Saturday, noon - 2:30 pm (Saturday until 3 pm); Dinner, Monday -Saturday, 5:30 pm - 10 pm; Friday & Saturday, 5:30 pm - 10 pm. Reservations are usually required.
Main course price range: $20 - $30.

Meli Melo

362 Greenwich Avenue, 629.6153

Tiny jewel of a restaurant with French casual foods such as yummy onion soup and crepes. Our favorite, however, is their croque monsieur. The fresh fruit sorbets are to die for. These are the best sorbets you will have in town. The Owner, Chef Marc Penvenne, is very gracious as well as talented. The weekend breakfast menu consists mainly of delicious omelets.

Hours: every day, 10 am - 10 pm. No reservations.
Main course price range: $5 - $11.

RESTAURANTS

DINING OUT

Meigas

10 Wall Street, Norwalk, CT, 203.866.8800

At press time the owner of the popular Meson Galecia announced a name change to Meigas, a new chef and Spanish menu. Although we have not had a chance to test the new restaurant, the chef, Luis Bollo, comes with good credentials and we look forward to trying his food.

Hours: (Check for new hours). Closed Monday and most holidays. Lunch, Tuesday - Sunday, noon - 3 pm; Dinner, Tuesday - Thursday & Sunday, 6 pm - 9:30 pm; Friday & Saturday until 10:30 pm.

Directions: I-95 N to Exit 16, Left off the exit, L on Wall, entrance on Hugh St.

Mhai Thai

280 Railroad Avenue, 625.2602

If you are hungry for Thai food, you will be delighted with this choice. The cuisine is authentic, the service gracious, and the decor is attractive. We love their green curries.

Hours: Lunch, Tuesday - Friday, noon - 2 pm; Dinner, Tuesday - Thursday, 5:30 pm - 9:30 pm, Friday & Saturday, 5:30 pm - 10:30 pm, Sunday, 5:30 pm - 9 pm.

Main course price range: Lunch, $8 - $17; Dinner, $16 - $22.

Mirage Café

531 North Main Street, Port Chester, NY, 914.937.3497

Funky decor with excellent French-Caribbean food. Their menu changes often. Try the wonderful steak au poivre or steak diable. Their lemon grass shrimp, and Southwestern tuna are also good choices.

Hours: Dinner only. Sunday - Tuesday, 6 pm - 12 pm; Wednesday & Thursday, 6 pm - 1 am; Friday & Saturday, 6 pm - 2 am. Reservations in advance are recommended, especially for weekends.

Main course price range: $17 - $24.

RESTAURANTS

DINING OUT

Moonstruck

50 Greenwich Avenue, 861.6500

www.moonstruckchocolate.com

A chocolate shop selling expensive but wonderful chocolates. They also serve first-rate coffee (they used to be the Coffee Tree). They have Häagen- Dazs ice cream as well as milkshakes. There are a few tables. It's a great place to relax before or after shopping.

Hours: Monday-Friday, 6:30 am - 6 pm; Saturday, 7 am - 7 pm; Sunday, 7:30 am - 5 pm.

Morton's of Chicago

377 North State Street (Swiss Bank Center), Stamford, CT, 324.3939

A carnivore's paradise. If the menu presentation doesn't turn you into a vegetarian, you will find the steak as good as it gets. We especially liked the tenderloin brochette with diable sauce and Godiva hot chocolate cake. A popular place for men in suits.

Hours: Dinner, Monday - Saturday, 5 pm - 11 pm; Sunday, 5 pm - 10 pm.

Main course price range: $21 - $35.

Directions: I-95 N to exit 8, immediate L on Atlantic, immediate L on State.

Ocean 211

211 Summer Street, Stamford, CT, 973.0494

www.culinarymenus.com

Their creative preparations of fresh fish have earned them acclaim as one of the best seafood restaurants in the area. Not only is the food good, but we also like the sophisticated atmosphere of this attractive townhouse in the heart of downtown Stamford.

Hours: Lunch, weekdays, noon - 2:30 pm;

Dinner, Monday - Thursday, 5:30 pm - 9:30 pm,

Friday & Saturday until 10:30 pm.

Main course Price range: Lunch, $12 - $18; Dinner, $20 - $30.

Directions: I-95 N to exit 8, L on Atlantic, L on Broad, L on Summer.

Ocean Drive

128 Washington Street, South Norwalk, 203.855.1665

A very modern restaurant for "hip" patrons (the front window comes out in nice weather) with an exciting seafood menu and a lively bar.

Hours: Lunch, Wednesday - Friday, noon - 3 pm; Dinner, Sunday - Thursday, 5 pm - 10 pm; Friday & Saturday, until 11 pm.

Prices: Dinner main courses from $17 - $26.

Directions: I-94 North to exit 14, R on Fairfield (first street), bear left at fork on to Washington.

Ole Molé

130 High Ridge Road, Stamford, CT, 461.9962

This small restaurant with its rather unimposing exterior is the best Mexican restaurant in our area. Their authentic cuisine is fresh and healthy. Be sure to try their Molé Poblano. There is very limited seating, so come early or plan to make this a take-out dinner.

Hours: Tuesday - Thursday, 11:30 am - 9:30 pm; Friday & Saturday, until 10 pm; Sunday, 4 pm - 9 pm.

Main course prices: $6 - $12.

Directions: Merritt Parkway N to exit 35, R on High Ridge (restaurant is in shopping center across from Borders Books).

Paesano's Deli

146 Mason Street, 625.0040

Open weekdays for breakfast. Fast friendly service. Limited seating.

Hours: Monday - Saturday, 7 am - 5 pm; Sunday, 8 am - 4 pm.

Pantanal

29 North Main Street, Port Chester, NY, 914.939.6894

The best Brazilian restaurant in the area. Try their speciality meat dish, Rodizio. The trick here is to not eat your weight in their delicious cheese bread (Pao de Queijo) before your meal.

Hours: Lunch, Tuesday - Friday, noon - 3 pm; Dinner, weekdays, 5 pm - 11:30 pm; Lunch/Dinner, weekends, noon - 11:30 pm.

Main course price range: Weekday specials, lunch, $9 - $11 (lunch buffet $8); Dinner, $14 - $22.

RESTAURANTS

DINING OUT

Panda Pavilion

137 West Putnam Avenue, 869.1111

We go here all the time. We always feel at home at this well-priced Chinese restaurant with friendly service. Try the delicious sesame chicken, spicy broccoli, orange beef or the house special bean curd. Free delivery for orders of $20 and over.

Hours: Monday - Thursday, 11:30 am - 10 pm;

Friday, 11:30 am - 11 pm;

Saturday, noon - 11 pm; Sunday, noon - 10 pm.

(Lunch is served until 3 pm).

Main course price range: Lunch, $6 - $10; Dinner, $10 - $28.

(La) Panetiere

530 Milton Road, Rye, NY, 914.967.8140

www.lapanetiere.com

Westchester County's best. Extremely good classic French food only fifteen minutes away. Attractive Provençale dining room. Try their roast lamb or duck.

Hours: Lunch, weekdays, noon - 2:30 pm; Dinner, Monday-Friday, 6 pm - 9:30 pm; Saturday seatings at 6 pm and 8:30 pm; Sunday (dinner menu only), 1 pm - 3 pm and 5 pm - 8:30 pm. Advanced reservations recommended, no minimum. Jackets required, ties preferred.

Main course price range: Lunch, $17 - $24 (or price fixed menu at $31); Dinner, $25 - $36 (Tasting menu at $85).

Directions: I-95 S to exit 19, R on light to Milton Rd.

TIPS: SEPTEMBERFEST

Be sure this festival, sponsored by the United Way, is marked on your calendar. You and your family will have a wonderful time. You will find rides, kids activities, food and live entertainment. Call 869-2221 for details.

RESTAURANTS

DINING OUT

Paradise Bar & Grill

78 Southfield Avenue (Stamford Landing), Stamford, CT, 323.1116

www.paradisebarandgrille.com

Located on the water at the Stamford Landing, near Dolphin Cove. Eating here is like stepping into a tropical island restaurant. In summer you can dine open-air on the boardwalk. Try the many charcoal-broiled fish entrees. The seafood pizzas are also worth trying. Children are welcome.

Hours: Sunday brunch, 11:30 am - 3 pm; Lunch, Monday, Thursday, Saturday, noon - 5 pm ; Dinner, Monday - Thursday and Sunday, 5 pm - 9 pm; Friday & Saturday, open until 10 pm.

During the winter, closed Sunday & Monday evenings and Saturday lunch. In the summer reservations are accepted for eight or more. In the winter, reservations are accepted for two or more.

Main course price range: Lunch, $11 - $20; Dinner, $12 - $28.

Major credit cards accepted.

Directions: I-95 N to exit 7, R on Greenwich Avenue, next light is intersection of Greenwich Avenue/Selleck/Southfield. Stamford Landing is .2 miles on the left.

Pasquale Ristorante

2 Putnam Avenue (border of Greenwich), Port Chester, NY, 914.924.7770

This family style restaurant serves well seasoned southern Italian Cuisine in a friendly and relaxing atmosphere.

Hours: Closed Monday; Tuesday - Thursday, noon - 10 pm;
Friday, noon - 11 pm; Saturday, 3 pm - 11 pm; Sunday, 1 pm - 9 pm.

Main course Prices: $11-$18

RESTAURANTS

DINING OUT

Pasta Nostra

116 Washington Street, Norwalk, CT, 203.854.9700

www.PastaNostra.com

This warm, lively, simple restaurant has a European feel. Its menu is original and mighty good. The swordfish with corn salsa is a standout as are the ravioli dishes. Beware of several quirks: reservations are usually necessary but owner, Chef Bruno requires a $25 credit card deposit in case you don't show or don't cancel by 3 pm. American Express cards are not accepted.

Hours: Wednesday - Saturday, 5:30 - closing.

Directions: I-94 North to exit 14, R on Fairfield (first street), bear left at fork on to Washington.

Main course prices: $20 - $37.

Pasta Vera

48 Greenwich Avenue, 661.9705

www.PastaVera.com

A casual Italian restaurant noted for its homemade pastas. It is usually quiet enough to have a good conversation. It's also a great place for a late lunch. First-time visitors should try their homemade ravioli. Unfortunately, their service can be inconsistent.

Hours: Monday - Thursday, 9:30 am - 10 pm; Friday & Saturday, until 10:30 pm; Sunday, 4 pm - 9 pm. In the winter, their Sunday hours are noon - 9 pm. Lunch is served until 3 pm. Open all holidays, with no vacation closings. Reservations are accepted for parties of six or more.

Main course price range: Lunch, $9 - $13; Dinner, $10 - $18.

Penang Grill

55 Lewis Street, 861.1988

Casual dining with Pan-Asian foods. Try the yummy spicy mango chicken.

Hours: Monday - Thursday, 11 am - 10 pm; Friday & Saturday, 11 am - 11 pm; Sunday, noon - 10 pm. Lunch menu is served until 3 pm. Table space is limited. No reservations accepted.

Main course price range: Lunch, $7 - $8; Dinner, $12 - $20.

DINING OUT

Piero's

44 South Regent Street, Port Chester, NY, 914.937.2904

Casual, off-the-beaten-path Northern Italian. The friend who introduced us to this small restaurant was concerned that putting it in our guide would make it even harder to get reservations. Once you try the house red wine and veal saltimbocca or scampi, you will understand.

Hours: Lunch, Tuesday - Friday, noon - 2:30 pm; Dinner, Tuesday - Thursday, 5 pm - 9:30 pm; Friday, 5 pm -10:30; Saturday, 2 pm - 10:30 pm; Sunday, 2 pm - 9:30 pm.

Main course price range: $13 - $21. Visa and MasterCard only.

Directions: US-1 S thru Port Chester, R on Westchester, L on South Regent.

Pizza Express

160 Hamilton Avenue, 622.1693

A friendly, small neighborhood store that takes pride in treating their customers "like family." They have free delivery and will fax you their menu. Try their homemade raviolis.

Hours: Monday - Saturday, 10 am - 10 pm; Sunday, 11 am - 10 pm.

Pizza Factory

380 Greenwich Avenue, 661.5188

Not everyone can agree on the best pizza joint, but Pizza Factory's pizza is always competing for the top of the list. Be sure to try their gorgonzola salad and four cheese pizza. They have table service and carry out.

No credit cards or delivery. They will accept a Greenwich check.

Hours: Open every day, 11:30 am - 9 pm (Friday & Saturday until 9:30 pm or later).

Pizza Glenville

243 Glenville Road, 532.1691

Glenville residents, as well as people all over town, love Glenville Pizza. It is one of the few places serving by the slice. No deliveries. No credit cards, but they will accept a check.

Hours: Closed Mondays; Tuesday - Saturday, 10:30 am - 10:30 pm; Sunday, noon - 10 pm.

RESTAURANTS

DINING OUT

Pizza Hut
19 Glenville Road, 531.4411
They may be a chain, but we still like their pan pizza.
Major credit cards accepted. No deliveries.
Hours: Sunday - Thursday, 11 am - 10 pm (Sunday from noon); Friday & Saturday, 11 am - 11 pm.

Pizza Post
522 East Putnam Avenue, 661.0909
A local favorite.
No deliveries. No credit cards, but they accept checks.
Hours: Monday - Thursday, 11 am - 10 pm; Friday & Saturday, 11 am - 11 pm; Sunday, noon - 10 pm.

Planet Pizza
28 Railroad Avenue, 622.0999
Traditional New York City-style pizzeria in a central Greenwich location next to the theater. Try their "Penne Planet." Clean, well-lighted dining area. They will deliver.
Hours: Sunday - Thursday, 10 am - 11 pm; Friday & Saturday, 10 am - 12 pm.

Polpo
554 Old Post Road # 3, Greenwich, 629.1999
This out-of-the-way Italian Restaurant is a popular Greenwich destination for those in the know. It is located in a charming 100-year old stone house. The ambiance is warm and diners always seem to be in a festive mood. The restaurant has a dress code; business casual is okay. This is a great place to have Dover sole.
Hours: Monday - Thursday, 11:45 am - 10 pm; Friday, until 11 pm, Saturday, 1 pm - 11 pm, Sunday, 3 pm - 10 pm.
Main course prices: Dinner, $19 - $36.

Porterhouse

124 Washington Street, South Norwalk, CT, 203.855.0441
www.PorterhouseRestaurant.com
A little loud and slow, but the great steaks and desserts, served in a warm, friendly, woody atmosphere, will make you a regular. They have an excellent wine list, but be sure to try their delightful fresh-brewed tea. The lamb, calamari with chili sauce, and porterhouse steaks are all delicious.
Hours: Dinner, Tuesday - Thursday, 5 pm - 10 pm; Friday & Saturday, 5 pm - 11 pm, Sunday, 4:30 pm - 9 pm. Closed Monday.
Main course price range: $18 - $36.
Directions: I-94 North to exit 14, R on Fairfield (first street), bear left at fork onto Washington.

Putnam Restaurant

373 Greenwich Avenue, 869.4683
This inexpensive and informal home-town restaurant has been in business since 1955. We hope it stays. It was recently redecorated. Their menu is like a diner's with a large number of choices. Choose one of their specials, which are often the best. Only the desserts leave us less than enthused. They are a good place for a traditional breakfast. We are glad they do not seem compelled to play music so loudly that conversations are difficult.
Hours: Open every day from 7 am - 10 pm.
Main course price range: $4 - $13.

Quattro Pazzi

245 Hope Street, Stamford, 964-1801
A wonderful pasta restaurant tucked away in the Glenbrook area of Stamford. This place hits the spot when we want to have a hearty bowl of pasta with friends. Try the fettuccini a la Mitty. This restaurant is small and popular, so expect some noise.
Hours: Lunch, Tuesday - Friday, 11:30 am - 3 pm; Dinner, Tuesday - Friday, 5 pm - 10 pm; Saturday, 5 pm - 11 pm; Sunday, 5 pm - 9 pm.
Main course price range: Lunch, $10 - $15; Dinner, $13 - $20.
Directions: I-95 N to exit 8, stay straight on South State Street, L on Canal, R on Tresser (US-1), L on Glenbrook Rd, continue straight onto Hope.

RESTAURANTS

DINING OUT

Rebeccas

265 Glenville Road, 532.9270

One of the best restaurants in town. This Manhattan-chic restaurant run by a husband and wife team is tucked in mid-country Greenwich. It serves modern American cuisine with a French flair. Rebecca Kirhoffer has assembled a sophisticated wine list to match her husband Chef Reza Khorshidi's awesome food. The restaurant has a sleek modern look, complete with a large window that allows you to see the kitchen. Although we loved the tuna with mustard, be sure to try their signature dishes: two soups in one bowl or the three ravioli appetizer followed by the lobster with lemons (completely out of the shell and easy to eat) for your main course. Other main courses to try are the grilled Dover sole with lemon sauce or the squab with pomegranate sauce.

Hours: Closed Monday. Lunch, Tuesday - Friday, lunch, 11:30 am - 2:30 pm; Dinner, Tuesday - Thursday, 5:30 pm - 9:30 pm; Friday & Saturday, 5:30 pm - 10:30 pm; Sunday 5:30 pm - 9:30 pm. Be sure to make a reservation well in advance (a month's notice wouldn't hurt), although you might be able to drop in and eat at the bar.

Main course price range: Lunch, $18 - $32, Dinner, $28 - $45.

River Cat Grill

148 Rowayton Avenue, Rowayton, CT, 203.854.0860

The sister restaurant to the popular Boxing Cat Grill. Like the Boxing Cat, there is an eclectic menu with great flavors. We liked their spicy chowder and crispy tuna. Be sure to try the ginger crusted salmon or jumbo shrimp, as well as their large selection of wines by the glass. The atmosphere is sophisticated with good service, and you can hear your dinner companions speak.

Hours: Lunch, Wednesday - Friday, 11:30 am - 5 pm; Saturday, 11:30 am - 3:30 pm; Sunday, 11:30 - 3:30; Dinner, Monday - Saturday, 5:30 pm - 10 pm (open to 11 pm on Friday & Saturday); Sunday, 4:30 pm - 9:30 pm. The bar stays open later.

Main course price range: $12 - $32. They do not accept Diner's or Discover cards.

Directions: I-95 N, exit 12, Rte 136 toward Rowayton.

RESTAURANTS

DINING OUT

Roger Sherman Inn

195 Oenoke Ridge Road (Route 124), New Canaan, CT, 203.966.4541

www.rogershermaninn.com

Built in the 1700's, it is one of the oldest and prettiest inns in Fairfield County. The Swiss owners serve continental cuisine with Swiss specialties. Try their vegetable lasagne, fricassee of lobster and scallops, pepper steak or the chef's signature chicken. Be sure to order the chocolate souffle in advance. It is superb. On Sunday evenings they serve raclette and fondue ($34 per person). The inn is well equipped for elegant parties. It can accommodate groups from 8 to 180 guests. Ask to see a copy of their typical wedding banquet menu.

Hours: Breakfast, weekdays, 7 am - 10 pm, Saturday & Sunday, 8 am - 10 pm; Lunch, Tuesday - Saturday, noon - 1:45 pm; Sunday brunch, noon - 1:45 pm (not available January - March);

Dinner, Monday - Saturday, 6 pm - 8:45 pm; Sunday, 6 pm - 7:45 pm. It's wise to make reservations in advance.

Main course price range: Dinner, prix fixe at $50 per person or á la carte. Brunch, prix fixe at $32 per person.

Directions: Merritt N exit 37, L onto Rte 124 N - 2 miles, Rte 124 makes a right at Cherry Street. Next left (light) - on Main continue on 124 for 1 mile. Inn is on the right.

Rowayton Seafood Company

89 Rowayton Avenue, Norwalk, CT, 203.866.4488

www.RowaytonSeafood.com

Small and popular, informal and relaxed, just right for summer dining. A good place to bring land-locked visitors for lobster and a view of the water. Just in case you don't want lobster, try their seafood stew, grilled tuna or fresh oysters.

Hours: Open every day. Lunch, 11:30 am - 3 pm; a limited menu is sometimes available from 3 pm - 5 pm; Dinner, 5 pm - 10 pm (Friday & Saturday until 11 pm). On weekends, be sure to make reservations well in advance.

Main course price range: Lunch, $11 - $20; Dinner, $18 - $32; Lobster by the pound.

Directions: I-95 N to exit 12, Rte 136 towards Rowayton for 1.5 miles to stop sign, 500 yards the right.

RESTAURANTS

DINING OUT

Silvermine Tavern

194 Perry Avenue, Norwalk, CT, 203.847.4558

www.SilvermineTavern.com

A 15 - 20 minute drive from Greenwich, this eighteenth century Colonial inn, situated right on the river, is a very good choice for Sunday brunch. The reasonably-priced buffet has a selection of dishes to delight every one. We especially enjoyed their french toast, yogurt with strawberry preserves and their justifiably famous buns. The atmosphere is informal and children are always welcome. The inn is very spacious, but it is also popular, so arrive early. For lunch try their seafood angel hair pasta. For dinner try their herb-crusted rack of lamb.

Hours: Lunch, Monday - Saturday (closed Tuesday), noon - 2:30 pm; Sunday Brunch, 11 am - 2:30 pm. Dinner, Monday - Saturday (closed Tuesday), 6 pm - 9 pm; Sunday, 3:30 pm - 8:30 pm; Friday & Saturday, live jazz, 9 pm - 11 pm. Reservations for brunch are given only for parties of seven or more.

Main course price range: Sunday brunch is $21 for adults, $9.95 for children ages 5-10, children under 5 are free; Lunch, $8 - $14; Dinner, $19 - $29.

Directions: Merritt Parkway N to Exit 40A, R on Main Street, R on Perry Avenue. R on Silvermine Road.

Skylight Café (by Mary & Martha's Catering)

YWCA, 259 East Putnam Avenue, 869.6501

A well-priced, bright and sunny eatery where you can enjoy a continental breakfast, a healthy lunch or just grab a freshly baked muffin. Try their chicken or tuna salad sandwich. Once a month they serve afternoons tea. Call for dates and reservations. Children are always welcome!

Hours: weekdays, 8:45 am - 4 pm (Fridays in the summer, they close at 3 pm); no credit cards.

RESTAURANTS

DINING OUT

Sky Top Restaurant

Westchester County Airport, White Plains, NY, 914.428.0251
We happened to be there just at sunset and we were delighted to find delicious continental food, pleasant service and a pretty view of our local airport.
Hours: Lunch, Monday - Saturday, 11 am - 4 pm;
Dinner, Monday - Saturday, 4 pm - 9 pm.
Reservations are accepted.
Main course price range: Lunch, $7 - $14; Dinner, $16 - $29.
Directions: King Street N to Rye Lake Road.

Smokey Joe's Bar-B-Q

1308 East Main Street (US-1), Stamford, CT, 406.0605
Formerly Buster's, it still has the best Texas Bar-B-Q this side of Fort Worth. Casual and inexpensive, Smokey Joe's offers a great variety of meats, gumbos and side dishes, in a cafeteria-style restaurant setting. The servings (on paper, not porcelain) are large, especially the Texan size. Order their beef brisket and pulled pork, with a side of collard greens and sweet potato fries.
Hours: Monday - Thursday, 11:30 am - 9:30 pm; Friday & Saturday, 11:30 am - 10:30 pm; Sunday, 11:30 am - 9:30 pm.
Main course price range: Sandwiches, $3 - $8;
 two-meat combos, $10 - $14.
Directions: I-95 N to exit 9, R on US 1.

SoNo Seaport Seafood

100 Water Street, South Norwalk, CT, 203.854.9483
A very informal spot on the water to have lobster or fish and chips. Bring your children. Nice outside deck with raw bar.
Hours: Open every day. November - April, 11 am - 9 pm; May - October, 11 am - 10 pm.
Reservations accepted for parties of six or more.
Main course price range: $6 - $17.
Directions: I-95 N, exit 14, turn right. Go straight to intersection of Washington and Water, R before the bridge. Restaurant is 100 yards on the left in SoNo Square.

RESTAURANTS

DINING OUT

Sonora

179 Rectory Street, Port Chester, NY 914.933.0200

www.SonoraRestaurant.com

On this out-of-the-way corner is a popular, lively restaurant serving "Latin-American food with a French flair." Several of chef Rafael Palomino's cookbooks are for sale in the restaurant. Try the quesadillas for starters followed by one of their many fish entrees or the peanut chicken.

Hours: Closed Monday; Lunch, Tuesday -Friday, noon - 3 pm; Dinner, Sunday-Thursday, 5 pm - 10pm, Friday & Saturday, 5 pm - 11 pm.

Directions: Post Road to Main Street in Port Chester. R on Rectory.

Splash Café Inn at Long Shore

260 South Compo Road, Westport, CT, 203.454.7798

www.DecaroRestaurantGroup.com

A Baang relative with the same delicious eclectic Pacific Rim menu. A lovely setting on the water, with a variety of spicy fish entrees. The lobster sushi is to die for. You will also like the sea bass and Shanghai beef. Located in a town park, the Inn has a great outdoor terrace right along the water with a bar and good live music. It's a great place to watch the sunset. The bar is open late.

Hours: Sunday Brunch, 11 am - 3 pm; Dinner, Tuesday - Saturday, 5:30 pm - 10 pm (Friday & Saturday until 11 pm), Sunday, 5 pm - 9 pm. Open later in the summer. During the summer, Lunch is served on Friday & Saturdays, from 11:30 - 2:30.

Main course price range: Dinner, $21 - $38, Lunch, $9 - $15.

Directions: I-95, exit 17, 2 lights to stop sign, L onto Riverside Avenue, R onto Bridge. R at first light after bridge, R at 1st light (look for golf course).

Starbucks

301 Greenwich Avenue, 661.3042

60 East Putnam Avenue, 629.0432

1253 East Putnam Avenue, Riverside, 698.1790

Hours: Monday - Saturday, 6 am - 10 pm

(Friday & Saturday until 11 pm); Sunday, 7 am - 9 pm.

Stonehenge Inn

Route 7, Ridgefield, CT, 203.438.6511

Well-respected eclectic French food in an attractive 16-room inn set on ten acres. Order one of the fantastic souffles at the beginning of your meal. If you forget, try the raspberry creme souffle. For the adventurous, the buffalo steak entree is excellent.

Hours: Closed Mondays. Dinner, Tuesday - Saturday, 6 pm - 9 pm; Sunday, 4 pm - 8 pm; Sunday brunch, noon - 2:30 pm. An advance reservation is always a good idea.

Main course price range: Dinner, $18 - $34; Brunch, $30 prix fixe.

Major credit cards accepted.

Directions: Merritt Parkway N to exit 39B, Take Rte 7N for 13 miles, Inn on the L.

Subway Sandwich

28 Greenwich Avenue, 622.1515

www.Subway.com

Here's where to find the famous sandwiches.

Hours: Every day, 9 am - 11 pm.

Sundown Saloon

403 Greenwich Avenue, 629.8212

www.SundownSaloon.com

This informal restaurant serves both traditional and imaginative Western food. Try the brisket sandwich or BBQ ribs. Enjoy a banana split for dessert. Be sure to order the lemonade. The friendly staff—and crayons for writing on the tablecloths—make this a good choice for the whole family. After work this is a popular meeting place for working adults.

Hours: Lunch, every day, 11:30 am - 5 pm; Dinner, every day, 5 pm - 11 pm (Friday & Saturday until midnight). Does not accept reservations.

Main course price range: Lunch, $8 - $13. Dinner, $14 - $20.

RESTAURANTS

DINING OUT

Tamarind

112 North Main Street, Port Chester, NY, 914.939.9103
A trendy martini bar and restaurant serving Asian fusion with a distinctly Indian slant. We highly recommend one of their many kababs. While dining here, it's easy to imagine you are relaxing in the tropics.
Hours: Open every day, Lunch, noon - 3 pm; Dinner, Sunday - Thursday, 4 pm - 10 pm; Friday & Saturday, 4 pm - 7 pm.
Main course price range: $13 - $20.

Tandoori (Taste of India)

163 North Main Street, Port Chester, NY, 914.937.2727
It's so nice to have a good Indian restaurant close to Greenwich. Try their fixed-price buffet lunch, weekdays. Their chicken tikka masala and shrimp malabar are favorites. We always order sweet lasse.
Hours: Sunday brunch, noon - 2:30; Lunch, Monday - Saturday, buffet, noon - 2:30 pm; Dinner, every day, 5:30 - 10 pm.
Main course price range: Lunch buffet, $10; Dinner, $10 - $19; Brunch, $12.

Telluride

245 Bedford St, Stamford, CT 357.7679
www.culinarymenus.com/telluride.htm
An interesting variety of fresh, made-to-order food in a casual, friendly, western mountain ambiance. We recommend the sauteed mountain trout, fresh from Colorado and coated in cornmeal.
Hours: weekdays, 11:30 am - 11pm; Saturday 5 pm - 11 pm;
Sunday 5 pm - 10 pm.
Main Course Prices: Lunch $8 - $15, Dinner $9 - $30
Directions: I-95 North to Exit 8 - Atlantic St. At the light at the end of the ramp go left onto Atlantic St. Follow for ½ mile until it becomes one way. This is Bedford Street. Telluride is one block up on the right. They have parking in the front and the rear but it is still difficult to find a spot.

RESTAURANTS

DINING OUT

Terra Ristorante Italiano
156 Greenwich Avenue, 629.5222

Walking along Greenwich Avenue, it's hard to escape the wonderful smells coming from their wood-burning ovens serving up Northern Italian food. A lively, hip trattoria. We recommend the Gamberoni appetizer or the chicken, both made in their special oven. If you want to escape the noise, dine on the terrace.

Hours: Lunch, Monday - Saturday, noon - 2:30 pm; Dinner, Monday - Saturday, 5:30 pm - 10:30 pm; Sunday dinner, 6 pm - 9:30 pm.

Main course price range: Lunch, $11 - $22. Dinner, $11 - $32.

That Little Italian Restaurant
228-230 Mill Street, Byram, 531.7500

Tucked away on a small street in the Byram section of Greenwich, this attractive restaurant just keeps getting better. The place to go when you want good pasta without going to a fancy restaurant. This is one spot where it isn't too noisy to have a conversation.

Hours: Lunch, weekdays, 11:30 -2:30; Dinner, every day, 5 pm - 10 pm (Friday & Saturday until 11 pm).

Reservations are accepted for parties of 6 or more.

Main course price range: $9 - $19.

Thataway Café
409 Greenwich Avenue, 622.0947

www.ThatawayCafe.com

A casual restaurant situated at the end of the Avenue. Try the popcorn shrimp, quesadillas, mixed grill or fish specials. The outdoor patio is the place to be in the summertime.

Hours: Lunch, Monday - Sunday, 11:30 am - 5 pm; Dinner, Monday - Thursday 5 pm - 11 pm (Friday & Saturday until Midnight); Sunday brunch, 11 am - 3 pm. Live seasonal entertainment - call for days and times. Reservations are accepted for parties of 6 or more on Monday through Thursday.

Main course price range: Lunch, $8 - $15. Dinner, $15 - $23.

RESTAURANTS

DINING OUT

Thomas Henkelmann
(at the Homestead Inn), 420 Field Point Road, 869.7500
www.ThomasHenkelmann.com
Nestled in Belle Haven, in a lovely, formal inn with antiques and a garden setting; there is a restaurant with delicious contemporary French food. The owner and chef, Thomas Henkelmann, is regarded as one of the best chefs in the USA.
Hours: Breakfast, weekdays, 7 am - 9:30 am; weekends, 8 am - 10 pm; Lunch, weekdays, noon - 2:30 pm; Dinner, every day, 6 pm - 9:30 pm; Closed the first two weeks in March. Closed Sundays from mid-July through August.
Main course price range: Breakfast, $10 - $16; Lunch, $35 - $55; Dinner, $55 - $75.
Reservations should be made well in advance.

Upper Crust Bagel Company
197 Sound Beach Avenue, Old Greenwich, 698.0079
A good place to sit down and chat while having a deli sandwich and a fruit smoothie. They have tasty old-fashioned kettle-boiled and hearth-baked bagels, as well as gourmet spreads and coffees.
They accept checks but no credit cards.
Hours: weekdays, 6 am - 4pm; Saturday, 7 am - 4 pm; Sunday, 7 am - 3pm.

Valbella
1309 East Putnam Avenue, Riverside, 637.1155
www.ValbellaRestaurant.com
Excellent Italian food, good service and a dressy decor. There is something wonderful on the menu for everyone. Try their lobster cocktail, sea bass with Dijon mustard sauce and chocolate souffle. They have a spectacular wine cellar with 850 wines to choose from. Truly a town favorite and our vote as the best Italian restaurant in town. If only it were less noisy....
Hours: Lunch, weekdays, noon - 3 pm; Dinner, Monday - Saturday, 5 pm - 10 pm; Closed on Sunday. Reservations required.
Main course price range: Lunch, $15 - $20; Dinner, $24 - $40.

RESTAURANTS

DINING OUT

Versailles

315 Greenwich Avenue, 661.6634

A very French bistro with excellent pastries. Just the right place to meet a friend for lunch. The good food and atmosphere are reminiscent of our Paris favorites.

Hours: Monday - Thursday, 7:30 am - 9:30 pm; Friday, 7:30 am - 9:30 pm; Saturday, 8 am - 10 pm; Sunday, 8 am - 8 pm. Breakfast is served until 11 am, Lunch until 3 pm (Sunday brunch until 5 pm).

Main course price range: Breakfast, $8 -10; Lunch, set menu at $17 or $11 - $15; Dinner, $18 - $25.

Viscardi's Colonial Inn

220 Sound Beach Avenue, Old Greenwich, 637.0367, 637.4634

An institution in Old Greenwich for over 30 years—perfect when you want excellent value and a wholesome meal. The Viscardi family makes this restaurant a warm, friendly place for your family. Usually quiet enough to have a conversation.

Hours: Open every day, Monday - Saturday, 11:30 am - 10 pm; Sunday, 4 pm - 8 pm. Summer and Sunday hours vary; it's a good idea to call first.

Main course price range: Lunch, $6 - $17; Dinner, $12 - $18.

Vuli

Stamford Mariott, 2 Stamford Forum (Atlantic Street), 323-5300

The gimmick of this restaurant is that it rotates (very slowly) on top of the Mariott Hotel. Unfortunately, its views do not show much of downtown Stamford. Although some of our friends like this restaurant, we found the prices high, the decorations neo-bordello and the food (as well as the service) uneven in quality. Live jazz on Friday evenings and Saturday evenings they have a small swing band and dancing.

Hours: Lunch, weekdays, 11:30 am - 3:30 pm; Sunday Brunch, 11 am - 3:30 pm; Dinner, weekdays, 5 pm - 10 pm, Saturday, 5 pm - 11 pm, Sunday, 4 pm - 10 pm.

Main course price range: Lunch, $15 - $24, Dinner, $21- $45.

Directions: I-95 N to exit 8, L on Atlantic

RESTAURANTS

DINING OUT

Wendy's

420 West Putnam Avenue, Greenwich, 869.9885

This is the only fast food burger place with a drive-through in Greenwich.

Hours: Monday - Saturday, 10 am -11 pm, Sunday, 10 am - 11 pm.

Whole Foods

90 East Putnam Avenue, 661.0631

www.wholefoods.com

This mostly organic grocery store has a first class deli. On a recent evening, I served their lemon-pepper rotisserie chicken, sesame green beans, mixed green salad and corn bread. Everyone loved it!

Hours: Open everyday, 8 am - 9 pm.

Willett House

20 Willet Avenue, Port Chester, NY, 914.939.7500

www.TheWillettHouse.com

A steak house serving good steaks and seafood in a meticulously restored turn-of-the-century granary building. We like the porterhouse steak and Maine lobster. Fun atmosphere and good steaks, but pricey. Its nickname is the "Wallet House."

Hours: Lunch, weekdays, 11:45 am - 3 pm; Saturday, noon - 3 pm. Dinner, Monday - Thursday, 3 pm - 10 pm; Friday, 3 pm - 11 pm; Saturday, 3 pm - 11 pm; Sunday, 4 pm - 9 pm.

Main course price range: Lunch, $9 - $25; Dinner, $19 - $49. Everything is á la carte, so salads and side dishes are extra, making this a good place to go on an expense account.

RESTAURANTS

DINING OUT

Winfields

Hyatt Regency, 1800 East Putnam Avenue, Old Greenwich, 637.1234

www.Hyatt.Greenwich.com

Set in a beautifully converted publishing building. Not a typical hotel nor typical hotel fare. The Hyatt demonstrates what good hotel dining can be. The indoor garden with water, flowers and very high ceilings gives the feeling of dining outdoors—even in the middle of the winter. The food is first-rate. We especially like their Sunday brunch.

Hours: Open every day and all holidays. Breakfast every day, 6:30 am - 10:30 am; Lunch every day except Sunday, 11 am - 5 pm (Sunday brunch, 11:30 am - 2:30 pm). Dinner every evening, 5 pm - 10 pm. Reservations are accepted and are a good idea, especially for Sunday brunch.

Main course price range: Breakfast, $4 - $15; Lunch, $10 - $19; Dinner, $12 - $26; Brunch price fixed at $38 per person, although on important holidays it may be higher.

Xaviars

506 Piermont Avenue, Piermont, NY, 845.359.7007

www.xaviars.com

Rockland County's best. Just twenty-five minutes from Greenwich across the Tappan Zee Bridge. This intimate, romantic restaurant serves contemporary continental cuisine. It is the Hudson Valley's most celebrated restaurant. It is located in Piermont which has a number of very good art galleries—don't miss the Piermont Flywheel Gallery and Win Zibeon's paintings—so arrive in time to peruse them first. Don't even consider going without making reservations well in advance.

Hours: Lunch, noon - 2 pm, Friday and Sunday; Dinner, Wednesday - Friday, 6pm - 8:45 pm; Saturday seatings 6 pm or 9 pm, Sunday, 5 pm - 8 pm.

Main course price range: Lunch, price fixed at $32 or $35; Dinner, price fixed, $60 for 3 courses, $80 tasting menu with 7 courses, $120 tasting menu with wine; Sunday lunch, price fixed, $32.

No credit cards are accepted, only cash or check.

Directions: I-95 S to I-287 W, cross the Tappan Zee Bridge and take first exit for Rte 9W West, left when you see the signs to Piermont, follow the road downhill to the Hudson River and turn right.

DINING OUT

Zanghi

201 Summer Street, Stamford, CT 327.3663

Chef Nicola Zanghi has done it again. His mouth-watering, contemporary cuisine is drawing raves. The decor is sophisticated and chic. The service couldn't be more attentive. Go early for the 3-course prix fixe menu. The theaters and movies are a short stroll away. We especially liked the whiskied pan stew and if you are in the mood for sweet breads or liver, be sure to try it here.

Hours: Dinner, Monday - Thursday, 5:30 pm - 9:30 pm;
Friday & Saturday, 5:30 pm - 10 pm.
Pre-theater prix fixe menu at $33.50 from 5:30 pm - 6:45 pm.
Main course price range: $19 - $35.
Directions: I-95 N to exit 8, L on Atlantic, L on Broad, L on Summer.

TIP: ONLY GEESE HONK IN GREENWICH
Residents know that Greenwich is a place to relax, unwind and enjoy life. Yes, we still need to get places on time, but we drive with consideration. Honking–except in dangerous situations–is taboo. If someone is honking inappropriately, it is probably a car with an out-of-town license plate. We like to say "in Greenwich only the geese honk"

SCHOOLS

ADULT CONTINUING EDUCATION

There are a great variety of language schools and other continuing education resources in and around the town. The following are some of our favorites. For additional information on art, dance or music instruction, see the appropriate section under CULTURE or contact the Greenwich Arts Council (see CULTURE, ART). For cooking schools, see COOKING. For Sports Instruction, see FITNESS & SPORTS.

Alliance Française
299 Greenwich Avenue, 629.1340
An ideal way to learn or refresh your French.

Allegra Dance Studio
37 West Putnam Avenue, 629.9162
Adult classes in ballroom dancing. Open all year.

Dick Conseur's Ballroom Dancing
Mary and Richard Conseur
596 Stillwater Road, Stamford, CT 06902, 325.1332
If you suddenly need to look confident on the dance floor, give them a call. Discreet private lessons for ballroom or country and western dancing.

Fairfield University
Fairfield, CT, 203.254.4220, 4000
www.fairfield.edu
Fairfield is a major university with a 200-acre campus and great offerings in almost every conceivable subject. Definitely worth a call to get their catalog. They have over 1,000 continuing education students.
Directons: I-95N to exit 22; L at 2nd stop sign; R onto Barlow;
at light, L onto N. Benson.

SCHOOLS

ADULT CONTINUING EDUCATION

Garden Education Center

Montgomery Pinetum, Bible Street, Cos Cob, 869.9242
www.gecgreenwich.org
The Center's new horticulture buildings provide classrooms and workrooms for a variety of programs and lectures. Founded in 1957, the center is not only a strong educational facility, but also provides a good framework for new residents to make friends. They are closed during the summer.

Greenwich Adult and Continuing Education

625.7474,
http://gps.lhric.org
This amazing program offers a wide range of courses taught at the high school, with interesting teachers. It is always priced right. Registration is in January and August/September. Be sure to call for a catalog; you are bound to see several courses you can't resist.

Greenwich Library

101 West Putnam Avenue, 622.7900   www.greenwich.lib.ct.us
The most utilized library in the State of Connecticut. It is also a popular spot for those who want to learn about the Internet. See the complete description of the Library system under GREENWICH, ENJOYING GREENWICH. With its $40 million building development, it can only get more impressive. You can access the library's catalog on the Internet.
Hours: weekdays, 9 am - 9 pm (June - August until 5 pm);
Saturday, 9 am - 5 pm; Sunday, 1 pm - 5 pm (October through April).
Closed on major holidays.

Loretta Stagen Floral Designs

81 Commerce Street, Stamford, CT 323.3544
www.lorettastagen.com
She provides innovative flower arrangements and party decorations for corporate events and weddings. She also offers classes and workshops in flower arranging. For five or more students, she will create a special class in their area of interest. Her web site has interesting links to wedding sites.

SCHOOLS

ADULT CONTINUING EDUCATION

Manhattanville College
Purchase, NY, 914.694.2200, 800.328.4553
www.mville.edu, asp@mville.edu
A local college with a very attractive campus.
Be sure to check out their course offerings.
Directions: King St. N to Anderson Hill Rd., L onto Rte 120 (Purchase St.).

Norwalk Community Technical College
Norwalk, CT, 203.857.7080
www.ncc.commnet.edu
A surprisingly large selection (more than 300 courses) of adult education courses on a variety of subjects. Nice, modern facilities. They also offer courses at satellite locations in Stamford, Greenwich and Darien.
Directions: Exit 13 off I-95 N.

Silvermine School of Art
New Canaan, CT, 203.966.6668 ext. 2
www.silvermineart.com
Programs for adults and youngsters alike. For art instruction, it can't be beat.
Directions: Merritt Pkw N, exit 38; R onto Rte 123 N; straight until Rte 106 junction; R onto 106 N; at stop sign, R onto Silvermine Rd; one mile on R.

SUNY - Purchase
735 Anderson Hill Road, Purchase, NY, 914.251.6500
www.purchase.edu, conted@purchase.edu
Purchase College is a part of the State University of New York. It has beautiful grounds and controversial modern buildings. Check out their adult education offerings.
Directions: King St. N to Anderson Hill Rd., R into SUNY.

SCHOOLS

ADULT CONTINUING EDUCATION

UCONN Stamford
Connecticut Information Technology Institute
One University Place, Stamford, CT, 251.8400
www.stamford.uconn.edu
Close by in Stamford is an exciting new facility where the University of Connecticut offers undergraduate programs plus professional and technical continuing education courses.
Directions: I-95 N to exit 7, L on Washington, L on Broad.

TIP: SoNo ARTS CELEBRATION
In early August South Norwalk has an exciting art festival with over 150 juried artists as well as an interesting mix of performances on five stages. The festival runs from 10 am to midnight and is appropriate for children as well as adults.
Call 203.866.7916 for details.

SCHOOLS

PRESCHOOL

For early childcare, see CHILDREN, CHILDCARE.

Preschool programs are usually very popular. You should contact the school well in advance to make sure you have reserved a place. Usually programs are half-day until the child is four years old.

Banksville Nursery School

12 Banksville Road, 661.9715

Children, ages 3 - 4. Creative movement classes. Morning and afternoon sessions available. Closed during the summer.

Bridges

Old Greenwich Civic Center, Harding Road, 637.0204

Children, ages 2 - 4. New theme each month. Morning and afternoon sessions.

Brunswick Preschool

Ridgeview Avenue, 625.5800

Boys, ages 4 - 6. Admission to pre-K usually ensures admission to the school. Co-ed summer camp for children ages 4 - 5.

Children's Day School

139 East Putnam Avenue, 869.5395

Children, infants - 5 years. All-day, year-round childcare and preschool located in the Second Congregational Church. Stresses cooperation and integration of projects.

Christ Church Nursery School

254 East Putnam Avenue, 869.5334

Children, ages 2 - 4. Blend of enrichment and free play. Kindergarten alternative, 9 am - 1:30 pm.

SCHOOLS

PRESCHOOL

Convent of the Sacred Heart Early Learning Program
1177 King Street, 531.6500
Girls, ages 3 - 4; Half-day program for 3-year-olds optional; 4-year-olds, full day. Grounded in the Catholic tradition, although 35% of students are not Catholic.

Family Center
40 Arch Street, 869.4848
www.familycenters.org
Children, ages 3 - 4. An all-day, year-round childcare and preschool. 5:30 pm pick-up available. Learn-through-discovery approach.

Giant Steps Head Start at Wilbur Peck Court
629.6286 Ages: 3 - 4

Kids Corner Head Start at Armstrong Court
869.2730 Ages: 3 - 4

First Church Preschool
108 Sound Beach Avenue, Old Greenwich, 637.5430
Children, ages 3 - 4. Hours: 9 am - 11:30 am or 12:30 pm - 3 pm. Some preference is given to church members. Summer camp program for ages 3 - 4.

First Presbyterian Church Preschool
37 Lafayette Place, 869.7782
Children, ages 2½ - 4. Morning and afternoon classes.
Also 2 x 2 program, 2 days per week. Enrichment programs change every 6 - 8 weeks. Art Scampers summer camp for ages 3 - 6.

Greenwich Academy
200 North Maple Avenue, 625.8990
Girls, ages 4 - 5. Morning and afternoon sessions.
Admission to pre-K usually ensures admission to the school.

SCHOOLS

PRESCHOOL

Greenwich Catholic School

471 North Street, 869.4000

Children, ages 4 - pre-K. Pre-K is a structured program with academics for 4-year-olds. Little Angels is a play group for younger children. Admission to these programs does not ensure admission to the school.

Greenwich Country Day

Old Church Road, 622.8529

Starting at age 3. Admission to pre-K usually ensures admission to the school. Summer camp for children ages 4 - 5.

Greenwich Kokusai Gakuen

Worldwide Children's Corner

521 East Putnam Avenue, 629.5567, 618.0790

Children, ages 2½ - 5 years. Full-day program.

Greenwich Preschool Clinic

Riverside Elementary School

90 Hendrie Avenue, 637-5412

Greenwich runs a preschool for ages 3-4.

Greenwich Preschool Program, 637-2892

Reform Synagogue Hilltop Preschool

257 Stanwich Road, 629.0018

Children, ages 1 - 4. Jewish traditions stressed. Special program for parents with one and two-year-olds, to introduce them to their first school experience.

Fun-for-Ones for age 1, Mommy-and-Me for age 2.

Half-day preschool classes for ages 2 - 4.

North Greenwich Nursery School

606 Riversville Road, 869.7945

Children, ages 3 - 4. Half-day program with optional extended-day available. Computers integrated into program. US Gymnastic Academy is at the same location and can provide afternoon classes.

SCHOOLS

PRESCHOOL

Putnam Indian Field School
101 Indian Field Road, 869.0982, 661.4629
Children, ages 2½ - 5. Summer camp program for ages 3 - 5.

Round Hill Nursery School
466 Round Hill Road, 869.4910
Children, ages 2 - 4. Fifty years of giving children a love of going to school. Computer training and special teachers for music and art.

St. Catherine's
6 Riverside Avenue, Riverside, 637.9549
Children, ages 2 - 4. Age 2, 1 - 3 pm; ages 3 - 4, 9 am - 12:30 pm.

St. Agnes Preschool
247 Stanwich Road, 869.8388
Children, ages 2 yrs 9 mos - 5. Flexible 3, 4 or 5-day a week programs. Half-day programs with extended-day options. Summer camp program.

St. Paul's Christian Nursery School
286 Delavan Avenue, 531.5905
Children, ages 3 - 4; 9 am - 11:30 am. Religious values stressed.

St. Paul's Day School
200 Riverside Avenue, Riverside, 637.3503
Children, ages 2 - 5. Nonsectarian, with enrichment program for older children. Summer camp program for ages 3 - 6.

St. Savior's Nursery School
350 Sound Beach Avenue, Old Greenwich, 698.1303
Children, ages 2 yrs 5 mos - 5. Nondenominational.
Summer camp program for ages 3 - 5.

Selma Maisel Nursery School
Temple Sholom, 300 East Putnam Avenue, 622.8121
Children, ages 2 - 5. "Mommy & Me" program for 2 and under. Programs with Judaic content.

SCHOOLS

PRESCHOOL

Tiny Tots
97 Riverside Avenue, Riverside, 637.1398
Children, ages 2 - 5. Residential setting. One of the oldest nursery schools in town. Summer camp program for ages 2 - 6.

Whitby School
969 Lake Avenue, 869.8464
Children, ages 1 - 5 years. This is the oldest American Montessori school. Summer camp program for ages 2 - 6.

YMCA Rainbow Connection Preschool
40 Gold Street, Byram, 869.3381
Children, ages 2 years 9 months - 5 years, 8:30 am - 1:15 pm. Follows public school calendar. Offers enrichment curriculum.

YWCA 1-2-3 Grow/Beginnings
259 East Putnam Avenue, 869.6501 x 221
Children, ages 15 months - 3 years; toddlers, 9 am - 11:30 am; age 2, 9 am - 11:30 am or noon - 2:30 pm.

YWCA Tinker Tots
259 East Putnam Avenue, 869.6501 x 241
Children, ages 2 - 4. Half-day program for age 2; ages 3 - 4, full-day, 7:30 am - 6 pm. Enrichment programs. Summer camp.

SCHOOLS

PRIVATE/PAROCHIAL

Greenwich has an abundance of excellent private schools. Typical annual tuition is $9,000 to $15,000, depending upon the grade. Private schools typically have more applicants than they have spaces. It is prudent to apply early. Private schools often have one or more open houses for parents of prospective attendees. Many offer extended-day programs or early drop-off for their preschoolers.

Brunswick School
100 Maher Avenue, 625.5800
www.brunswickschool.org
Boys, pre-K (age 4) through 12th grade.

Convent of the Sacred Heart
1177 King Street, 531.6500
www.cshgreenwich.org
Girls, pre-K (age 4) through 12th grade.

Eagle Hill
45 Glenville Road, 622.9240
www.eaglehillschool.org
Co-ed, ages 6 - 16. A school for bright children with learning disabilities. Day and 5-day boarding. Student faculty ratio is 4:1.

Greenwich Academy
200 North Maple Avenue, 625.8900
www.greenwichacademy.org
Girls, pre-K (age 4) through 12th grade.

Greenwich Country Day
Old Church Road, 622-8510
www.greenwichcds.org
Co-ed, pre-K (age 3) through 9th grade.

Greenwich Catholic School
471 North Street, 869.4000
www.rc.net/bridgeport/gcs
Co-ed, pre-K (age 4) through 8th grade.

SCHOOLS

PRIVATE/PAROCHIAL

Greenwich Japanese School
270 Lake Avenue, 629.9039
www.gwjs.org
Co-ed, grades 1 - 9.

Stanwich School
257 Stanwich Road, 869.4515
www.stanwichschool.org
Founded by Patricia Young, the former head of the lower school at Greenwich Academy, our newest school has opened its cheerful classrooms. Plans for additional grades are in place. Co-ed, K to 2.

Whitby School
969 Lake Avenue, 869.8464
www.whitbyschool.org
Co-ed, grades pre-K - 8. Founded in 1958, it is one of the oldest Montessori schools in the country. During the summer Whitby conducts a drama day camp for ages 8- 16.

SCHOOLS

PUBLIC SCHOOLS

www.greenwich.k12.ct.us

Greenwich public schools rank among the best in the nation and are consistently ranked the best in Fairfield County. In addition to their other fine programs, Greenwich schools have outstanding ESL (English as a Second Language) programs for all grades K - 12.

The elementary schools serve students in grades K - 5, the middle schools serve students in grades 6 - 8 and the high school serves students grades 9 - 12.

Schools open for students around Labor Day and close in the middle of June.

Board of Education

290 Greenwich Avenue

Call 625.7400 for school district information.

Call 625.7447/6 for brochures and pamphlets.

Before and After-School Child Care Programs

Ten of the elementary schools offer before and after-school programs for enrolled students. These programs are paid for by the parents. These programs are on-site at the elementary schools. Children can usually be dropped off at 7:30 am and must be picked up by 6 pm. There is often a waiting list so apply early. Some of the schools also offer enrichment programs where children can take computer or other classes. Call your elementary school to see what programs they sponsor. For other programs, see CHILDREN, CHILDCARE or SCHOOLS, PRESCHOOL.

Kindergarten

To register for kindergarten, your child must have reached the age of five on or before January 1 of his or her kindergarten year. Parents must provide a birth certificate and proof of residence. Your child must also have a complete physical examination and a record of immunizations.

SCHOOLS

PUBLIC SCHOOLS

School Closings

If schools are closed for snow, or if opening is delayed, listen to Greenwich Radio WGCH (1490) and WSTC (1400). Announcements begin at 6:30 am. You may also find information on channel 72.

School Bus Information

625.7449

Call for information on school bus pick-up times and locations. If your child is young and other children are not nearby, you can often get the school bus to stop in front of or near your home. Bus service is provided for students who live beyond:

Grades K - 5, one mile from the school;
Grades 6 - 8, one and a half miles from school;
Grades 9 - 12, two miles from school.

Public School Web Site:

www.greenwich.k12.ct.us

SCHOOLS

PUBLIC ELEMENTARY

Cos Cob Elementary School
300 East Putnam Avenue, Cos Cob, 869.4670
Dominic Butera, Principal (490 students, 8.45 am -3.15 pm)

Glenville Elementary School
33 Riversville Road, 531.9287
Ellen Flanagan, Principal (452 students, 8.30 am - 3.00 pm)

Hamilton Avenue Elementary School
184 Hamilton Avenue, 869.1685
Carol Sarabun, Principal (304 students, 8.15 am - 2.45 pm)

International School at Dundee
55 Florence Road, Riverside, 637.3800
Douglas Fainelli, Principal (8.45 am - 3.15 pm)

Julian Curtiss Elementary School
180 East Elm Street, 869.1896
Nancy Carbone, Principal (363 students, 8.15 am - 2.45 pm)

New Lebanon Elementary School
25 Mead Avenue, Byram, 531.9139
Connee Dawson, Principal (257 students, 8.15 am - 2.45 pm)

North Mianus Elementary School
309 Palmer Hill Road, Riverside, 637.9730
Frank Arnone, Principal (454 students, 8.45 am - 3:15 pm)

North Street Elementary School
381 North Street, 869.6756
Elisabeth Burfeind, Principal (526 students, 8:45 am - 3:15 pm)

SCHOOLS

PUBLIC ELEMENTARY

Old Greenwich Elementary School
285 Sound Beach Avenue, Old Greenwich, 637.0150
Marjorie Sherman, Principal (415 students, 8.45 am - 3.15 pm)

Parkway Elementary School
141 Lower Cross Road, 869.7466
Sandra Mond, Principal (427 students, 8.45 am - 3.15 pm)

Riverside Elementary School
90 Hendrie Avenue, Riverside, 637.1440
John Grasso, Principal (520 students, 8.45 am - 3.15 pm)

TIP: KIDS' TIME
The Performing Arts Center at Purchase College, in addition to their superb adult concert series, has a series of sensational performances designed for children. One series for ages 4-9 and one is for ages 9 and up. Check it out www.ArtCenter.org or contact them at 914.251.6200.

SCHOOLS

PUBLIC MIDDLE SCHOOLS

Central Middle School
9 Indian Rock Lane, 661.8500
James Bulger, Principal (526 students, 7.45 am - 2.35 pm)

Eastern Middle School
51 Hendrie Avenue, Riverside, 637.1744
Benjamin Davenport, Principal (554 students, 7.45 am - 2.35 pm)

Western Middle School
Western Junior Highway, 531.5700
Donald Strange, Principal (516 students, 7.45 am - 2.35 pm)

PUBLIC HIGH SCHOOLS

Arch School
289 Delavan Avenue, 532.1956
Barbara Varanelli, Program Administrator (8.00 am - 2.00 pm)
The Arch School is an alternative high school for students who need special attention.

Greenwich High School
10 Hillside Road, 625.8000
Elaine Bessette, Headmistress (1991 students, 7.30 am - 2.15 pm)

TIP: COLLEGE SELECTION GUIDANCE
Mary Leinbach has helped many public and private Greenwich students select the right college and prepare for college interviews. Her $200 fee goes to the First Congregational Church's College and University Loan Fund and is tax-deductible.
Call Mary at 531.9434

SENIORS

INTRODUCTION

Seniors in Greenwich typically stay actively involved in the community, often serving on town boards, the RTM, and philanthropic organizations. Many of our volunteer organizations are run by the retired presidents and leaders of major companies. This wealth of talent of our senior leaders is a significant reason Greenwich is America's number one town. Most senior citizens continue living in their own homes by utilizing the many services the town has available.

CLUBS AND ORGANIZATIONS

Glenville Senior Citizens
Western Greenwich Civic Center
Contact: Thomas Roberto, President - 661.9594

Greenwich Old Timers Athletic Association
PO Box 558, Greenwich 06836
David Theis, President - 869.4857
Contact: Griff Harris, Jr., Secretary - 869.9200

Greenwich Seniors Club
Sheila Shea Russo, Executive Director - 531.4345
Rosemary Pugliese, Membership - 531.8600

Retired Men's Association
YMCA
50 East Putnam Avenue
Joseph Robinson, President - 698.2220
Contact: Bill Eustis, Program Chairman - 637.4512

SENIORS

COMPUTERS & THE INTERNET

Computer Training

The internet and e-mail are sparking a communications revolution among seniors who find it the easiest way to stay connected with their family and interests. In addition to the extensive list of computer courses given by Greenwich Continuing Education, and other resources described in SCHOOLS, ADULT CONTINUING EDUCATION, there are several senior-specific computer programs.

DeCaro Associates

3 Sweet Briar Lane, Cos Cob, 921.4757
Noted Greenwich web site designers, responsible for many of Greenwich's best web sites, help seniors with computer problems at discounted prices.

Greenwich High School Computer Teaching Club

(Student Activities office) 625.8000
Weekly classes where students provide one-on-one tutoring to seniors.

Norwalk Community-Technical College

Norwalk, CT, 203.857.7060 or 203.857.7080
This community college allows seniors age 62 and older to audit any course free of charge. For more details on the college see the entry in SCHOOLS, ADULT CONTINUING EDUCATION.

SeniorNet

622.3990/3989
This program, underwritten by telephone and computer companies, has over 240 locations nationwide and offers low-cost computer training for people age 50+. The SeniorNet program admits eight students per class. They meet twice weekly for four weeks. It offers courses at the Greenwich and Stamford Senior Centers.

SENIORS
HOUSING

According to the town's 1998 Plan of Conservation and Development, the Housing Authority has 291 independent living units for seniors with low income and who are over 62. The town also owns Nathaniel Witherell SNF (skilled nursing facility), with 200-beds on Parsonage Road which offers many outstanding programs for its residents. Admission preference is given to Greenwich residents, but because the facility is almost always 100% occupied, it is wise to call 869.4130 for an application well in advance of expected need.

(The) Mews
½ Bolling Place, 869.9448
Assisted living for seniors 55 and over. The Mews is a managed-care residential community in the heart of downtown Greenwich, very close to the town's Senior Center. Rooms and suites are available at affordable rates.

Hill House
10 Riverside Avenue, 637.3177
37 one-bedroom apartments for the well elderly. Residence is open to any able-bodied person over age 62 who meets income guidelines.

Resources for Respite Care
This guide published by the Junior League of Greenwich includes websites, sources for financial assistance, support groups as well as other resources for people caring for elderly or disabled loved ones. It is distributed by Community Answers as well as the Greenwich Hospital.

SENIORS

INFORMATION & REFERRAL

For information on medical resources, see the HEALTH section.

Commission on Aging

622.3992

Located in the Senior Center, the Commission on Aging provides information and written materials on a variety of issues of interest to seniors. Commission staff provides information and referral services and locates resources.

Hours: weekdays, 9 am - 4 pm.

Community Answers

622.7979

This volunteer group will guide you to the right number for your need. See their more complete description under INFORMATION, SOURCES.

Greenwich Hospital

863.4444

Provides community outreach by offering support groups, health screenings and community health education.

Infoline

In Connecticut dial 211 (outside CT 260.522.4636)

www.infoline.org

A 24-hour confidential information, referral, advocacy and crisis help line. Caseworkers have information about hundreds of services, including health, transportation, housing, safety, employment, support services, counseling, financial/legal services and activities.

Municipal Agent for the Aged

622.3805

Assists seniors in accessing programs, benefits and services.

SENIORS

SERVICES & ACTIVITIES

Call-A-Ride
37 Lafayette Place, 661.6633
Non-profit organization. Residents 60 years or older can call for a ride to anywhere in Greenwich for any purpose. Please give them 24 - 48-hours notice.
Hours: weekdays, 9 am - noon and 12:30 pm - 3:15 pm

Friendly Connections
20 Bridge Street, 661.8841
Family Centers, Inc. provides two Friendly Connections programs:
Telephone Groups
This program brings seniors—or those who have difficulty getting out—together on the telephone for a variety of recreational, support and discussion groups. All groups are conducted over the phone and are facilitated by a moderator. There are more than 50 groups scheduled each month. They are a great way to meet new friends and stay connected.
Friendly Callers
Professionally-trained volunteers make daily calls to elderly, homebound or isolated individuals. Telephone Reassurance provides an opportunity to have a friendly chat, stay in-touch and feel safer at home. They can also provide medication reminders and a "safety check," when requested. Calls are made every day from 9 am - 9 pm.

Friendly Visitors
622.6455
This program, run by the Town Department of Social Services, provides trained volunteers to visit seniors.

Home Hair Styling Services
Maria Barbosa, 203.445.0140
If you are not feeling well enough to go out to have a manicure or to have your hair styled, call Maria. She cuts both men and women's hair and will make you have a good hair day.

SENIORS

SERVICES & ACTIVITIES

Jewish Family Services of Greenwich

One Holly Hill Lane, 622.1881

www.jfsgreenwich.org

A free service for Greenwich residents over 60 providing grocery shopping for the homebound; also, carpentry, minor plumbing and snow shoveling.

Kindness Counts

Teacher leader, Jonathan Guyot Smith, 531.5700

www.KindnessCounts.com

A Western Middle School student-run program. Students prepare and deliver meals to residents in senior housing facilities.

Meals-on-Wheels

869.1312

Non-profit organization prepares and delivers to homes of anyone recovering from illness or an accident, regardless of age.

$7 per day for two meals, one hot and one cold.

Hours: weekdays 8 am - 1 pm

Senior Center

299 Greenwich Avenue, 622.3990

Stop in to see the monthly bulletin board of activities. There are a lot of activities going on! Recent listings included: "Qigong" Chinese exercises, chess and bridge instruction, a luncheon cruise, trips to the opera, ice cream socials, painting, shopping center trips and a brown bag auction. Free classes (in conjunction with Greenwich Continuing Education) were being held in line dancing, writing short stories, writing your memoirs and sewing.

Hours: weekdays, 9 am - 4 pm.

Supermarketing for Seniors

One Holly Hill Lane, 622.1881

One of the wonderful Jewish Family Service programs to help homebound older residents. They will arrange grocery shopping on a weekly basis, and this kind service is free.

SENIORS

SERVICES & ACTIVITIES

TAG (Transportation Association of Greenwich)
13 Riverside Avenue, 637.4345
Non-profit organization operates a fleet of 15 specially modified vehicles. They drive elderly and disabled people of all ages to health, social and educational organizations in Greenwich and neighboring communities.
TAG operates Monday - Saturday, 6 am - 8 pm.

USE - Senior Center Job Placement Service
Job Placement Service, 629.8031
Utilize Senior Energy, a volunteer employment referral service for area residents over 50. It is a good resource for everything from painters to babysitters.
Hours: weekdays, 9:30 am - 12:30 pm.

Weekend Lunch Bunch
Greenwich Hospital, 863.3690
Anyone age 55 or older can enjoy a $4.50 4-course meal in the cafeteria.
Hours: Saturday & Sunday, noon - 2 pm.

YMCA Exercise Programs
50 East Putnam Avenue, 869.1630
The Y offers a number of programs tailored to the needs of seniors, including walking, stretching, resistance training and swimming.

TIP: GREENWICH POPS CONCERT
For a lovely evening, pack a picnic and head to the Roger Sherman Baldwin Park for one of Pops concerts sponsored by the Greenwich Arts Council and the Department of Parks & Recreation. The park opens for picnics at 6 pm and the concerts start at 7:30 pm. Call 622.3998 for details.

SHOPPING

INTRODUCTION

Greenwich Avenue is an active, vibrant shopping and dining center. Without a doubt you will enjoy a stroll down the Avenue. Most likely you will be greeted with friendly smiles and you will certainly enjoy window shopping even if you are not in the mood to buy. Old timers in Greenwich often lament the changes to the Avenue. It certainly is true that some of the mom and pop stores have had to leave because of high rents. Space on the Avenue rents for approximately $75 to $90 per square foot. This means that a 2,000 square foot store would rent for about $13,000 a month. We encourage you to support the individual entrepreneurs that remain. Sound Beach Avenue in Old Greenwich is another wonderful shopping street, more reminiscent of how Greenwich Avenue used to be. You will also note that many interesting shops are on side streets in Greenwich and Old Greenwich as well as in Cos Cob, Riverside and Glenville. We are lucky to have such a variety. While some towns have had their downtown shopping areas deserted because of nearby malls, Greenwich shopping just grows stronger and prettier.

A note on Hours: Many stores change their hours with the season—longer hours around Christmas and shorter during the summer. They also experiment with different hours. The hours noted for each store are therefore an indication only and should not be taken as absolute.

A note on Customer Service: Although no store is perfect, the independently owned stores in town often offer the most consistently superior customer service. That is, after all, their key to competing with the chains. If you find a rude salesperson, it may be an inexperienced part-time person. If you find a store with consistently bad service please let us know.

For **Repairs**, see HOMES, WHERE TO GET THINGS REPAIRED.

SHOPPING

BY SPECIALTY

Antiques
Antique & Artisan
    Center
AT Proudian
B & D Johnson
    Antiques
Colby & Stuart
    Antiques
Donald Rich Antiques
Federalist
Greenwich Oriental
Art
Guild Antiques
Harborview Center for
    Antiques
Henri-Burton French
    Antiques
Hiden Galleries
Louis Louis Antiques
Manderly Antiques
Main Street Cellar
Michael Kessler
    Antiques
Provinces de France
Quai Voltaire
    Antiquites
Rue Faubourg St.
    Honré
Shippan Center for
    Arts & Antiques
Stamford Antiques
Stamford Antiques
    Center
Vallin Galleries

ART - Galleries
Gallerie SoNo
Meserve Coale Gallery
Portland Place Gallery
Cavalier Galleries
Flinn Gallery
Greenwich Gallery
Lois Richards
    Galleries

ART - Supplies
Barney's Place
Friedman

ART - Framing
Barney's Place
Left of The Bank
Red Studio

Automobile Needs
Hank May's Goodyear

Boating
Greenwich Kayak
    & Canoe Co.
Landfall Navigation
Rex Marine Center

Books
Barnes & Noble
Borders Books
Gift Shop at Christ
    Church
Diane's Books
    of Greenwich
Inspirations
Just Books
Parker's
Waldenbooks

CHILDREN - Clothing, Shoes & Gifts
April Cornell
Babies "R" Us
Baby & Toy
    Superstore
Baby Gap
Beame & Barre
Best & Co.
Buy Buy Baby
Candy Nichols
Candy Nichols Loft
Children's Classics
Chilly Bear
Flight of Fancy
Gap Kids
Imaginarium
Laura Ashley
L'Enfance Magique
Little Eric
Petit Patapon
Talbots Kids

SHOPPING

BY SPECIALTY

CHILDREN - Furniture & Equipment
Amish Outdoor Living
Babies "R" Us
Baby & Toy
        Superstore
Bellini
Buy Buy Baby
Go To Your Room
Great Outdoor Toy
        Company
Kid's Supply Co.
Wendy Gee!

CLOTHING - Men
Allen's of Nantucket
Cashmere
Banana Republic
Decker's
Gap
J Crew
Richard's
Van Driver

CLOTHING - Women
Allen's of Nantucket
Cashmere
Ann Taylor
Anthropologie
April Cornell
Avant-Tout
Banana Republic
Cashmere Inc.
Chancy D'Elia
Dorothy Mann
Elsebe
Gap
Helen Ainson
J Crew
J. McLaughlin
Nancy T's
Patricia Gourlay
Razook's
Richard's
Saturnia
Sophia's Great Dames
Sound Beach
        Sportswear
Tahiti Street
Talbots
Tetonia
TSE Cashmere
Wendy's Closet

CONSIGNMENT - Furniture, Sliver, Jewelry
Commission Mart
Consign It
Estate Treasurers of
        Greenwich
Silk Purse

CONSIGNMENT - Clothing
Act II Consignment
Consigned Designs
Roundabout

Cosmetics
Parfumerie Douglas

Dancewear
Beame & Barre

Department Stores
Bloomingdales
Filenes
Kohl's
Lord and Taylor
Macy's
Neiman Marcus
Nordstrom
Saks Fifth Avenue

SHOPPING

BY SPECIALTY

Electronics - Audio/Visual, Computer, Cameras & Electronics
Audiocom
Bang & Olufsen
CompUSA
Computer Supercenter
Greenwich Photo,
    Card & Gift
Kiev USA
Performance Imaging
Radio Shack
Ritz Camera Center

Florists, Nurseries & Garden Accessories
Cos Cob Farmer's
    Market
Gift Shop at Greenwich
    Hospital
Greenwich Orchids
Greenwich Nursery
Ivy Urn
Kenneth Lynch & Sons
McArdle Florist & Garden Center
Old Greenwich Flower Shop
Riverside Florist & Gifts
Sam Bridge Nursery & Greenhouse
Secret Garden
Shanti Bithi
Tulips Greenwich

FOOD - Ethnic & Spices
Fuji Mart
Penzey's Spices
Scandia Food and Gift

FOOD - Fish
Bon Ton
Fjord Fisheries Market
Lobster Bin

FOOD - Fruit, Vegetables & Cheese
Cos Cob Farmer's
    Market
Farmer's Market
Farmer's Markets
Greenwich Farmer's
    Market
Greenwich Fruit and
    Produce
Hay Day
Purdy's Farm and
    Nursery
Schultz's Cider Mill
Silverman's Farm
White Silo Farm
Whole Foods

FOOD - Grocery
Food Emporium
Food Mart
Round Hill Store (The)
Stew Leonard's
Stop & Shop Home
    Shopping
Trader Joe's
Whole Foods
Whole Foods Home
    Delivery

FOOD - Meat
Harrington's of
    Vermont
Manero's Meat Shop
Village Prime Meats

SHOPPING

BY SPECIALTY

FOOD -Bakeries
Arnold Bakery Outlet
Black Forest
Beyond Bread
Di Mare Pastry Shop
Kneaded Bread
Sal's Pastry Shop
St. Moritz
Sweet Art
Sweet Lisa's
    Exquisite Cakes
Upper Crust Bagel
Versailles

FOOD - Chocolates & Candy
Darlene's Heavenly
        Chocolates
Moonstruck
Papery (The)
Sweet Spot

FOOD - Ice Cream
Baskin-Robbins
Capriccio
Carvel
Häagen-Dazs
Longford's
Meli-Melo

FOOD - Wine
Connecticut Wines
        & Liquors
Horseneck Liquors
Var Max Liquor Pantry
Wine World on Elm

Gifts, Dishes & Crystal
Baccarat
Cadeaux
Clementine's
Confetti Card & Gift
    Shop
Gift Shop at Bruce
    Museum
Gift Shop at Christ
    Church
Gift Shop at Green-
    wich   Hos-
    pital
Gift Shop at Hyatt
    Hotel
Goldenberry
Green
Greenwich Exchange
    for Women's Work
Greenwich Photo, Card
    & Gift
Hoagland's of
    Greenwich
House Warmings
Inspirations
Ivy Urn
Michaelangelo of
    Greenwich
Nesting
Quelques Chose
Rinfret Home &
    Garden
Sophia's Great Dames
Tallow's End
Tuscany

HEALTH - Equipment, Furniture & Products
Care Center (The)
Dave's Cycle and
    Fitness
Greenwich Health
    Mart
Neal's Yard (Natural
    Remedies)
Omni Fitness
Relax the Back
Serenity Path
Vitamin Shoppe
Whole Foods

HOME - Accessories
Anthropologie
Bed, Bath & Beyond
Home Works
HomeGoods
Laura Ashley
Lynnens
Nordic Stove & Fire-
    place Center
Pier One Imports
Post Road Iron Works
Pottery Barn
Restoration Hardware
Rinfret Home &
    Garden
Rue Faubourg St.
    Honré
Simon Pearce

SHOPPING

BY SPECIALTY

HOME - Appliances
Complete Kitchen
Cook & Craft
Harris Restaurant
	Supply
Reo Appliances
Bed, Bath & Beyond

HOME - Furniture (indoor & outdoor)
Amish Outdoor Living
Baker Furniture
Bombay Furniture
Duxiana
Ethan Allen
Federalist
IKEA
Lillian August
Patio.com
Pier One Imports
Pottery Barn
Restoration Hardware
Safavieh
Smith & Hawken
Stickley - Audi
	Company
United House
	Wrecking
Village Clock Shop

HOME - Hardware, Lighting & Decorating
Accessory Store
Ceramic Design
Country Floors
Fashion Light Center
Feinsod
Floor Covering
	Warehouse
Greenwich Hardware
Home Depot
Home Depot Expo
Klaff's
Laura Ashley
Light Touch
McDermott Paint &
	Wallpaper
Ring's End Lumber
Safavieh
Stuttig
Super Handy
	Hardware
Waterworks

Jewelry
Betteridge Jewelers
Carolee Jewelry
Lux Bond & Green
Penny Weights
Steven B. Fox Fine
	Jewelry
Tiffany & Co.

Lingerie
Patricia Gourlay
Victoria's Secret

Luggage
Dinoffer
Innovation Luggage

Magazines & Papers
Avenue News
Marks Brothers
	Stationers
Ronnie's News
Zyn's News

Malls & Shopping Centers
Clinton Crossing
	Premium Outlets
Liberty Village
Ridgeway Shopping
	Center
Stamford Town Center
Westbrook Factory
	Stores
Westchester Mall
Woodbury Commons

Music, Videos & DVDs
Atelier Constantin
	Popescu
Clinton's Pianos
Music Source (The)
Sam Goody
Video Station

SHOPPING

BY SPECIALTY

Office Supplies & Equipment
Marks Brothers
      Stationers
Staples

Outlets
C.R. Gibson Factory
      Store
Clinton Crossing
   Premium Outlets
Decker's
Exposures Catalog
      Outlet
J. McLaughlin Outlet
Liberty Village
Lillian August Home
      Outlet Store
Strauss Warehouse
      Outlet
Westbrook Factory
      Stores
Woodbury Commons

Parties & Entertaining
Fiesta Place
Party City
Party Paper & Things
Strauss Warehouse
      Outlet
Tallows End

Pets
House of Fins
Pet Pantry

Pharmacies
CVS 24-Hr Pharmacy
Finch Pharmacy
Grannick's Pharmacy
Kerr's Village
      Pharmacy
North Street Pharmacy

Sewing & Needlework
Nimble Thimble
Village Ewe

SHOES & Accessories - Men & Women
Ann Taylor
Grossman's Shoe Store
Kate Spade
Mephisto
Nine West
Richards
Shoes N More
Talbots

Sporting Equipment & Clothing
All Sports Apparel
Axis Boardsports
Bedford Sportsman
Beval Saddlery
Bruce Park Sports
Chilly Bear
Compleat Angler
Custom Golf of
      Connecticut
Darien Golf Center
Darien Sport Shop
Dave's Cycle &
      Fitness
De Mane's Golf Inc.
Eastern Mountain
      Sports
EuroChasse
Greenwich Bicycles
Gordon's Gateway to
      Sports
Griffin & Howe
Hickory & Tweed
International Soccer
      World
Orvis
Outdoor Traders
Pub Games Plus
Recreation Showroom
Rex Dive Center
Riders Up
Rink & Racquet
Sportif Ltd.
Sportsman's Den
Tack Room
Threads & Threads

SHOPPING

BY SPECIALTY

Stationery & Cards

C.R. Gibson Factory
  Store
Celia's Hallmark
Confetti Card & Gift
  Shop
Greenwich Photo, Card
  & Gift
l Papiro
Marks Brothers
  Stationers
Packages Plus-N-More
Papery (The)
Saint Clair
Staples

Thrift

ELDC
Goodwill
Hospital Thrift Shop
Merry-Go-Round
Neighbor-to-Neighbor
Rummage Room
Salvation Army

Toys

Baby & Toy
  Superstore
Dianne's Doll Shoppe
Fun House
Hobby Center
Imaginarium
Kay-Bee Toys
Right Start
Smart Kids Company
Toys "R" Us
Whimsies Doll House
  & Minature Shop

SHOPPING

BY NEIGHBORHOOD

Armonk, NY
Hickory & Tweed
Schultz"s Cider Mill
Village Prime Meats

Bedford Hills, NY
Bedford Sportsman

Byram
Arnold Bakery Outlet
De Mane's Golf Inc
Dianne's Doll Shoppe
Go To Your Room
Greenwich Kayak &
      Canoe Co
Kiev USA

Chappaqua, NY
Wendy Gee!

Clinton, CT
Clinton Crossing
      Premium Outlets

Cos Cob
Commission Mart
Confetti Card & Gift
      Shop
Cos Cob Farmers
      Market
Darlene's Heavenly
      Chocolates
Dave's Cycle and
      Fitness
ELDC   Cos Cob
Fjord Fisheries Market
Food Mart
Gordon"s Gateway to
      Sports
Hobby Center
Nesting
Packages Plus-N-More
Party Paper & Things
Serenity Path
Sportsman's Den
Sweet Lisa's Exquisite
      Cakes

Darien, CT
Compleat Angler

Darien Golf Center
Darien Sport Shop
Helen Ainson
Orvis
Ring's End Lumber
Trader Joes
Village Clock Shop

Easton, CT
Silverman's Farm

Elizabeth, NJ
IKEA

Flemington, NJ
Liberty Village

Glenville
Finch Pharmacy
Super Handy
      Hardware

Greenwich - Back Country
Connecticut Wines
and Liquors
North Street Pharmacy
Purdy's Farm and
      Nursery
Riders Up
Round Hill Store (The)
Sam Bridge Nursery &
      Greenhouse

SHOPPING
BY NEIGHBORHOOD

Greenwich - Downtown

Act II Consignment
Allen's of Nantucket
Cashmere
Ann Taylor
Anthropologie
April Cornell
AT Proudian
Audiocom
Avant-Tout
Avenue News
B & D Johnson
        Antiques
Baby Gap
Baccarat
Baker Furniture
Banana Republic
Bang & Olufsen
Barney's Place
Baskin-Robbins
Beame & Barre
Best & Co.
Betteridge Jewelers
Black Forest
Bon Ton
Bruce Park Sports
Cadeaux
Candy Nichols
Candy Nichols Loft
Carolee Jewelry
Cashmere Inc.
Cavalier Galleries
Ceramic Design
Chancy D'Elia
Chilly Bear
Clementine's

Complete Kitchen
Computer Supercenter
Consign It
Consigned Designs
Country Floors
Diane's Books
Dinoffer
Donald Rich Antiques
Dorothy Mann
Duxiana
Elsebe
EuroChasse
Farmers Markets
Fashion Light Center
Federalist
Flight of Fancy
Flinn Gallery
Food Emporium
Gap
Gap Kids
Gift Shop at Bruce
        Museum
Gift Shop at Christ
        Church
Gift Shop at Greenwich
        Hospital
Goldenberry
Goodwill
Grannick's Pharmacy
Green
Greenwich Bicycles
Greenwich Exchange
        for Women's Work
Greenwich Farmer's
        Market
Greenwich Fruit &
        Produce
Greenwich Gallery
Greenwich Hardware

Greenwich Health
        Mart
Greenwich Nursery
Greenwich Orchids
Greenwich Oriental
        Art
Greenwich Photo, Card
        & Gift
Griffin & Howe
Grossman's Shoe Store
Guild Antiques
Häagen-Dazs
Harrington's of
        Vermont
Henri-Burton French
        Antiques
Hoagland's of
        Greenwich
Horseneck Liquors
Hospital Thrift Shop
House of Fins
Il Papiro
Innovation Luggage
Inspirations
Ivy Urn
J Crew
J. McLaughlin
Just Books
Kate Spade
Kay-Bee Toys
Kid's Supply Co.
Landfall Navigation
Laura Ashley
L'Enfance Magique
Light Touch
Lillian August
Little Eric
Lobster Bin

SHOPPING
BY NEIGHBORHOOD

Lois Richard's
Galleries
Louis Louis Antiques
Lux Bond & Green
Lynnens
Manderly Antiques
Manero's Meat Shop
Marks Brothers
Stationers
McArdle Florist &
Garden Center
McDermott Paint &
Wallpaper
Meli-Melo
Mephisto
Merry-Go-Round
Meserve Coale Gallery
Michael Kessler
Antiques
Michaelangelo of
Greenwich
Moonstruck
Nancy T's
Neal's Yard (Natural
Remedies)
Neighbor-to-Neighbor
Nine West
Omni Fitness
Outdoor Traders
Papery (The)
Parfumerie Douglas
Patio.com
Patricia Gourlay
Performance Imaging
Pet Pantry
Petit Patapon
Pier One Imports
Post Road Iron Works

Provinces de France
Quai Voltaire
Antiquites
Radio Shack
Razooks
Red Studio
Relax the Back
Renata Horstman
DePepe
Restoration Hardware
Richards
Right Start
Rinfret Home &
Garden
Rink & Racquet
Ritz Camera Center
Ronnie's News
Roundabout
Rue Faubourg St.
Honre'
Saint Clair
Saks Fifth Avenue
Sam Goody
Saturnia
Secret Garden
Shoes N More
Simon Pearce
Smart Kids Company
Sophia's Great Dames
Sportif Ltd.
St. Moritz
Steven B. Fox Fine
Jewelry
Stop & Shop Home
Delivery
Stuttig
Sweet Art
Tahiti Street

Talbots
Talbots Kids
Tallow's End
Threads & Threads
Tiffany & Co.
TSE Cashmere
Tulips Greenwich
Tuscany
Van Driver
Versailles
Victoria's Secret
Video Station
Waldenbooks
Waterworks
Wendy's Closet
Whimsies Doll House
& Minature Shop
Whitney Shop
Whole Foods
Wine World on Elm
Zyn's News

Harriman, NY
Woodbury Commons

New Canaan, CT
Beval Saddlery
Main Street Cellar
Penny Weights
Silk Purse
Smith & Hawken

New Rochelle, NY
Home Depot Expo

SHOPPING
BY NEIGHBORHOOD

Norwalk, CT
Axis Boardsports
Barnes & Noble
C.R. Gibson Factory
    Store
CompUSA
Decker's
Exposures Catalog
    Outlet
Gallerie SoNo
J. McLaughlin Outlet
Klaff's
Lillian August Home
    Outlet Store
Penzey's Spices
Portland Place Gallery
Pub Games Plus
Reo Appliances
Rex Dive Center
Rex Marine Center
Scandia Food and Gift
Toys "R" Us

Old Greenwich
All Sports Apparel
Baskin-Robbins
Beyond Bread
Care Center (The)
Children's Classics
Cook & Craft
CVS 24-Hr Pharmacy
Feinsod
Food Mart
Fuji Mart
Fun House
Gift Shop at Hyatt
    Hotel
House Warmings

Kerr's Village
    Pharmacy
Left of The Bank
Nordic Stove &
    Fireplace Center
Old Greenwich Flower
    Shop
Quelques Chose
Rummage Room
Sound Beach
    Sportswear
Staples Old
    Greenwich
Sweet Spot
Tetonia
Upper Crust & Bagel
    Company
Village Ewe

Orange, CT
Recreation Showroom

Port Chester, NY
Carvel
Farmer's Market
Friedman
Hank May's Goodyear
Harris Restaurant
    Supply
Home Depot
Home Works
Kneaded Bread
Kohl's
Nimble Thimble
Party City
Strauss Warehouse
    Outlet
Var Max Liquor Pantry
Vitamin Shoppe

Ridgefield, CT
Amish Outdoor Living

Riverside
Atelier Constantin
    Popescu
Celia's Hallmark
Colby & Stuart
    Antiques
Di Mare Pastry Shop
Estate Treasurers of
    Greenwich
Food Emporium
Hay Day
Imaginarium
International Soccer
    World
Music Source (The)
Riverside Florist &
    Gifts

Rye, NY
Parker's
Longford's

Scarsdale, NY
Bellini
Buy Buy Baby

Sherman, CT
White Silo Farm

SHOPPING

BY NEIGHBORHOOD

Stamford, CT
Accessory Store
Antique & Artisan
    Center
Baby & Toy
    Superstore
Bed Bath & Beyond
Bombay Furniture
Borders Books
Clinton's Pianos
Custom Golf of
    Connecticut
Eastern Mountain
    Sports
Ethan Allen
Fiesta Place
Filene's
Floor Covering
    Warehouse
Harborview Center for
    Antiques
Hiden Galleries
HomeGoods
Landmark Document
    Services
Lord & Taylor
Macy's
Pottery Barn
Ridgeway Shopping
    Center
Safavieh
Sal's Pastry Shop
Salvation Army
Shanti Bithi
Shippan Center for Arts
    & Antiques

Stamford Antique
    Mall
Stamford Antiques
    Center
Stamford Town Center
United House
    Wrecking

Westbrook, CT
Westbrook Factory
    Stores

Westport, CT
Great Outdoor Toy
    Company
Stew Leonard's
Tack Room

White Plains, NY
Bloomingdale's
Neiman Marcus
Nordstrom
Stickley - Audi
    Company
Westchester Mall

Wilton, CT
Kenneth Lynch &
Sons
Vallin Galleries

Yonkers, NY
Babies "R" Us

SHOPPING

BY STREET NUMBER

East Putnam Avenue

- 7 Greenwich Oriential Art
- 12 Country Floors
- 17 Threads and Threads
- 19 Just Books
- 25 Horseneck Liquors
- 36 Dorothy Mann
- 45 J. McLaughlin
- 45 Patricia Gourlay
- 45 Razooks
- 51 Elsebe
- 55 Cashmere Inc.
- 61 Cos Cob Farmers Market
- 71 Greenwich Photo, Card & Gift
- 79 Neal's Yard
  (Natural Remedies)
- 90 Whole Foods
- 115 Performance Imaging
- 120 AT Proudian
- 122 B & D Johnson Antiques
- 124 Food Mart
- 132 Confetti Card & Gift Shop
- 134 Manderly Antiques
- 213 Packages Plus-N-More
- 217 Gordon's Gateway to Sports
- 220 Nesting
- 239 Serenity Path
- 245 Commission Mart
- 248 Neighbor-to-Neighbor
- 254 Gift Shop at Christ Church
- 340 Greenwich Fruit & Produce
- 397 Darlene's Heavenly
  Chocolates
- 403 Party Paper & Things
- 405 Hobby Center
- 533 ELDC
- 600 Patio.com
- 1050 Hay Day
- 1064 Colby & Stuart Antiques
- 1072 International Soccer World
- 1075 Music Source (The)
- 1139 Atelier Constantin Popescu
- 1162 Estate Treasurers of
  Greenwich
- 1212 Fuji Mart
- 1239 CVS 24-Hr Pharmacy
- 1239 Food Emporium
- 1241 Imaginarium
- 1249 Riverside Florist & Gifts
- 1263 Celia's Hallmark
- 1263 Di Mare Pastry Shop
- 1265 Radio Shack
- 1297 Staples
- 1374 Nordic Stove &
  Fireplace Center
- 1800 Gift Shop at Hyatt Hotel

SHOPPING

BY STREET NUMBER

West Putnam Avenue
6 Greenwich Gallery
15 Duxiana
22 Provinces de France
23 Donald Rich Antiques
23 Waterworks
24 Mephisto
26 Ronnie's News
30 Louis Louis Antiques
40 Greenwich Bicycles
42 Right Start
44 Michael Kessler Antiques
44 Rue Faubourg St. Honré
48 Roundabout
101 Flinn Gallery
160 Food Emporium
161 Stop & Shop Home Delivery
168 Fashion Light Center
340 Griffin & Howe
345 Post Road Iron Works
354 Landfall Navigation
475 Greenwich Nursery
480 Anthropologie

Greenwich Avenue
Cross Street:
Putnam Avenue
16 Meserve Coale Gallery
30 Greenwich Health Mart
41 Sportif Ltd
42 Marks Brothers Stationers
47 Goldenberry
50 Moonstruck
54 Lois Richards Galleries
59 Avant-Tout

SHOPPING

BY STREET NUMBER

Greenwich Avenue

Cross Street:

Amogerone

72 Innovation Luggage
75 Kay-Bee Toys
82 Ritz Camera Center
85 Clementine's
86 Bang & Olufsen
88 Grossman's Shoe Store
89 Baskin-Robbins
92 April Cornell
96 Parfumerie Douglas
100 Candy Nichols
100 Candy Nichols Loft
103 Green
107 Barney's Place
113 Tahiti Street
117 Betteridge Jewelers
118 Complete Kitchen
120 Nine West

Greenwich Avenue

Cross Street:

Lewis

126 J Crew
140 Tiffany & Co.
145 Sam Goody
151 Talbots
158 Stuttig
160 Video Station
165 Talbots Kids
169 Lux Bond & Green
173 Waldenbooks
175 Hoagland's of Greenwich
195 Greenwich Hardware
200 Ann Taylor
200 Baker Furniture
200 Laura Ashley
200 Victoria's Secret
205 Saks Fifth Avenue
225 Pier One Imports
236 Baccarat
236 L'Enfance Magique

SHOPPING

BY STREET NUMBER

Greenwich Avenue

Cross Street:
Elm

239 Restoration Hardware
244 Chancy D'Elia
250 Cadeaux
251 Shoes N More
254 Banana Republic
255 Flight of Fancy
260 Beame & Barre
264 Baby Gap
264 Gap
264 Gap Kids
268 Papery (The)
271 Kate Spade
271 Petit Patapon
277 Grannick's Pharmacy
278 Lynnens
279 Whitney Shop
289 Best & Co
289 TSE Cashmere

Greenwich Avenue

Cross Street:
Havemeyer

311 Allen's of Nantucket
    Cashmere
315 Versailles
321 Audiocom
325 Simon Pearce
343 Bon Ton
344 Dinoffer
353 Michaelangelo of Greenwich
354 Zyns News
359 Richards

SHOPPING

BY STREET NUMBER

Greenwich Avenue
Cross Street:
Grigg/Fawcett
360 Tuscany
362 Meli-Melo
365 Federalist
365 Il Papiro
367 Relax the Back
374 Haagen-Dazs
375 Sweet Art
375 Avenue News
375 Wendy's Closet
378 Quai Voltaire Antiquites
382 Henri-Burton French
     Antiques
383 St. Moritz
384 Guild Antiques
398 EuroChasse
401 Chilly Bear
405 Cavalier Galleries

SHOPPING

35 mm
31 East Elm Street, 629.3566
Extremely competent staff. Leave your film here—you will like the results. There is an after-hours drop off at the front door.
Hours: weekdays, 8:30 am - 6 pm; Saturday, 10 am - 3 pm.

Accessory Store
69 Jefferson Street, Stamford, CT 327.7128
Dealers and decorators use this store and you should, too. They have a large selection of lamp shades and chandelier parts. They also have many lamps, display stands and more, all at great prices.
Hours: Monday - Saturday, 10:30 am - 5:30 pm; Sunday, noon - 5 pm.
Directions: I-95 N to Exit 8, R on Canal (second light), L on Jefferson. Store is next to Antique and Artisan Center but uses the same address.

Act II Consignment Shop
48 Maple Avenue, 869.6359
In a lovely old stone house behind the Second Congregational Church. There are five rooms of gently worn women's, men's and children's clothing. Also bric-a-brac and small household items.
Store Hours: Wednesday, 10 am - 5 pm;
Thursday and Saturday 10 am - 1:30 pm.
Consignment Hours: Wednesday noon - 3 pm; Thursday 10 am - 1 pm.
Closed June through September.

All Sports Apparel
146 Sound Beach Avenue
Old Greenwich, 698.3055
www.AllSportsApparel.com
Apparel for most sports, even yoga. Team licensed products including hats and jerseys. They also carry field hockey and lacrosse equipment.
Hours: Monday - Wednesday, 10 am - 6 pm; Thursday and
Friday, 10 am - 8 pm; Saturday, 9 am - 5 pm.

Allen's of Nantucket Cashmere
311 Greenwich Avenue, 629.1925
www.NantucketCashmere.com
Casual cashmere sweaters for men and women. Other casual women's attire.
Hours: Monday - Saturday, 9 am - 6 pm; Sunday, noon - 5pm.

SHOPPING

Ann Taylor
200 Greenwich Avenue, 661.6455
www.AnnTaylor.com
High end casual.
Hours: weekdays, 9 am - 6 pm; Saturday, 9 am - 5 pm.

Amish Outdoor Living
346 Ethan Allen Highway (Rte 7), Ridgefield, CT, 203.431.9888
Amish craftsmen from around the country supply this shop. Indoor
and outdoor tables and chairs are handcrafted and of fine quality. Sue
Knight, the manager, cares about the people who make it and the people
who buy it. Your children will love the outdoor playhouses and you
will like the reasonable prices and look of the sturdy children's furni-
ture.
Hours: Monday - Saturday, 9 am - 5 pm; Sunday, noon - 5 pm;
Closed Wednesdays.
Directions: Merritt Parkway N to exit 39 (or I-95 N to exit 15) (Norwalk),
N about 13 miles on Route 7.

Anthropologie
480 West Putnam Avenue, 422.5421
www.anthropologie.com
An eclectic group of faddish retro items. This large store carries a little
of everything from women's panties to books to doorknobs.
Hours: Monday-Saturday, 10 am - 7 pm (Thursday until 8 pm);
Sunday, 11 am - 5 pm.

Arnold Bakery Outlet
10 Hamilton Avenue, Byram (between I-95 exits 2 and 3),
531.4770
That good smell wafting onto I-95 just before Greenwich comes from
the Arnold Bakery. Their bread is available at local grocery stores, but
for a wide selection of bread at bargain prices visit the factory outlet
shop.
Hours: Monday - Wednesday, 8 am - 6 pm; Thursday - Friday, 6 am - 6
pm; Saturday, 8 am - 6 pm; Sunday, 10 am - 5 pm.

SHOPPING

April Cornell
92 Greenwich Avenue, 661.3563
www.aprilcornell.com
This small boutique for ladies and girls apparel is one of 65 such stores across the USA. They also carry screen-printed linens, pottery and gift ware. They have a nice selection of mother-daughter matched dresses.
Hours: Monday - Saturday, 10 am - 6 pm; Sunday, noon - 5 pm.

AT Proudian
120 East Putnam Avenue, 622.1200
They have been in the oriental rug business in Greenwich a long time and have a good reputation.
Hours: Monday - Saturday, 10 am - 5 pm.

Atelier Constantin Popescu
1139 East Putnam Avenue, Riverside, 637.7421
Sells, repairs and rents string instruments.
Hours: weekdays, 10 am - 6 pm; Saturday, 10 am - 2 pm.

Audiocom
321 Greenwich Avenue, 552.5224
www.AudiocomHiFi.com
Previously in Old Greenwich since 1968. They sell high quality audio and video equipment.
Hours: weekdays, 10 am-5:30 pm, excluding holidays;
Saturdays, 10 am - 5 pm.

Avant-Tout
59 Greenwich Avenue, 861.5826
Hand-knit sweaters made to order. French and Italian dresses for all occasions.
Hours: Monday - Sunday, 10 am - 6 pm.

Avenue News
375 Greenwich Avenue, 629.2429
A popular shop with magazines on every topic.
Hours: Sunday - Thursday, 5:30 am - 9 pm;
Friday & Saturday until 10 pm.

SHOPPING

Axis Boardsports

132 Washington Street, South Norwalk, 203.866.6444

A store devoted to skateboards, skateboard accessories, snowboards and wakeboards.

Hours: Open everyday, noon - 8 pm (Friday and Saturday until 10 pm).

Directions: I-95N to exit 14, R off exit, Go down the hill and bear left at the first light on to Washington street.

B & D Johnson Antiques

122 East Putnam Avenue, 618.6009

A large showroom, primarily English furniture.

Hours: Monday-Saturday, 10 am - 5 pm.

Babies R US

2700 Central Park Ave., Yonkers, NY, 914.722.4500

Mega baby store selling toys, bedding, furniture.

Worth the drive: There is a street approximately 20 minutes away in Westchester County, NY called Central Park Avenue. Baby stores are along both sides of the street.

Hours: Monday-Saturday, 9:30 am - 9:30pm, Sunday, 10 am - 7 pm.

Directions: I-95 S to exit 21, I-287 W to exit 8 (Westchester Avenue towards White Plains), follow NY-119 to Bronx River Parkway S, from Bronx River Parkway take ramp towards Scarsdale/Ardsley, R on Ardsley Rd, L on NY-100 S/Central Park Avenue.

Baby & Toy Superstore

11 Forest Ave., Stamford, 327-1333

www.babyandtoy.com

Baby and teen furniture and accessories at reasonable prices. A good place for pregnant couples to register.

Hours: Monday - Saturday, 9:30 am - 5:30 (Thursday until 8pm); Sunday, noon - 5 pm.

Directions: I-95 N to exit 8, L at light, pass 3 lights, L on Forest.

Baby Gap

264 Greenwich Avenue, 625.0662

www.BabyGap.com

A department in the back of Gap Kids for infants up to about 36 months.

Hours: Monday - Saturday, 9 am - 7 pm (Thursday until 8 pm); Sunday, 10 am - 5 pm.

SHOPPING

Baccarat
236 Greenwich Avenue, 618.0900
www.baccarat.fr
French luxury crystal. A table set with their crystal is very special.
They also have a selection of pretty vases and gift ware.
Hours: Monday - Saturday, 10 am - 6 pm (Thursday - 7 pm)

Baker Furniture
200 Greenwich Avenue, 862.0655
www.BakerFurniture.com
Now you can buy directly what once was the exclusive province of
interior designers. Furniture, fabrics and accessories with a timeless
elegance.
Hours: Monday - Saturday, 10 am - 6 pm; Sunday, noon - 5 pm.

Banana Republic
254 Greenwich Avenue, 622.9199
www.BananaRepublic.com
They sell the Gap's higher end casual career clothing. Most of the clothes
are rather trendy.
Hours: Monday - Saturday, 10 am - 7 pm; Sunday, 11 am - 6 pm.

Bang & Olufsen
86 Greenwich Avenue, 625.3388
www.Bang-Olufsen.com
They have been creating music and audio systems for over 75 years.
Their Danish designs are so attractive they are on display at the Museum of Modern Art. In their store you will find stereos, speakers, tele-
visions and telephones.
Hours: Monday -Saturday, 10 am - 6 pm (Thursday until 8 pm);
Sunday noon - 5 pm

Barnes & Noble
360 Connecticut Avenue (Grade A Plaza), Norwalk, CT
203.866.2213
www.bn.com
This is the closest of their super-stores and like all of their stores,
stocked with a multitude of volumes on all subjects.
Hours: Monday - Saturday, 9 am - 11 pm; Sunday, 9 am - 9 pm.
Directions: I-95 N to exit 13, R on US 1.

SHOPPING

Barney's Place
107 Greenwich Avenue, 661.7369
British Art as well as fine art, craft and drafting supplies.
Hours: Monday - Saturday, 9 am - 5:30 pm.

Baskin-Robbins
89 Greenwich Avenue, 869.4098
146 Sound Beach Avenue, Old Greenwich, 637.0480
www.BaskinRobbins.com
31 flavors and more.
Greenwich Hours: Monday-Saturday, 11 am - 10 pm;
Sunday, 11 am - about 8 pm.
Old Greenwich Hours: Monday - Sunday, 10:30 am - 10:30 pm.

Beame & Barre
260 Greenwich Avenue, 622.0591
Dance wear to suit even the most discriminating ballerina's tastes.
Plus exercise wear, skating attire and costumes.
Hours: weekdays, 10 am - 5:30 pm; Saturday, 10 am - 5 pm.

Bed Bath & Beyond
Ridgeway Shopping Center, Stamford, CT, 323.7714
www.BedBathandBeyond.com
A huge store with everything you would expect.
Hours: Monday-Saturday, 9 am - 9 pm; Sunday, 9:30 - 6 pm.

Bedford Sportsman
25 Adams Street, Bedford Hills, NY, 914.666.8091
Specializes in freshwater fly-fishing equipment. A good resource for New York watershed streams.
Hours: Tuesday - Saturday, 9:30 am - 5:30 pm.
Directions: North Street to Banksville Road, becomes Rt 22. R at the end of Rt 22 into Bedford Village. L of village green, still on Rt 22 past Bedford Golf & Tennis Club, past Ripawam School. Take L fork; across from RR Ctr.

SHOPPING

Bellini Juvenile Designer Furniture

495 Central Park Avenue, Scarsdale, NY , 914.472.7336
Well-made baby and teen furniture.
Hours: Monday-Saturday, 10 am - 6 pm, Sunday, noon - 5 pm.
Directions: I-95 S to 287 W to exit 4 (RT-100A), L off Ramp towards
Hartsdale. At 3rd main intersection R on Central Park Avenue.

Best & Co

289 Greenwich Avenue, 629.1743
This is a sophisticated children's department store serving children
from infancy through the early teenage years. In addition to clothing,
the store offers layette registry, home furnishings for children and gifts.
They have a department in Bergdorf Goodman in New York City.
Hours: Monday - Saturday, 9:30 - 5:30

Betteridge Jewelers

117 Greenwich Avenue, 869.0124
www.betterridge.com
Third generation family-owned business. Buying, selling and collecting some of the finest jewelry for 104 years. The shop specializes in
timepieces, rare and exceptional stones, jewels and pearls, plus a broad
collection of classic and contemporary jewelry and silver to suit a diverse clientele.
Hours: Tuesday - Saturday, 9 am - 5 pm.

TIP: BABY STORES ON CENTRAL PARK AVENUE

It's worth the drive to visit these baby stores which
you will find along both sides of the street: Central
Park Avenue is approximately 20 minutes away in
Scarsdale, NY (Westchester County). You'll find everything you need for your children. Bring a lot of
energy–it's going to be an exhausting day!
Directions: I-95 S to 287 W to exit 4 (RT-100A), L off
Ramp towards Hartsdale. At 3rd main intersection R
on Central Park Avenue.

SHOPPING

Beval Saddlery

50 Pine Street, New Canaan, CT, 203.966.7828

www.beval.com

English saddlery and clothing. They do a good job of fitting a saddle to you and your horse.

Hours: Monday-Saturday, 9 am - 5 pm (Thursday until 8 pm).

Directions: Merritt Parkway N to Exit 37, L onto Route 124. At light (gulf station on right), L on Cherry Street. Go straight through the light, Cherry Street will turn into Pine Street.

Beyond Bread

216 Sound Beach Avenue, Old Greenwich, 637.2543

Wonderful croissants, brioche and fresh baguettes. Outstanding holiday and special order pies. Get there early.

Hours: Open every day except Monday, Tuesday-Friday, 6 am - 4 pm; Saturday, 6 am - 9 pm; Sunday, 6 am - 1 pm.

Black Forest

52 Lewis Street, 629.9330

www.blackforestpastryshop.com

German-style bakery. Don't miss the Black Forest Cake and Chocolate Mousse Bombe, Summer Fruit Tarts, delicious wedding cakes.

Try Bread Ventures' chocolate-cherry bread on the weekend.

Hours: Monday - Saturday, 7:30 am - 6 pm; Monday closes at 5 pm; Sunday, 8 am - 1 pm.

Bloomingdales

175 Bloomingdale Road, White Plains, NY, 914.684.6300

www.Bloomingdales.com

A large stand-alone store, with lots of parking.

Hours: Monday-Saturday, 10 am - 8 pm (Monday & Thursday until 9:30); Sunday, 11 am - 7 pm.

Directions: I-95 S to I-287 W to exit 8 (Westchester Avenue), L on Bloomingdale.

SHOPPING

Bombay Furniture
Stamford Town Center, 327.9116
Furniture that creates an English look on a low budget. Be prepared to assemble it.
Hours: Monday- Friday, 10 am - 9 pm; Saturday, 10 am - 8 pm; Sunday, noon - 6 pm.
Directions: I-95 N to exit 8, L on Atlantic, R on Tresser, L onto ramp.

Bon Ton
343 Greenwich Avenue, 869.0462
www.lobsterscanfly.com
This is a reliable fish store. They have high quality fish as well as prepared seafood specialties and a full line of Russian caviar.
Hours: Monday - Saturday, 7 am - 6 pm.

Borders Books
1041 High Ridge Road, Stamford, CT, 968.9700
www.borders.com
When you need to visit a mega-bookstore, this store is nearby. There is a nice coffee shop with good treats.
Hours: Monday - Saturday, 9 am - 11 pm; Sunday, 9 am - 9 pm.
Directions: Merritt Pkw N to exit 35, R on High Ridge.

Bruce Park Sports
104 Mason Street, 869.1382
Team uniforms and equipment for most sports.
Hours: weekdays, 10 am - 6 pm (Thursday - 7:30);
Saturday, 10 am - 5:30 pm; Sunday, 10 am - 3:30 pm.

Buy Buy Baby
1019 Central Park Avenue, Scarsdale, NY, 914.725.9220
Everything for children ages 0-3. Large store—wear comfortable shoes!
Hours: Monday-Saturday, 9:30 am - 9:30 pm; Sunday, 10:30 am - 6pm
Directions: I-95 S to 287 W to exit 4 (RT-100A), L off Ramp towards Hartsdale. At 3rd main intersection R on Central Park Avenue.

CVS 24-Hour Pharmacy
Thru-Way Shopping Center, 1239 East Putnam Avenue, Old Greenwich 698.4006

SHOPPING

C.R. Gibson Factory Store

39 Knight Street, Norwalk, CT, 203.840.3353

It's fun to have an outlet in our area for their fine quality photo albums, stationery and gift wrap.

Hours: Monday - Saturday, 9 am - 5 pm

Directions: I-95 N to exit 16 onto East Avenue to Wall Street, R at Meson Galecia Restaurant onto Knight.

Cadeaux

250 Greenwich Avenue, 629.8595

www.CadeauxArt.com

Antique prints, vintage posters and fine home furnishings.

Hours: Monday - Saturday, 10 am - 6 pm.

Candy Nichols and The Loft

100 Greenwich Avenue, 622.1220

www.CandyNichols.com

www.TheLoftAtCandyNichols.com

This successful children's store is run by two local moms. They know what kids in our schools think is "cool" and they tailor their merchandise to suit them. Candy Nichols has children's clothing and accessories from infants to girls size 6 and boys size 7. The Loft is a specialty store for older children, girl's sizes 7-14 and boy's 8-20. They have Quiksilver, Roxy and Lilly shops within the store.

Hours: Monday-Saturday, 9:30 am - 5:30 pm, Sunday noon - 5 pm.

(The) Care Center

29 Arcadia Road, Old Greenwich, 637.3599

www.YourCareCenter.com

A home medical equipment company with just about everything you need to recover from a short illness or long term care. They specialize in scooters, power wheelchairs, seat lift chairs and courteous service.

Hours: weekdays, 8:30 am - 5:30 pm; Saturday, by appointment.

Carolee Jewelry

19 East Elm Street, 629.1515

www.carolee.com

Classy costume jewelry. Pearls are her signature. She bought Jackie Kennedy's famous three-strand pearl necklace.

Hours: Monday - Saturday, 10 am - 5:30 pm.

SHOPPING

Carollines Studio
24 Byfield Lane, 661.6340 or 2267
Carol O'Neil is a master gilder with over 25 years experience. She specializes in the restoration of fine furniture, and decorative and painted pieces, including mirrors and frames. Hours by appointment.

Cashmere Inc.
55 E. Putnam Avenue, 552.1059
They have a wide selection of sweaters, dresses, scarves, gloves and friendly help.
Hours: Monday - Saturday, 9:30 am - 5:30 pm.
Open Sundays noon - 5 pm in December.

Cavalier Galleries
405 Greenwich Avenue, 869.3664
www.cavaliergalleries.com
Ronald Cavalier specializes in painting and sculpture by contemporary artists working in a representational style. You may already have smiled at one of the gallery's life-like sculptures on a sidewalk in Greenwich or Stamford.
Hours: Monday - Thursday, 10:30 am - 6 pm;
Friday & Saturday, 11 am - 9 pm; Sunday, noon - 5 pm.

Celia's Hallmark
Riverside Commons Shopping Center (1263 East Putnam), 637.3844
Complete line of Hallmark cards and gift items.
Hours: weekdays, 9 am - 8 pm, Saturday - 6 pm,
Sunday, 10 am - 2 pm.

Ceramic Design
26 Bruce Park Avenue, 869.8800
The store is larger than it appears. They have a good selection of tiles and knowledgeable help.
Hours: Monday-Friday, 9 am - 5 pm; Saturday, 10 am - 4 pm.

SHOPPING

Chancy D'Elia
244 Greenwich Avenue, 869.0654
One of the oldest stores in Greenwich opened in February 1934. For years this friendly staff has been helping local residents find the right apparel for all occasions. Moderately priced.
Hours: Monday - Saturday, 9 am - 5:30 pm.

Children's Classics
254 Sound Beach Avenue, Old Greenwich, 698.3255
A delightful collection of first-rate children's clothing. Greenwich mothers frequent this shop for basic as well as beautiful garments.
Hours: Monday - Saturday, 9:30 am - 5:30 pm.

Chillybear
401 Greenwich Avenue, 622.7115
www.chillybear.com
A store for the hip young adolescent. Filled with the latest garb as well as skateboards, in-line skates and accessories.
Hours: Monday - Saturday, 10 am - 6 pm; Sunday, noon - 5 pm.

Clementines
85 Greenwich Avenue, 869.9787
www.MyClementine.com
French and English household and gift items. Fun store to browse in.
Hours: Monday - Saturday, 9 am - 5 pm.

Clinton Crossing Premium Outlets
Route 81, Clinton, CT, 860.664.0700
www.premiumoutlets.com
The largest outlet center in Connecticut, they have seventy upscale stores. If you have time, have dinner at the nearby Inn at Chester, 318 West Main Street (Rts 145 & 81), Chester, CT, 860.526.9541 or at the top-rated French Restaurant Du Village, 59 Main Street (at Maple Street), Chester, CT, 860.526.5301.
Summer Hours: Monday - Saturday, 10 am - 9 pm;
Sunday, 10 am - 8 pm.
Winter Hours: Sunday - Wednesday, 10 am - 6 pm;
Thursday - Saturday, 10 am - 9 pm.
Directions: I-95 N exit 63.

SHOPPING

Clinton's Pianos

225 Atlantic Street, Stamford, 975.2905, 800.791.0982
www.clintonspianos.com
A great number of pianos, grand, upright, player and digital. They stock new and used pianos such as Steinway, Boston, Baldwin, Boshdorfer, Chickering, Yong Chang, Wurlitzer, Kohler & Campbell. They also do tuning, repair and rentals. They can help you arrange piano lessons.
Hours: Monday, Friday & Saturday, 10 am - 5 pm; Tuesday, Wednesday & Thursday, 10 am - 7 pm; Sunday, noon - 5 pm.
Directions: I-95 N to exit 8 (Atlantic Street), L on Atlantic.

Colby & Stuart Antiques

1064 East Putnam Avenue, 637.4523
Attractive, quality English and American late 18th and early 19th century antiques. Expect nice pieces but not bargains. They will make reproductions to fill in a collection or design. They have some estate jewelry.
Hours: Monday - Saturday, 10 am - 5 pm; Sunday, noon - 4 pm.

Commission Mart

245 East Putnam Avenue, Cos Cob, 869.5512
Furniture and collectibles. A collection of American art. Still some good finds.
Hours: Monday - Saturday, 9:30 am - 5:30 pm; Sunday, noon - 5 pm.

Compleat Angler

987 Post Road, Darien, CT, 203.655.9400
www.compleat-angler.com
A large selection of fly-fishing and light tackle spin-fishing equipment as well as outdoor clothing. Ask about their lessons and guide service.
Hours: Monday - Saturday, 9:30 am - 6 pm (Thursday until 8 pm); Sunday, 11 am - 4 pm.

Complete Kitchen

118 Greenwich Avenue, 869.8384
www.TheCompleteKitchenLLC.com
This shop caters to passionate cooks who want the best.
Hours: Monday - Saturday, 9:30 am - 6 pm.

SHOPPING

CompUSA

US 1, Grade A Plaza, Norwalk, CT, 203.852.7005
20 Tarrytown Road, White Plains, NY, 914.761.5111
If you know the computer equipment you want, this is a good place to find it.
Hours: Monday - Saturday, 10 am - 9 pm; Sunday, noon - 6 pm.
Directions to White Plains: I-95 S to I-287 W, I-287 exit 5, L over hwy, L on Tarrytown (100S/119E).
Directions to Norwalk: I-95 N to exit 13, R on US 1.

Computer Super Center

103 Mason Street, 661.1700
For friendly help and expert advice try the Super Center.
Hours: Monday - Saturday, 10 am - 9 pm; Sunday, noon - 6 pm.

Confetti Card & Gift Shop

132 East Putnam Ave, Cos Cob, 661.2022
Delightful cards and good selection of wrapping paper. The owners are some of the nicest people you will meet.
Hours: Monday - Saturday, 9 am - 6 pm, open Sunday during holidays.

Connecticut Wines and Liquors

1071 King Street, 531.8135
A selection of over 500 wines from around the world.
Hours: Monday - Saturday, 9 am - 8 pm.

Consigned Designs

115 Mason Street (Village Square off Mason Street), 869.2165
Designer consignments for women and children.
Hours: Monday- Saturday, 10 am - 5 pm.

Consign It

115 Mason Street, 869.9836
This shop is a good place to consign and a good place to buy. Not a lot of display room, as a result they are often light on furniture. During the summer months, they are able to display a wider variety by using an outdoor tent. A good source for pre-owned jewelry, silver and china. Fairly priced. If you have jewelry you'd like to consign, this is the place.
Hours: Monday - Saturday, 10 am - 5 pm. Closed Sunday.

SHOPPING

Cook and Craft

27 Arcadia Road, Old Greenwich, 637.2755
www.CookAndCraft.com
A unique shop with high quality kitchen essentials. The cookware, knives, utensils, gadgets, cookbooks and gourmet pantry items are selected by the owner, an ex-chef of ten years. They have a bridal registry.
Hours: Tuesday -Saturday, 10 am - 5:30 pm

Cos Cob Farmer's Market

61-63 East Putnam Avenue, Cos Cob, 629.2267
Fresh fruit, vegetables and flowers at very reasonable prices.
Hours: Monday - Saturday 8 am - 7 pm; Sunday 9 am - 6 pm.

Country Floors

12 East Putnam Avenue, 862.9900
www.countryfloors.com
A large store with a good selection of all styles and prices. One of 6 stores throughout the USA.
Hours: Monday-Friday, 9 am - 5:30 pm; Saturday, 9 am - 5 pm.

Custom Golf of Connecticut

2770 Summer Street, Stamford, CT, 323.7888
Wide variety of golf clubs for sale or rent and some clothing. They do repairs and re-gripping.
Hours: weekdays, 8 am - 6 pm (Thursday until 8 pm in summer); Saturday, 9 am - 5 pm.
Directions: I-95 N to Atlantic Street exit 8, L on Atlantic (becomes Bedford), past Stop & Shop, L and next L onto Summer.

Darien Golf Center

233 Post Road, Darien, CT, 203.655.2788
Excellent selection of golf equipment and men's clothing.
Hours: weekdays, 8 am - 5:30 pm; Saturday, 8 am - 5 pm; Sunday, 9 am - 4 pm.
Directions: I-95 N to exit 13, L on Post Rd.

SHOPPING

Darien Sport Shop

1127 Post Road, Darien, CT 203.655.2575

www.DarienSport.com

Good-looking sports attire. They also carry a limited supply of Boy and Girl Scout uniforms.

Hours: Monday to Saturday, 9 am - 5:30 pm; Thursday until 8:30 pm.

Directions: I-95 N to exit 11, turn toward Darien, keep left and merge on US-1 (Post Road).

Darlene's Heavenly Chocolates

397 East Putnam Avenue (Cos Cob Plaza), Cos Cob, 622.7077

Our favorite chocolate shop in town. Not only are the chocolates delicious, Darlene always makes you feel glad you shopped there. Ask her about special chocolate deliveries.

Hours: Monday - Saturday, 10:30 am - 6 pm; Expanded holiday hours.

Dave's Cycle and Fitness

78 Valley Road, Cos Cob, 661.7736

www.davescycle.com

A good source for bike rentals and exercise equipment.

Hours: Monday - Wednesday, Friday, 10 am - 6 pm; Thursday, 10 am - 8 pm; Saturday, 9 am - 5 pm; Sunday, noon - 4 pm.

Decker's

696 West Avenue, Norwalk, CT 203.857.4584

Off-price clothing store, especially good for cashmere sweaters.

Hours: Monday - Saturday, 10 am - 5:30 pm; Sunday, noon - 5 pm.

Directions: I-95 N to exit 15, US-7 N to exit 1, right on Cross, R on Belden, R on West.

De Mane's Golf, Inc.

35 Chapel Street, 531.9126

Golfers in-the-know visit Rick's shop for custom clubs and repairs.

Hours: Tuesday - Friday, 10 am - 6 pm; Saturday, 11 am - 4 pm.

SHOPPING

Diane's Books of Greenwich

8A Grigg Street, 869.1515

A family book store with a faithful and devoted following. You will find a wealth of children's books, a good travel book section and, best of all, a knowledgeable, resourceful sales staff. This is a must-visit bookstore.

Hours: weekdays, 9:30 am - 5 pm; Saturday, 9 am - 4 pm. July and August, 9:30 am - 5pm.

Diane's Doll Shoppe

227 Mill Street, 531.3370

www.dianesdollshoppe.com

A darling collection of play and collector dolls. Sweet faces so lifelike, they encourage you to pick them up and cuddle them. A delight for collectors and the little girl in your life.

Hours: Tuesday - Saturday, 10 am - 5 pm.

Di Mare Pastry Shop

Riverside Commons Shopping Center (1263East Putnam), 637.4781

www.DimarePastryShop.com

The hot spot to order your child's birthday cake. They have a large selection of themes & characters to decorate children's cakes (computerized and handmade).

Hours: Monday - Saturday, 8 am - 6:30 pm; Sunday, 8 am - 3pm in winter; in the summer, noon - 1 pm.

Dinoffer

344 Greenwich Avenue, 622.8238

Luggage, briefcases, handbags, wallets and photo albums. High quality, high end.

Hours: Monday - Saturday, 9:30 am - 6 pm.

Open Sundays 11 am - 5 pm, between Thanksgiving and Christmas.

Donald Rich Antiques

23 West Putnam Avenue, 661.6470

He has a large showroom of English and American antiques.

Hours: Tuesday - Saturday, 10 am - 5 pm.

SHOPPING

Dorothy Mann
36 East Putnam Avenue, 622.8588
Sophisticated business, evening and casual clothing. An exceptionally friendly staff to go with their exceptionally good taste.
Hours: weekdays, 10 am - 6 pm; Saturday, 10 am - 5:30 pm.

Duxiana Beds
15 West Putnam Avenue, 661.7162
www.Duxiana.com
Made in Sweden with several layers of springs, Dux beds are guaranteed for 20 years and cost between $4,000 and $8,000 for a king size bed and between $2,000 and $3,000 for a single. Owners of these beds tell us they are worth the cost.
Hours: Monday - Saturday, 10 am - 6 pm; Sunday, noon - 5 pm.

Eastern Mountain Sports
952 High Ridge Road, Stamford, CT 461.9865
www.ems.com
75 stores in 15 different states. A general purpose sports store with an emphasis on camping, climbing and kayaking. A good place to find out about climbing and kayaking instruction.
Hours: Monday - Saturday, 10am - 9pm; Sunday, noon - 6 pm; call for holiday hours.
Directions: Merritt Parkway North to exit 35. R on High Ridge.

ELDC (Early Learning Development Center)
522 East Putnam Avenue, Cos Cob, 869.0464
Generous donors seem to always leave small items and fine clothing. When one of our editors broke his arm, he needed to cut his jacket sleeve open to accomodate the cast. At ELDC he found a handsome Brooks Brothers blazer for $10. He liked it so much that even after the cast was removed, he had the sleeve repaired. He continues to wear it. A recent find: Wedgewood vase.
Hours: Monday - Saturday, 9:30 am - 4:30 pm; donations, 10 am - 3 pm.

Elsebe
51 East Putnam Avenue, 869.4760
Elegant casual and business attire from well known designers. Elsebe, the owner, gives great personal attention. She is very good at helping you find just the outfit you need.
Hours: Monday - Saturday, 10 am - 5:30 pm.

SHOPPING

Estate Treasures of Greenwich

1162 East Putnam Avenue, Riverside, 637.4200

An antique consignment shop which has a wide selection of jewelry and china. A good source for silver services and serving pieces. A large number of tables and desks, although some are high quality reproductions (always marked as reproductions).

Hours: Monday - Saturday, 10 am - 5:30 pm; Sunday, noon - 5:30 pm.

Ethan Allen

2046 West Main, Stamford CT, 325.2888

www.EthanAllen.com

This 30,000-square-foot store is the company's largest to date. Its collections are divided between informal and classic. They carry just about everything for a home, including a large selection of furniture, window treatments, area rugs and accessories.

Hours: Monday - Saturday, 10 am - 6 pm (Tuesday & Thursday, until 8 pm); Sunday, noon - 5 pm.

Directions: Just over the Greenwich border on US 1.

EuroChasse

398 Greenwich Avenue, 625.9501

www.eurochasse.com

Two floors of fascinating gifts and fashionable men's and women's sporting apparel. If you plan to hunt in Europe, this is a must. They also have serious fly fishing equipment.

Hours: Monday - Saturday, 10 am - 5 pm.

Exposures Catalog Outlet

87 Water Street (Sono Square), South Norwalk, CT, 203.866.5259

Excellent prices on their decorative accessories, photo albums and pretty frames.

Hours: Monday - Saturday, 10 am - 5:30 pm; Sunday, noon - 5 pm

Directions: I-95 N to exit 14, R on West, bear left at fork onto North Main, cross intersection with Washington street, L on Haviland, R on South Water.

SHOPPING

Farmer's Market

604 North Main Street, Port Chester, NY, 914.935.1075

When you are looking for fresh fruit and vegetables at off hours, this store, located next to Carvel in the circle between Greenwich and Port Chester, is a good bet. In addition their prices are very reasonable.

Hours: Monday - Saturday, 8 am - 7 pm; Sunday, 9 am - 6 pm.

Farmer's Markets

From mid-May to mid-October, farmers come to the local area, set up stands and sell their produce. It is usually picked the day it is sold and couldn't be fresher. At some of the stalls you can also find homemade items such as breads, jellies and cheese. Farmer's markets have become so popular that Greenwich residents dash to nearby towns on days the Greenwich Market is closed. Each market has its own character.

Saturday: Greenwich, Horseneck Parking Lot (across from the Boys & Girls Club), 9:30 am - 1:30 pm.

Monday: Stamford, Columbus Park, 10 am - 3 pm.

Wednesday: Darien, CVS Parking Lot, noon - 6 pm.

Thursday: Stamford, Columbus Park, 10 am - 3 pm.

Fashion Light Center

168 West Putnam Avenue, 869.3098

A handy local resource for bulbs, lampshades, lamps, chandeliers and repairs.

Hours: Monday - Saturday, 9 am - 5:30 pm.

Federalist

365 Greenwich Avenue, 625.4727

Not antiques, but only experts would know it. The shop is filled with fine reproductions of 18th century furniture and accessories.

Hours: Monday - Saturday, 10 am - 6 pm; Sunday, noon - 5 pm.

Feinsod

268 Sound Beach Avenue, Old Greenwich, 637.3641

www.servistar.com

A friendly, well-stocked hardware store run by people who take customer service that extra step. They even repair storm windows and screens.

Hours: Monday - Saturday, 8 am - 5:30 pm; Sunday, 10 am - 4 pm.

SHOPPING

Fiesta Place
902 E Main Street, Stamford 203.961.0034
They sell party favors including pinatas of all kinds
Hours: weekdays, 10 am - 7 pm, Saturday, 10 am - 6 pm

Fjord Fisheries Market
137 River Road, Cos Cob, 661.5006
www.fjordcatering.com
Fresh fish and friendly service. Imported smoked salmon and herring
from Norway.
Hours: Monday - Saturday, 8 am - 7 pm; Sunday, 10 am - 6 pm.
(In the winter they close at 5 pm.)

Filene's
Stamford Town Center 357.7373
Hours: Monday & Tuesday, 10 am - 9 pm; Wednesday, Thursday, Friday, 9 am - 9 pm; Saturday, 9 am - 8 pm; Sunday, 11 am - 7 pm.
Directions to Stamford Town Center: I-95 N to exit 8, L on Atlantic, R on Tresser, L onto ramp.

Finch Pharmacy
3 Riversville Road, Glenville, 531.8494
Friendly pharmacy in the heart of Glenville.
Hours: weekdays, 8 am - 6 pm; Saturday, 9 am - 6 pm. Closed Sunday.

Flight of Fancy
255 Greenwich Avenue, 661.1188
Children love this shop because it carries the latest in accessories and clothing. They carry Lilly Pulitzer apparel.
Hours: Monday - Saturday, 9:30 am - 6 pm; Sunday, noon - 5 pm.

Flinn Gallery
At Greenwich Library, 101 West Putnam Avenue, 622.7900
This attractive gallery, sponsored by the Friends of Greenwich Library, has rotating exhibits selected by a jury. In addition the Gallery hosts the annual juried exhibition of the Greenwich Art Society.

SHOPPING

Floor Covering Warehouse
112 Orchard Street, Stamford, CT, 323.3113
Tucked away, yet close to Greenwich, this family-owned carpet store has good prices and good service.
Hours: Tuesday-Friday, 9 am - 4:45 pm; Saturday, 9 am - 3:30 pm.
Directions: I-95 N to exit 7; R on Greenwich Avenue, R on Homestead, L on Orchard.

Food Emporium
160 West Putnam Avenue, 622.0374
www.foodemporium.com
A good general purpose grocery. It stays open late, even on weekends.
Hours: weekdays, open 24 hours-a-day; Saturday, 7 am - midnight; Sunday, 7 am - 9 pm.

Food Mart
120 Post Road (East Putnam Road), Cos Cob, 629.2100
26 Arcadia Rd, Old Greenwich, 637.1701
www.porricellis.com
Both stores are full-service supermarkets which have been family owned and operated for the past 51 years. They are neighborhood meeting spots where regulars highly praise their family service and excellent meat, fish and produce departments. Their deli makes some of the best sandwiches in town.
Hours: Monday - Sunday, 7 am - 7 pm (Friday until 8 pm, Sunday until 6 pm); closed most holidays.

Friedman, A.I.
431 Boston Post Road, Port Chester, NY, 914.937.7351
Discount art and craft supply store frequented by many local artists. Their custom framing hours may be different.
Hours: weekdays, 9 am - 8:30 pm; Saturday, 9 am - 6 pm; Sunday, 10 am - 6 pm.

Fuji Mart
1212 East Putnam Avenue, Old Greenwich, 203.698.2107
An authentic Japanese grocery. Buy a bag of frozen gyoza.
Hours: Tuesday - Friday, 10:30 am - 6:30 pm (Saturday until 7 pm); Sunday, 10 am - 6 pm.

SHOPPING

(The) Funhouse

236 Sound Beach Avenue, Old Greenwich, 698.2402

This is a store where you may happily take your children. They have a great variety of small, inexpensive items. Parents fill their party bags here. Good place to find a unique or hard-to-find gift. The staff couldn't be more friendly. They will suggest age-appropriate gifts, sure to please.

Hours: weekdays, 10 am - 6 pm; Saturday, 10 am - 5 pm;
Sunday, 11 am - 4 pm. Closed in August

Gallerie SoNo

68 Water Street, South Norwalk, 203.831.8332

They represent contemporary artists. They also frame the work they sell. Prices range from $400 to $10,000.

Hours: Tuesday by appointment; Wednesday & Thursday, 10 am - 6 pm; Friday & Saturday 10 am - 9 pm; Sunday noon - 5 pm.

Directions: I-95N to exit 14, R off exit, go down the hill on Fairfield Avenue, bear left at the first light on to Washington Street, R on Water (just before the bridge).

Gap

264 Greenwich Avenue, 622.5190

www.Gap.com

The Gap targets customers between the ages of 20 and 30. Its merchandise is divided between career clothing and trendy attire. Its lower price line is sold at Old Navy (an anchor store in the Ridgeway Shopping Center). Banana Republic carries their higher end casual career clothing.

Hours: Monday - Saturday, 9 am - 7 pm (Thursday until 8 pm);
Sunday, 10 am - 5 pm.

Gap Kids

264 Greenwich Avenue, 625.0662

www.GapKids.com

Sporty clothes for children from about 3 years old up to about 12.

Hours: Monday - Saturday, 9 am - 7 pm (Thursday until 8 pm);
Sunday, 10 am - 5 pm.

SHOPPING

Gift Shop - at Bruce Museum
1 Museum Drive, 869.0376

www.brucemuseum.com

This attractive, high-quality store is filled with unique gifts from around the world. Merchandise complements the Museum's current exhibits. Many items in the store have educational value. The selection of books is excellent. Be sure to attend their holiday gift bazaar.

Hours: Tuesday - Saturday, 10 am - 4:30 pm; Sunday, 1 am - 4:30 pm. Closed Mondays.

Gift Shop - at Christ Church
254 East Putnam Avenue, 869.9030

This is the "in" place to go when you need a special gift with meaning. Marijane Marks and her helpful staff have a fine selection of books, gifts, jewelry and greeting cards. During holidays, gifts cascade out of the shop, making the store a joy to visit.

Hours: Monday - Saturday noon - 5 pm; Sunday 10 am - 1 pm;

Gift Shop - at Greenwich Hospital
5 Perryridge Road, 863.3371

www.greenhosp.chime.org

They have a wide array of gifts for patients, including pretty planters and beautiful nightgowns. The items selected by the volunteer staff have made this shop a place to go whether or not you are visiting in the hospital. Selections are well-priced and tax free. All profits go the hospital.

Hours: weekdays, 9:30 am - 8 pm; Saturday, 11 am - 6 pm; Sunday, noon - 6 pm.

Go To Your Room
234 Mill Street, Byram, 532.9701

Children's rooms do not have to be boring. Fernando Martinez, an Argentine furniture designer, creates colorful, whimsical furniture which will make any child smile.

Hours: Monday - Saturday, 10:30 am - 5 pm.

SHOPPING

Goldenberry

47 Greenwich Avenue, 863.9522

www.goldenberry.com

Traditional teas, never out of fashion, are more popular than ever in Greenwich. This English importer can supply all of your tea party needs. Put together a gift basket from their selection of English teas, marmalades and biscuits.

Hours: Monday - Saturday, 10 am - 5:30 pm.

Goodwill Industries of Western CT, Inc.

At the Greenwich Recycling Center, Holly Hill Lane

203.576.0000   800.423.9787

www.goodwillwct.com

A large trailer with a friendly person ready to receive your donations is conveniently parked just inside our town "dump." Goodwill needs clothing, shoes, toys, tools, kitchenware, linens and small appliances in "saleable" condition. This is recycling in the true sense of the word.

Hours: Weekdays, 8 am - 3 pm; Saturday, 8 am - noon.

Gordon's Gateway to Sports

217 East Putnam Avenue (Mill Pond Shopping Center), 661.1824

Now in its 30th year of operation, this sports store is still going strong. They are well-known for their racquet sports. They will re-string your old racquet or lend you a new one to demo. They carry swimming attire for serious swimmers. They are experts at lacrosse equipment. During the winter they have an extensive ski department. Expect friendly service.

Hours: Monday - Thursday, 9 am - 8 pm; Friday, 9 am - 5:30 pm; Saturday, 9 am - 5 pm; Sunday, 11 am - 4 pm.

Grannick's Pharmacy & Medical Supply Company

277 Greenwich Avenue, 869.3492

They know and care about their customers. A good place to rent or buy medical equipment. Call for their delivery policy.

Hours: Monday - Saturday, 8:30 am - 7 pm (Saturday until 6 pm).

Great Outdoor Toy Company

9 Kings Highway, Westport, 203.222.3818

Interchangeable parts allow you to design fun redwood play sets.

Hours: Monday - Saturday, 9 am - 5 pm (closed Wednesday).

Directions: I95 N to Exit 17. L at exit, R on Sylvan Road, R on Rt 1, L on Kings Highway N.

SHOPPING

Green

103 Greenwich Avenue, 863.9120

www.GreenHomeFurnishings.com

Green is a specialty home furnishing store with a very artistic flair. No ordinary things here. They have an eclectic range of gifts, decorative textiles, lighting, occasional furniture and art.

Hours: Monday - Saturday, 9:30 am - 6 pm.

Greenwich Bicycles

40 West Putnam Avenue, 869.4141

www.GreenwichBikes.com

This store has all the right equipment. A very helpful web site to review before you shop for a bike.

Hours: Weekdays, 10 am - 6 pm; Saturday, 9:30 am - 5:30 pm

Greenwich Exchange for Women's Work

28 Sherwood Place, 869.0229

This small shop, whose mission is to help others help themselves, has reasonably-priced, handmade items by local residents. If you want to give a gift to a newborn or young child, you will like their handknit sweaters and smocked dresses.

Hours: Weekdays, 9 am - 2 pm.

Greenwich Fruit and Produce

340 Greenwich Avenue, 869.7903

This is a high quality fruit and vegetable shop with lots of variety. We like treating ourselves to their bouquets of lovely, inexpensive, fresh flowers. They always have a nice selection on the street just outside the shop.

Hours: Monday - Saturday, 8 am - 7 pm; Sunday, 9 am - 6 pm.

Greenwich Gallery

6 West Putnam Avenue, 622.4494

www.artnet.com/greenwich.html

This gallery specializes in 19th and early 20th century paintings. Besides being a pleasure to visit, this store also offers appraisal, restoration and framing services.

Hours: Monday - Saturday, 10 am - 5 pm.

Greenwich Hardware

195 Greenwich Avenue, 869.6750

Anyone moving into town will find this one of the most valuable resources. A great place to call when you have forgotten something: they will deliver it to you. Greenwich Hardware has a 10,000 sq. ft store on Banksville Home Center Complex. A great resource for back country residents: 914-234-2000.

Hours: Monday - Saturday, 8 am - 5:30 pm; Sunday, 9 am - 5 pm.

Greenwich Healthmart

30 Greenwich Avenue, 869.9658

A well-stocked health product store, including some foods and a great variety of vitamins and homeopathic remedies. Their cheerful service makes everyone feel well. Be sure to ask for their excellent newsletter.

Hours: everyday, 8:30 am - 5:30 pm (Sunday until 5 pm).

Greenwich Hospital Gift Shop Flowers

5 Perryridge Road, 863.3371

The gift shop keeps a selection of fresh flowers in vases. Call and they will immediately deliver a bouquet to your favorite patient.

Hours: Weekdays, 9:30 am - 8 pm; Saturday, 10 am - 6 pm;
Sunday, 12 am - 6 pm.

Greenwich Kayak & Canoe Co

42 Water Street (above Rudy's Bait & Tackle Shop), 351.3483

Maria Gourlay carries kayaks, canoes and accessories such as life jackets, paddles, pumps, chairs for canoes and instructional videos.

Hours: weekdays, 9 am - 5 pm; Saturday 9 am - 4 pm.

Greenwich Nursery

475 West Putnam Avenue, 622.0056

A resource for firewood. They will deliver.

Hours: weekdays, 8 am - 4 pm.

Greenwich Orchids

106 Mason Street, 661.5544

Grown in a local greenhouse, the orchids are exquisite. They have many varieties, some with unusual colors. They also make lovely flower arrangements.

Hours: Monday - Saturday, 9 am - 6 pm.

SHOPPING

Greenwich Oriental Art
7 East Putnam Avenue, 629.0500
A mixture of old and modern oriental art.
Hours: Monday-Saturday, 10 am - 5:30 pm

Greenwich Photo, Card & Gift
17 East Putnam Avenue, 869.4325
Many greeting cards designed to make you smile. Also a place to find photo frames and cameras. They will make holiday cards from your photos.
Hours: Weekdays, 8:30 am - 6 pm, Saturday until 5:30,
Sunday, 10 am - 4 pm.

Griffin & Howe
340 West Putnam Avenue, 618.0270
www.griffinhowe.com
Excellent sporting firearms, clothing and accessories. This is the place serious skeet and trap shooters buy their shotguns. They also have shooting schools and coaching.
Hours: Monday - Wednesday, 10 am - 6 pm; Thursday, 11 am -o 8 pm; Friday, 10 am - 6 pm; Saturday, 9 am - 5 pm.

Grossmans Shoe Store
88 Greenwich Avenue 869.2123
Their good selection of top of the line shoes has made them a favorite of several generations in Greenwich. Twice a year they have a half-price sale. It is a big draw, so arrive early.
Hours: Monday - Saturday, 9:30 am - 5:30 pm; Sunday, noon - 5 pm.

Guild Antiques
384 Greenwich Avenue, 869.0828
Owned by long term Greenwich residents, Regina and George Rich. They carry a large selection of English and American antiques.
Hours: Monday-Saturday, 10 am - 5 pm

Hank May's Goodyear
285 Boston Post Road (Route 1), Port Chester, NY, 914.937.0700
Eddie Jones, manager of this tire and service shop, can be trusted to give you the right information and great service.
Hours: Weekdays, 7 am - 6 pm; Saturday, 7 am - 5 pm.

SHOPPING

Harbor View Antiques Center
101 Jefferson Street, Stamford, CT, 325.8070
25,000 square feet of antiques.
Monday - Saturday, 10:30 am - 5:30 pm; Sunday, noon - 5 pm.
Directions: I-95 N to exit 8, R on Canal (at second light), L on Jefferson.

Harrington's of Vermont
83 Railroad Avenue, 661.4479
www.HarringtonHam.com
They sell their line of smoked meats, imported cheeses and a variety of jams, relishes, maple syrup and other gourmet products. If you need a ham for a party, this is the place. Try one of their ham sandwiches and you will know what we mean.
Hours: Monday - Saturday, 9:30 am - 5:30 pm; Sunday, 11 am - 4 pm.

Harris Restaurant Supply
25 Abendroth Avenue, Port Chester, NY, 914.937.0404
Commercial restaurant supplier which also allows the general public to buy supplies. Cooks go crazy here.
Hours: weekdays, 9 am - 4 pm; Saturday, 9 am - 2 pm.

Hayday
1050 East Putnam Avenue, Riverside, 637.7600
A sophisticated, gourmet country shop for fruits, vegetables and treats. Hayday carries hundreds of imported and American cheeses. Don't go in hungry!
Hours: Monday - Saturday, 8 am - 8 pm; Sunday, 8 am - 7 pm.

Helen Ainson
1078 Post Road, Darien, CT, 203.655.9841
www.HelenAinson.com
For over 20 years Helen Ainson has helped ladies in our area look their best at special occasions. When you discover you are soon to be "mother-of-the-bride," you will like their friendly, knowledgeable advice and fashions from over 150 manufacturers.
Hours: Monday - Saturday, 9:30 am - 5:30 pm (Tuesday & Thursday until 7 pm).
Directions: I-95 N to exit 11, one block north.

SHOPPING

Henri-Burton French Antiques

382 Greenwich Avenue, 661.8529

18th and 19th century French country antiques and accessories. A specialty is 19th century gold leaf mirrors.

Hours: Monday - Saturday, 10 am - 5 pm.

Hickory & Tweed

410 Main Street, Armonk, NY, 914.273.3397

www.hickorytweed.com

A ski store with a wide selection of skis to buy or rent. Good technical help.

Hours: Weekdays, 10 am- 5:30 pm (Thursdays open until 8 pm); Saturday, 9:30 am - 5:30 pm; Sunday, noon - 4 pm

Directions: 95S to 287 W to 684 N to Y38. Bear right to Rt 225, 2nd light R of Rt 128 (Main Street).

Hoagland's of Greenwich

175 Greenwich Avenue, 869.2127

A first-class gift shop owned for years by a Greenwich resident with exquisite taste. This is THE place for brides and grooms to register.

Hours: Monday - Saturday, 9 am - 5:30 pm.

Hobby Center

405 East Putnam Avenue (Cos Cob Plaza), Cos Cob, 869.0969

For years, kids in Greenwich have been rewarded for cleaning their room or finishing their homework with a trip to the Hobby House. Rockets and radio-controlled boats are current favorites.

Hours: Monday - Saturday, 9:30 am - 5:30 pm

Home Depot

600 Connecticut Avenue, Norwalk, CT, 203.854.9111

150 Midland Avenue, Port Chester, NY, 914.690.9755

www.homedepot.com

They have 40,000 brand names to choose from.

Hours: Monday - Saturday, 7 am - 10 pm; Sunday, 9 am - 6 pm.

Directions to the Norwalk store:

I-95 N to exit 13, R on US 1 (Connecticut Avenue).

Directions to the Port Chester store:

I-95S to exit 21, immediate R on Midland Avenue.

SHOPPING

Home Depot Expo
8 Joyce Road, New Rochelle, (914) 637.5600
If you are decorating or re-decorating your house, you owe it to yourself to go there to get ideas or to buy quality home accessories. Their contracting and design services can be slow.
Hours: Weekdays, 10 am - 9 pm; Saturday, 9 am - 9 pm; Sunday, 11am - 6 pm
Directions: I-95 exit 16, left at first light, go under RR at second light L, 100 yards on L.

HomeGoods
High Ridge & Cold spring Road, Stamford, 964.9416
www.HomeGoods.com
When you are ready to accessorize a room, this store is a must. Casual, fun items at great prices.
Hours: Monday - Saturday, 9:30 am - 9:30 pm; Sunday, 11 am - 6 pm.
Directions: Merritt Parkway N to exit 35, R on High Ridge

Home Works
509 North Main Street, Port Chester, NY 914.934.0907
When you want to redo your window draperies or upholster a chair, they are a good resource for your fabric.
Hours: Monday-Friday, 10 am - 5 pm.

Horseneck Liquors
25 East Putnam Avenue, 869.8944
www.horseneck.com
An excellent selection of wines from California and all over the world. Friendly, good advice. They will deliver and, if needed, gift-wrap for you.
Hours: Monday - Saturday, 9 am - 7 pm.

Hospital Thrift Shop
29 B Sherwood Place, 869.6124
Larger furniture items plus clothing and books are welcome here. Our finds: an old steamer trunk and a lovely white Laura Ashley graduation dress for $45!
Hours: Weekdays, 8:30 am - 4:30 pm; Saturday, 8:30 am - 1 pm. Closed Sunday.

SHOPPING

House of Fins
99 Bruce Park Avenue, 661.8131
Everything you need to make a successful aquarium, and good advice as well.
Hours: Monday - Saturday, 10 am - 7 pm; Sunday, noon - 5 pm.

Housewarmings
235 Sound Beach Avenue, 637.5106
Unique home furnishings and decorative accessories.
Hours: Weekdays, 10 am - 6 pm; Saturday, 10 am - 5 pm.

IKEA
1000 Center Drive, Elizabeth, NJ, 908.289.4488
www.Ikea.com
A huge store, with moderate prices and several grades of Scandinavian designed furniture and housewares. Popular with Europeans. There is a supervised children's play area. A good place to go when you are on a limited budget and need to furnish a home or dorm room quickly.
Hours: Monday - Saturday, 10 am - 9 pm; Sunday, 10 am - 6 pm
Directions: I-95 S across the George Washington Bridge to the New Jersey Turnpike exit 13A then follow signs.

Il Papiro
365 Greenwich Avenue, 661.2860
One of three stores. The others are in Palm Beach and New York City. They have Italian, handmade, decorated papers as well as desk accessories, and writing accessories.
Hours: Monday - Saturday, 10 am - 6 pm;
Open Sunday in November and December.

Images
202 Sound Beach Avenue, Old Greenwich, 637.4193
A high percentage of Old Greenwich residents trust their film to this shop. Among the many things they do, in addition to framing, are restore damaged photographs by removing scratches, tears and stains, enhance photographs to reduce red-eye or correct color and brightness, and, of course, enlarge, crop or add a border. No negative is required.
Hours: Monday - Saturday, 9 am - 6 pm. Winter hours may vary.

SHOPPING

Imaginarium
1241 East Putnam Avenue (Riverside Commons Shopping Center), Riverside, 637.7595
Our newest toy store was worth the wait. Warning—it is impossible to get little ones to leave!
Hours: Monday - Saturday, 10 am - 7 pm; Sunday, 11 am - 5 pm

Innovation Luggage
72 Greenwich Avenue, 869.5322
www.InnovationLuggage.com
A national chain carrying luggage, casual bags, business cases and travel accessories.
Hours: Monday - Saturday, 9 am - 6 pm (Open Saturday at 9:30 am); Sunday, noon - 5 pm.

Inspirations
135 Mason Street 629.8473
Gloria Aslanian has gifts and books that appeal to the Catholic, Jewish and Protestant faiths. If you are looking for a religious CD, children's game, or gift to cheer or inspire, she has a wide selection.
Hours: Tuesday - Friday, 10:30 am - 5:30 pm; Saturday 10 am - 2 pm; summer hours may vary.

International Soccer World
1072 East Putnam Avenue, Riverside, 637.3482
www.IntSoccWorld.com
This is the source for soccer clothing, supplies and equipment.
Hours: weekdays, 10 am - 6 pm; Saturday, 9 am - 5 pm; Sunday, 11 am - 3 pm.

Invisible Fencing
493 Danbury Road, Wilton, Stamford, 800.628.2264
www.caninefence.com
A safe way to keep your dog in your yard. Also works to keep your pet out of designated rooms in your home.
Hours: Monday - Saturday, 9 am - 6 pm.

SHOPPING

Ivy Urn
115 Mason Street (Village Square), 661.5287
www.ivyurn.com
A gift shop with attractive ornaments for gardeners.
Hours: Monday - Saturday, 10 am - 5 pm.

J Crew
126 Greenwich Avenue, 661.5181
www.JCrew.com
A large store with classic men and women's casual apparel. Wonderful service.
Hours: Monday - Saturday, 10 am - 7 pm (Thursday until 8 pm);
Sunday, noon - 5 pm.

Just Books
19 East Putnam Avenue, 869.5023
Just Books, Too
28 Arcadia Road, Old Greenwich, 637.0707
www.justbooks.org
Just Books is a haven for the sophisticated reader or someone looking for personal service. You can get a book delivered to a friend in Greenwich Hospital. Ask to be on their mailing list. The book reviews are interesting and keep you up-to-date with the literary world. They host many events to meet important authors. Be sure to frequent these charming bookstores.
Hours: weekdays, 9 am - 5:30 pm; Saturday, 9 am - 5 pm.

Kate Spade
271 Greenwich Avenue, 622.4260
www.KateSpade.com
Women's specialty shop selling chic handbags, shoes, and accessories.
Hours: Monday - Saturday, 10 am - 6 pm; Sunday, noon - 5 pm.

Kay-Bee Toy
75 Greenwich Avenue, 622.6081
A friendly store with tons of toys for kids who must have what is advertised on TV.
Hours: Monday - Saturday, 9 am - 7 pm; Sunday, 10 am - 6 pm.

SHOPPING

Kenneth Lynch & Sons

84 Danbury Road, Wilton, CT, 203.762.8363

www.klynchand sons.com

If you are looking for an elaborate fountain, pretty garden bench, statuary, topiary, weathervane or sundial, this will be paradise for you. The Lynch family has been crafting garden ornaments for over sixty years. Ornaments are made to order. Their extensive catalog is available for $10. Hours: Weekdays, 8 am - 5 pm.

Directions: Merritt Parkway N to exit 39 (Norwalk), N on Rte 7.

Kerr's Village Pharmacy

212 Sound Beach Avenue, Old Greenwich, 637.0593

A friendly local pharmacy with senior discounts and prescription delivery.

Hours: weekdays, 8 am - 6:30 pm; Saturday, 8:30 am - 6 pm.

Kid's Supply Co.

14 Railroad Avenue, Greenwich, 422.2100

www.KidsSupplyCo.com

It's a pleasure to visit this store selling beautiful, well-built, pricey kid's furniture and decorative accessories and linens.

Hours: weekdays, 9:30 am - 5:30 pm; Saturday, 10 am - 5 pm; Sunday noon - 4 pm.

Kiev USA

248 Mill Street, Byram, 531.0900

www.Kievusa.com

How lucky we are to have an in-town shop which can repair cameras such as Nikon, Zeiss and Leica. They also sell reconditioned cameras.

Hours: weekdays, 9:30 am - 5:30 pm; Saturday, 10 am - 5 pm (closed on Saturday during the summer).

Kinkos

48 West Putnam Avenue, 863.0099

www.kinkos.com

Pricey, but a great resource for copies to meet a deadline or when you need a passport photograph quickly. The Greenwich Kinkos is no longer open 24/7. The closest 24/7 Kinkos is 980 High Ridge Road, Stamford, CT 203.968.8100.

Hours: weekdays, 7 am - 9 pm.

SHOPPING

Klaff's

28 Washington Street, South Norwalk, CT, 800.552.3371
www.klaffs.com
A tremendous selection of indoor and outdoor lighting fixtures as well as a huge selection of door hardware, bathroom fixtures, and kitchen cabinets.
Hours: Monday - Saturday, 9 am - 5:30 pm; Thursday, 9 am - 8 pm.
Directions: I-95 N, exit 14. R at the top of the ramp, down hill, bear L at first light, go straight through 2nd light. Klaffs is one block R.

(The) Kneaded Bread

181 North Main Street, Port Chester, NY, 914.937.9489
Their freshly baked bread—all kinds— is delicious. Have a sandwich when you visit, but be sure to take home their Cinnamon Swirl. It makes great French toast.
Hours: Tuesday - Friday, 7 am - 6 pm; Saturday, 8 am - 4 pm; Sunday, 8 am - 1 pm.

Kohl's

431 Post Road (Shopping Center), Port Chester, NY 914.690.0107
www.Kohls.com
More of a J. C. Penny than a Caldor, they sell men and women's clothing and accessories as well as some household items at discounted prices.
Hours: Monday - Saturday, 8 am - 10 pm; Sunday, 10 am - 8 pm.
Directions: Follow US 1 through the main part of Port Chester.

Landfall Navigation

354 West Putnam Avenue, 661.3176
www.landfallnavigation.com
Henry Marx, the owner, is very knowledgeable and helpful. If you have a boat, he has what you need: charts, supplies or just information. Be sure to get a copy of his catalog.

Landmark Document Services

375 Fairfield Avenue, Stamford, 325.4300
www.landmarkprint.com
Our favorite place for larger volume printing. They are very careful and easy to work with. Their reasonable prices don't hurt, either.
Hours: weekdays, 8:30 am - 5:30 pm.

SHOPPING

Laura Ashley
200 Greenwich Avenue, 622.2382
www.LauraAshley.com
Conservative little girls clothing for ages 2 - 9. They also have home accessories and bedding.
Hours: Monday-Saturday, 10 am - 6 pm; Thursday until 7 pm; Sunday, noon - 5 pm.

Left of the Bank
185 Sound Beach Avenue, Old Greenwich, 637.4000
This quality framer does a lot of framing for local artists. Recently she has expanded her studio to include a gallery.
Hours: Tuesday - Saturday, 9 am - 5 pm.

L'Enfance Magique
236 Greenwich Avenue, 625.0929
Pretty French clothes accent this shop.
Hours: Monday - Saturday, 10 am - 5:30 pm; Sunday, noon - 5 pm.
Closed on Sundays, Memorial Day - Labor Day.

Liberty Village
1 Church Street, Flemington, New Jersey, 908.782.8550
www.premiumoutlets.com/location/liberty
Shop until you drop. There are more than 120 outlet stores in a number of outlet centers in Flemington. Sixty of the shops are in Liberty Village.
Hours: Sunday - Wednesday, 10 am - 6 pm; Thursday - Saturday, 10 am - 9 pm.
Directions: I-95 to I-287 W to I-287 S to Rte 202 W.

(The) Light Touch
12 Lewis Street, 629.2255
When you are looking for a lamp or lamp shade with character, be sure to stop in here.
Hours: Monday - Saturday, 10 am - 5:30 pm.

Lillian August
19 West Elm Street, 629.1539
Sofas, chairs and desks designed by Lillian August.
Hours: Monday - Wednesday, 10 am - 6 pm; Thursday - Saturday, 10 am - 7 pm; Sunday, noon - 5 pm.

SHOPPING

Lillian August Home Outlet Store

85 Water Street (Sono Square), South Norwalk, CT, 203.838.0153
www.lillianaugust.com
Sofas, chairs and desks designed by Lillian August.
Hours: Monday - Wednesday, 10 am - 6 pm; Thursday - Saturday, 10 am - 7 pm; Sunday, noon - 5 pm.
Directions: I-95 N to exit 14, R on West, bear left at fork onto North Main, cross intersection with Washington street, L on Haviland, R on South Water.

Little Eric

15 East Elm Street, 622.1600
A children's shoe store with high quality dress and play wear. A helpful sales staff eliminates the usual shoe shopping hassles.
Hours: Monday - Saturday, 10 am - 6 pm; Sunday 11 am - 5 pm.

Lobster Bin

204 Field Point Road, 661.6559
Just off Railroad Avenue. Plenty of fresh fish as well as parking.
Hours: Monday - Saturday, 8 am - 6 pm; Sunday, 9 am - 1 pm.

Locks and Keys (Charles Stuttig)

Charles Stuttig, 158 Greenwich Avenue, 869.6260
A fixture in Greenwich for many years, they provide a wide variety of locks and safes. Whether you have an emergency or just need a key replaced, they can be counted on and trusted.
Hours: weekdays, 7:30 am - 5:30 pm; Saturday, 8 am - 3 pm.

Lois Richards Galleries

54 Greenwich Avenue, 661.4441
www.loisrichards.com
We are pleased to see this gallery, which has many European artists, carrying the work of favorite Greenwich artists such as Margaret Bragg.
Hours: Monday - Saturday, 10 am - 5 pm; Sunday and evenings by appointment.

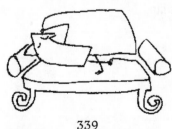

SHOPPING

Lord and Taylor

110 High Ridge Road, (at convergence of Long and High Ridge Roads) Stamford, CT, 327.6600

www.LordAndTaylor.com

A large full-service, stand-alone store, with easy parking and well priced, attractive fashions for men and women.

Hours: weekdays, 10 am - 9:30 pm; Saturday, 10 am - 8 pm; Sunday, 11 am - 7 pm.

Directions: Merritt Parkway to exit 34, R on Long Ridge, watch for sign on left.

Louis Louis Antiques

30 West Putnam Avenue, 629.1792

French Antiques

Hours: Tuesday - Saturday, 10 am - 5 pm.

Lux Bond & Green

169 Greenwich Avenue, 629.0900

www.LBGreen.com

They carry David Yurman jewelry and Steuben crystal.

Hours: Monday - Saturday, 9:30 am - 5 pm .

Lynnens

278 Greenwich Avenue, 629.3659.

www.Lynnens.com

Since 1980 this high end bed, bath, linen and nightwear store has been a real favorite of Greenwich residents. Their specialties are service and customizing linens.

Hours: Monday - Saturday, 10 am - 6 pm.

Macy's

Stamford Town Center, 964.1500

Hours: Monday & Tuesday, 10 am - 9 pm; Wednesday, Thursday, Friday, 9 am - 9 pm; Saturday, 9 am - 8 pm; Sunday, 11 am - 7 pm.

Directions to Stamford Town Center: I-95 N to exit 8, L on Atlantic, R on Tresser, L onto ramp.

SHOPPING

Main Street Cellar

120 Main Street, New Canaan, 203.966.8348
A mixture of antiques and interesting objects. There are other antique shops near-by that are worth checking too.
Hours: Monday-Saturday, 10 am - 5 pm.
Directions: Merritt Parkway N to exit 37, L on Rte 124/South Street, R on Elm, L on Main.

Manderly Antiques

134 East Putnam Avenue, 861.1900
Enter the shop from Millbank Avenue, "Mill Post Plaza", where there is easy parking. This shop, with its quality collection of antiques, many with animal motifs, will make you smile and want to buy.
Hours: Monday - Saturday, 10 am - 5 pm.

Manero's Meat Shop

559 Steamboat Road, 622.9684
www.maneros-greenwichct.com
You can still ask the butcher for your favorite cuts. Phone orders are welcome. Many of the best barbecues in town start here.
Hours: Weekdays, 9 am - 7 pm; Saturday 9 am - 9 pm;
Sunday, 9 am - 5:30 pm.

Marks Brothers Stationers

42 Greenwich Avenue, 869.2409
A Greenwich landmark shop with great customer service. Stop in to get your favorite newspaper or a new Mont Blanc fountain pen or anything in between. They are a complete office outfitter for supplies, equipment and furniture. They have the largest collection of writing instruments in Fairfield County.
Hours: Opens every day at 6:30 am; Monday until 5:45 pm;
Tuesday - Friday until 7 pm; Saturday until 5 pm; Sunday until 3 pm.

McArdle-MacMillen Florist & Garden Center

48 Arch Street, 661.5600, 800.581.5558
www.mcardles.com
Many pretty dinner tables are adorned with their arrangements. A good place to buy flowers (they have a large selection), corsages and plants. Come early on weekends during the garden season, as it is always busy —or place an order on their web site.
Hours: Monday - Saturday, 8 am - 5:30 pm; Sunday, open April, May, June, December 9 am - 2 pm.

SHOPPING

McDermott Paint & Wallpaper

35 Spring Street, 622.0699

If you are planning to do any of your own home painting, you can count on good advice and products from this long-time Greenwich shop. If you are trying to match a color, take a sample and they can duplicate it with their computer.

Hours: Monday - Saturday, 7:30 am - 5 pm.

(J.) McLaughlin

45 East Putnam Avenue, 862.9777

Primarily women's informal clothing.

Hours: Monday - Saturday, 10 am - 6 pm (Thursday until 7 pm).

(J.) McLaughlin Company Store

68 Water Street, south Norwalk, CT 203.838.8427

Primarily an outlet for women's informal clothing.

Hours: Monday - Saturday, 10 am - 6 pm; Sunday, noon - 6 pm.

Directions: I-95 N to exit 14, R on West, bear L at fork onto North Main, cross intersection with Washington Street, L on Haviland.

Mephisto Shoes

24 West Putnam Avenue, 869.9060

www.Mephisto.com

Casual shoes, made in France, costing about $300 a pair.

Hours: Monday - Saturday, 10 am - 6 pm

Merry-Go-Round

38 Arch Street, 869.3155

Thrift shop. Clothing and small objects are all neatly displayed. Our finds: two pretty framed watercolors, and a tennis skirt for $3.

Hours: Tuesday - Friday, 10 am - 3 pm; Saturday, 10 am - 2 pm; Closed July and August.

Meserve Coale Gallery

16 Greenwich Avenue, 661.9857

www.MeserveAndCoale.com

They specialize in 19th and 20th century works of impressionists, post-impressionists and modern artists. Prices range from $5,000 to $500,000. The gallery also offers appraisal, restoration and authentication assistance.

Hours: Tuesday - Saturday, 10 am - 5 pm. During July the hours are 1 am - 5 pm & Saturdays by appointment in August.

SHOPPING

Michael Kessler Antiques

44 West Putnam Avenue, 661.1212
www.MichaelKesslerAntiques.com
A small shop with pretty pieces. Primarily English antiques.
Hours: Tuesday-Saturday, 11 am - 5 pm.

Michelangelo of Greenwich

353 Greenwich Avenue, 661.8540, 800.677.4490
Wide selection of clocks, crystal, pewter, brass and silver which can be
engraved for personal or corporate gifts. They have produced awards
for the Super Bowl and the Pebble Beach Golf Tournament.
Hours: Tuesday - Friday, 10 am - 5:30 pm; Saturday 10 am - 5 pm.

Moonstruck

50 Greenwich Avenue, 861.6500
www.moonstruckCholocate.com
A chocolate shop selling expensive but wonderful chocolates. They also
serve great coffee (they used to be the Coffee Tree). They have Häagen
Dazs ice cream as well as milkshakes. There are a few tables. It's a
great place to relax during shopping.
Hours: weekdays, 6:30 am - 6 pm; Saturday, 7 am - 7 pm;
Sunday, 7:30 am - 5 pm.

(The) Music Source

1075 East Putnam Ave, Riverside, 698-0444
They carry a wide selection of sheet music as well
as strings and other small items.
Hours: Tuesday - Friday, noon - 5 pm; Saturday
10 am - 4 pm; closed Sunday & Monday.

Nancy T's

14 Lewis Street, 622.0347
www.Nancy-Ts.com
Designer fashions for ladies sizes 12 - 22. They have fashions from
over 30 designers including casuals by Tamotsu.
Hours: Monday - Saturday, 10 am - 6 pm; other hours by appointment.

SHOPPING

Neal's Yard (Natural Remedies)
79 East Putnam Avenue, 629.0885
An attractive shop stocking natural skin care and hair care products. They have an extensive range of herbs, essential oils and homeopathic remedies. Treat yourself to this shop.
Hours: Monday - Wednesday, 10 am - 5:30 pm; Thursday, 10 am - 8 pm; Friday & Saturday, 10 am - 5:30 pm.

Neighbor-to-Neighbor
Christ Church Annex, 248 East Putnam Avenue, 622.9208
This volunteer organization is greatly respected and appreciated in our Greenwich community. They have helped so many people in such a sensitive way. Donations of food, warm coats and clothing (in good condition) are always needed. The shop is restricted to people identified by our social service agencies as "in need" and the selections made in the nicely organized shop are free.
Hours: Weekdays, 8:30 am - 12:30 pm.

Neiman Marcus
Westchester Mall, 914.428.2000
www.NeimanMarcus.com
Hours: weekdays, 10 am - 8 pm; Saturday, 10 am - 7 pm; Sunday, noon - 6 pm.
Directions: I-95 S to I-287 W to exit 8 (Westchester Avenue), L on Bloomingdale or L on Paulding.

Nesting
220 East Putnam Avenue, Cos Cob, 422.6378
Meredith Bjork has collected whimsical gifts and furnishings for the home. If you need an artistic or unusual gift, check this out.
Hours: Tuesday - Saturday, 10 am - 6 pm.

Nimble Thimble
19 Putnam Avenue, Port Chester, NY, 914.934.2934
The resource for home sewing needs. Lots of fabrics, notions, and quilting supplies and sewing machines. This is the place to have your sewing machine repaired.
Hours: Monday - Saturday, 10 am - 5 pm.

SHOPPING

Nine West
120 Greenwich Avenue, 622.4655
www.NineWest.com
Quality women's footwear at an affordable price.
Hours: Monday - Saturday, 10 am - 6 pm (Thursday until 7 pm);
Sunday, noon - 5 pm.

Nordic Stove & Fireplace Center
1374 East Putnam Avenue, Old Greenwich, 637.4004
Everything you might want for your fireplace. Good customer service.
Hours: Tuesday - Friday, 9 am - 5 pm; Saturday, 9 am - 4pm. They are
open fewer hours in the summer.

Nordstrom
Westchester Mall, 914.946.1122
www.Nordstrom.com
Hours: Monday - Saturday, 10 am - 9:30 pm; Sunday, 11 am - 6 pm.
Directions: I-95 S to I-287 W to exit 8 (Westchester Avenue), L on
Bloomingdale or L on Paulding.

North Street Pharmacy
1061 North Street, 869.2130
Paul Fiscella and his wife have been running this neighborhood pharmacy for more than 20 years.
Hours: weekdays, 9 am - 6 pm; Saturday, 9 am - 5 pm.

Old Greenwich Flower Shop
232 Sound Beach Avenue, Old Greenwich, 637.0492
Fine flowers for over 40 years. Treat yourself to a weekend bouquet—
flowers are half price on Friday.
Hours: Monday - Saturday, 9 am - 5 pm.

Omni Fitness
20 Railroad Avenue, 422.2277
A wide selection of high-end fitness equipment at reasonable prices
and very nice people to work with.
Hours: Monday - Saturday, 10 am - 6 pm, Thursday, 10 am - 8 pm,
Sunday, 11 am - 5 pm.

SHOPPING

Orvis Company Store

432 Boston Post Road, Darien, 203.662.0844

www.orvis.com

Clothes, luggage and fishing equipment for the well-attired fisher. They also have a large book and video selection as well as a guide service.

Hours: Monday - Saturday, 10 am - 6 pm (Thursday until 8 pm); Sunday, 11 am - 3 pm.

Directions: I-95 N, exit 13, L on Post Road, mile on L.

Outdoor Traders

55 Arch Street, 862.9696

www.OutdoorTraders.com

Outfitters for just about any outdoor trip or trek.

Hours: weekdays, 10 am - 6 pm; Saturday, 9:30 am - 5:30 pm; Sunday, noon - 4 pm.

Packages Plus-N-More

Mill Pond Shopping Center, 213 East Putnam Ave, Cos Cob, 625.8130

One of the few places that carries Greenwich gift items including post-cards with local scenes. They not only ship packages for you, but will pick-up a package from your home upon request.

Hours: Monday - Saturday, 5:30 am - 6 pm; Sunday until 4 pm.

(The) Papery

268 Greenwich Avenue, 869.1888

www.ThePapery.Com

The Papery sells fine custom social stationery and invitations from a great variety of sources. If you want an out-of-the ordinary invitation you will have fun here. You will be sending more greetings to your friends when you see their large selection of high-end greeting cards. They also sell Madame Alexander dolls and Godiva Chocolates.

Hours: Monday - Saturday, 9:30 am - 6 pm (Thursday until 7 pm); Sunday, noon - 5 pm except July & August.

Party City

535 Boston Post Road,

Port Chester, NY, 914.939.6900

A giant store with an impressive inventory of party supplies. Like the Strauss Warehouse Outlet, they have a very large assortment of Halloween costumes during the season.

Hours: Monday - Saturday, 9:30 am - 9 pm; Sunday, 10 am - 6 pm.

SHOPPING

Party Paper and Things

403 East Putnam Avenue (Mill Pond Shopping Center), 661.1355
An excellent selection of high quality party paper goods, wrapping paper, disposable serving dishes and lots of balloons. They will deliver for a very modest fee.
Hours: Monday - Saturday, 10 am - 5:30 pm.

Patio.Com

600 East Putnam Avenue, Cos Cob, 869.3084
www.Patio.com
Primarily outdoor furniture.
Hours: Monday - Saturday, 10 am - 6 pm; Sunday noon - 5 pm.

Patricia Gourlay

45 East Putnam Avenue, 869.0977
Brides-to-be love this fine lingerie shop. This is also a good place to find the right bra. They are more conservative than their advertisements would indicate.
Hours: Monday - Saturday, 9:30 am - 5:30 pm

Penny Weights

124 Elm Street, New Caanan 966.7739
This is a great place to find an inexpensive piece of jewelry for a teenager. Most of the jewelry is silver. The sales staff is friendly and helpful. The prices are terrific.
Hours: Tuesday - Saturday, 10 am - 6 pm; Thursday until 8 pm;
Sunday, 12 pm - 5 pm. Closed Mondays.

Penzey's Spices

197 Westport Avenue, Norwalk, CT, 203.849.9085
Fresh spices make all the difference. Penzey's has a large selection of spices, spice blends and even extracts. Pretty wooden boxed sets of spices make appreciated hostess gifts.
Hours: weekdays, 9:30 am - 5:30 pm; Saturday, 9:30 am - 5 pm.
Directions: I-95 N to exit 16, L on East, R on US-1 (Westport Avenue), on L just past Stew Leonards.

SHOPPING

Performance Imaging
115 East Putnam Avenue, 862.9600
www.performanceimaging.net
Wow. If your are considering a home theater or home automation, this is a must-see place. Many people can show you pictures of how a theater might look, but here you can sit down in a variety of theaters just as if they were already installed in your home.
Hours: weekdays, 10 am - 6 pm; Saturday, 10 am - 5 pm; after hours, by appointment.

Pet Pantry
290 Railroad Avenue, 869.6444
Large store with a gigantic inventory. Friendly, helpful service.
Hours: weekdays, 8 am - 8 pm; Saturday, 8 am - 6 pm;
Sunday 9 am - 6 pm.

Petit Patapon
271 Greenwich Avenue, 861.2037
www.petitpatapon.com
Lovely playwear for young children. The whimsical and pastel-colored outfits will make you smile.
Hours: Monday - Saturday, 10 am - 6 pm; Sunday, noon - 5 pm

Pier One Imports
225 Greenwich Avenue, 622.4010
www.pier1.com
Affordable chain carrying everything for the home, from table linens - wicker furniture and throw pillows.
Hours: weekdays, 10 am - 8 pm; Saturday, 10 am - 7 pm;
Sunday, 10 am - 6 pm.

SHOPPING

Portland Place Gallery

25 South Main St, So. Norwalk, CT, 203.866.6013

They carry a wide selection of limited-edition original works of art from over 60 artists, as well as a variety of posters. They will mat and frame your selections.

Hours: Tuesday - Saturday, 10 am - 6 pm; Sunday, noon - 6 pm.

Directions: I-95N to exit 14, R off exit, Go down the hill on Fairfield Avenue, bear left at the first light on to Washington Street. At RR underpass R on to South Main.

Post Road Iron Works

345 West Putnam Avenue, 869.6322

Serving Greenwich for many years, they are the resource for ornamental welding. They also sell a good selection of fireplace accessories and weather vanes.

Hours: weekdays, 8 am - 5:30 pm; Saturday, 8 am - 3 pm.

Pottery Barn

Stamford Town Center, 324.2035

www.PotteryBarn.com

www.PotteryBarnKids.com

This fresh, appealing furniture is very popular in Greenwich. They have a strong emphasis on bed and bath as well as adorable furniture for children.

Hours: weekdays, 1o am - 9 pm; Saturday, 10 am - 8 pm;

Sunday, noon - 6 pm.

Directions: I-95 N to exit 8, L on Atlantic, R on Tresser, L onto ramp.

Provence de France

22 West Putnam Avenue, 629.9798

French Antiques

Hours: Monday - Saturday, 10 am - 5:30 pm.

SHOPPING

Pub Games Plus

176 Main Street, Norwalk, CT 203.846.5991
This is a store filled with adult games. Everything from darts to chess to dice & backgammon.
Hours: Monday - Saturday, 11 am - 6 pm (Monday until 7 pm, Saturday until 5 pm)
Directions: I-95 N to exit 15, US-7 N (towards Norwalk/Danbury) to exit 2, L onto CT-123/New Canaan Avenue, R onto Main/CT-123.

Purdy's Farm & Nursery

Upper King Street (1353 King Street), Greenwich, 531.9815
Greenwich used to have a lot of local farms. Most have disappeared, but Greenwich insiders keep Purdy's going strong. How can you resist very fresh from-the-farm produce at reasonable prices, sold by a friendly owner. In the fall, their pumpkins and cider are worth the trip.
Hours: Open everyday, 9 am - 5 pm, sometimes later.

Quai Voltaire Antiques

378 Greenwich Avenue, 618.9777
www.nartantiques.com
French antiques
Hours: Monday - Saturday, 10 am - 6 pm; Sunday, 1 pm - 5 pm.

Quelques Choses

259 Sound Beach Avenue, Old Greenwich, 637.5655
Tiny shop brimming with unique gifts.
Hours: Monday - Saturday, 10 am - 5 pm.

Radio Shack

1265 East Putnam Avenue (Riverside Commons Shopping Center), 637.5608
www.RadioShack.com
Although there are several locations in Greenwich and Port Chester, we like this one best. It's easy to park and up-to-date. If you need a telephone or telephone supplies, a strange battery, or you are not sure where to find some piece of electronic equipment, they will probably have it here.
Hours: Weekdays, 9 am - 9 pm; Saturday, 9 am - 7 pm; Sunday, 11 am - 5 pm.

SHOPPING

Razooks

45 East Putnam Avenue, 661.6603

www.razooks.com

An elegant shop with designer fashions for women. They have custom wedding gowns and wonderful choices for the bride's mother.

Hours: Monday - Saturday, 9:30 am - 5:30 pm.

Recreation Showroom

307 Racebrook Road, Orange, CT, 203.891.9633

www.RecreationShowroom.com

A variety of games and game tables including over 45 different pool tables on display. They also have a large assortment of camping equipment.

Hours: Monday-Saturday, 10 am - 6 pm(closed Wednesday); Thursday, 10 am - 8 pm; Sunday, 11 am - 4 pm.

Directions: I-95 N to exit 41, L on Marsh Hill Rd, R on US-1. L at next intersection on to Rte 114 (Racebrook Rd), the Recreation Showroom is on the right.

(The) Red Studio

39 Lewis Street, 861.6525

The frames are often works of art in themselves. They also sell prints and old drawings.

Hours: Monday - Saturday, 10:30 am - 6:30 pm.

Relax the Back

367 Greenwich Avenue, 629.2225

www.RelaxTheBack.com

For people seeking relief and prevention of back and neck pain, they offer attractive posture and back support products and self-care solutions.

Hours: Monday - Saturday, 10 am - 6 pm.

SHOPPING

Reo Appliances

233 East Avenue, East Norwalk, CT, 203.838.7925

www.reoappliances.com

Large selection of major appliances at competitive prices. Lots of personal service.

Hours: Monday - Saturday, 9 am - 5 pm; Thursday, 9 am - 7:30 pm. Closed Sunday.

Directions: I-95 N to exit 16, South on East Avenue

Restoration Hardware

239 Greenwich Avenue, 552.1040

www.restorationhardware.com

A very upscale, trendy, combination decorative hardware and home furniture store. It is just fun to walk through.

Hours: Monday - Saturday, 9 am - 8 pm (Thursday until 9 pm); Sunday, 11 am - 6 pm.

Rex Dive Center

144 Water Street, Norwalk, CT, 203-853-4148

www.RexDiveCenter.com

This the place to go for your Scuba equipment . You will be greeted by a friendly, knowledgeable staff. They provide lessons for beginners.

Hours: weekdays, 11 am - 7 pm; Saturday, 9 am - 5 pm; Sunday, noon - 5 pm.

Directions: I-95 N to Exit 14, R on Fairfield Avenue (which turns into Washington Street), R on Water.

Rex Marine Center

144 Water Street, Norwalk, CT, 203-853-4148

If you are looking for a small boat or boating paraphernalia, they are worth a visit.

Hours: weekdays, 11 am - 7 pm; Saturday, 9 am - 5 pm; Sunday, noon - 5 pm.

Directions: I-95 N to Exit 14, R on Fairfield Avenue (which turns into Washington Street), R on Water.

Richards of Greenwich

359 Greenwich Avenue, 622.0551

A Greenwich classic carrying fine quality men's and women's clothing from the world's leading designers.

Hours: Monday - Saturday, 7:30 am - 6 pm (until 9 pm on Thursdays).

SHOPPING

Riders Up

1061 North Street, 618.9286

This tack shop carries equipment for jumping, dressage and Western riding.

Hours: Closed Sundays in summer; Monday - Saturday, 10 am - 5:30 pm.

Ridgeway Shopping Center

2235 Summer Street, Stamford, CT

The anchor stores in this updated 400,000 square foot center are Marshall's and Old Navy. It does have a huge Bed, Bath and Beyond as well as a huge "Super Stop & Shop".

Hours: Monday - Saturday, 9:30 am - 9:00 pm. Bed, Bath is open Sunday, 9:30 am - 6 pm.

Directions: Merritt Parkway N to exit 34, R on Long Ridge which becomes Summer.

Right Start

42 West Putnam Ave., 422-2525

A good local resource for educational toys, books and videos. They also have car seats, strollers and much more. Mothers seem to congregate here.

Hours: Monday -Saturday, 10 am - 6 pm; Sunday, 11 am - 5 pm.

Rinfret Home and Garden

5 Lewis Street, 622.0204

Home accessories and unique gifts.

Hours: weekdays, 9:30 - 5:30; Saturday, 10 am - 5 pm.

Rink and Racquet

24 Railroad Avenue, 622.9180

Hockey (field & ice), Figure Skating, Baseball, Softball, Lacrosse, Rollerblades, Team uniforms.

Hours: weekdays, 9 am - 5:30 pm; Saturday, 9 am - 5 pm.

SHOPPING

Ring's End Lumber

181 West Avenue, Darien, 203.655.2525
www.RingsEnd.com
A large supplier of lumber, hardware and building materials. Good displays of kitchens and windows. If possible, shop on weekdays, they are very busy on the weekends.
Hours: weekdays, 7 am - 5 pm (Thursday until 8 pm); Saturday, 8 am - 5 pm
Directions: I-95 N to exit 10, L Noroton, R on West.

Ritz Camera Centers

82 Greenwich Avenue, Greenwich, 869.0673
www.ritzcamera.com
Part of a large chain of camera stores. They have an extensive selection of cameras and batteries for watches as well as cameras. They do one-hour photo developing.
Hours: weekdays, 8:30 am - 6:30 pm; Saturday, 10 am - 5 pm.

Riverside Florist & Gifts

Riverside Commons Shopping Center (1249 East Putnam Ave), 637.3093
Amazing service. Ask for Albert when you have a special request.
Hours: weekdays, 8 am - 7 pm, Saturday, 9 am - 5 pm,
Sunday, 10 am - 2 pm. Threads and Treads

Ronnie's News

26 West Putnam Avenue, 661.5464
A convenient place to find your favorite magazines and newspapers.
Hours: Weekdays, 6 am - 6 pm; Weekends, 6am - noon.

(The) Round Hill Store

Corner of Old Mill and Round Hill Road, 869.5144
This small country store opened in 1801, still provides milk, eggs and staples for the surrounding area. Try one of their delicious turkey sandwiches. Their customer base is about 50% of the people who work in the back country and 50% the people who live near-by.
Hours: weekdays, 6 am - 5 pm; Saturday, 7 am - 2 pm;
Summer, Monday -Saturday, 6 am - 6 pm.

SHOPPING

Roundabout
48 West Putnam Avenue, 552.0787
Clothes must be from a well-known designer, in perfect condition, and less than two-years-old to be consigned. The store also buys show and end-of-season stock from designers.
Hours: Monday - Saturday, 10 am - 5 pm

Rue Faubourg St. Honoré
44 West Putnam Avenue, 869.7139
For over 30 years this small shop has supplied antique lighting fixtures and fireplace accessories to Greenwich mansions and vintage homes.
Hours: Monday - Saturday, 9 am - 5 pm. Closed Sunday.

Rummage Room
191 Sound Beach Avenue, Old Greenwich, 637.1875
Notice the artistic window displays of this gem of a shop manned by cheerful volunteers. The shop is filled with clothing for young and old and interesting bric-a-brac. Our finds: a Marissa Christina sweater and a lace tablecloth.
Shop Hours: weekdays 10 am - 5 pm; Saturdays, 10 am - 1 pm.
Donation Hours: Monday - Thursday, 9 am - 5 pm;
Fridays, 9 am - 1 pm; Saturdays, 10 am - 1 pm.
Closed on Sundays and for the month of August.

Safavieh
248 Atlantic Street, Stamford, 327.4800
www.safavieh.com
Oriental rugs galore and lots of quality English, French and American reproduction furniture from firms such as Kindel, Baker, Widdicomb, Henredon and others. They have parking behind the store.
Hours: Monday - Wednesday, 10 am - 7 pm; Friday & Saturday, 10 am - 6 pm; Sunday 11 am - 5 pm.
Directions: I-95 N to exit 8 (Atlantic Street), L on Atlantic.

Saint Clair
23 Lewis Street, 661.2927
Going to Cartier's for fine stationery is not necessary if you live in Greenwich. This shop is the place for invitations and elegant stationery. Stop in and see the range of things they can do.
Hours: Tuesday - Saturday, 9:30 am - 5:30 pm. Closed Sunday and Monday.

SHOPPING

Saks Fifth Avenue
205 Greenwich Avenue, 862.5300
Stamford Town Center, 323.3100
www.SaksIncorporated.com
The traditional and trendy fashions you would expect.
Greenwich Hours: Monday - Saturday , 10 am - 6 pm,
Sunday, noon - 5 pm.
Town Center Hours: Monday & Thursday, 10 am - 8 pm; Tuesday,
Wednesday, Friday & Saturday, 10 am - 6 pm; Sunday, noon - 6 pm.
Directions to Stamford Town Center: I-95 N to exit 8, L on Atlantic, R
on Tresser, L onto ramp.

Sal's Pastry Shop
91 High Ridge Road (Bull's Head Shopping Center), Stamford,
CT, 323.0789
A family-owned and run Italian pastry shop. The owners take great
pride in their fresh cannolis. As an added bonus their prices are rea-
sonable.
Hours: Tuesday - Saturday, 8:30 am - 6:30 pm; Sunday 8 am - 2 pm.
Directions: Merritt Pkw N to High Ridge Exit, R on High Ridge.

Salvation Army
Truck pick-up: 800.958.7825
Stamford Thrift Shop, 896 Washington Blvd, 914.975.7630
A marvelous service is available for picking up furniture for donation.
Every time we have called, a courteous, strong man has arrived promptly
to take items destined to help people serviced by this most worthy
organization. 2 to 4 days notice is appreciated for pick-ups. A bin for
donations (of clothing only) is located inside our Recycling Center on
Holly Hill Lane.
Dispatcher Hours: Monday - Saturday, 7:30 am - 4 pm.

TIP: FINDING TAG SALES
The Friday and weekend *Greenwich Time* newspaper
lists tag sale locations. A popular Greenwich weekend pastime.
Greenwich Radio (869.1490) has a Saturday morning
trading post from 8 am - 9 am. A free way to find
items to buy or sell. They also announce tag sales.

SHOPPING

Sam Bridge Nursery & Greenhouse

437 North Street, 869.3418

www.sambridge.com

A family-run operation that has been welcoming Greenwich residents to their greenhouses since 1930. Many of the more than 100,000 plants available are grown in their own greenhouses. They offer classes on topics such as perennial gardening and pruning. You can select live or cut Christmas trees, which they will deliver to you when you are ready.
Hours: Closed Sunday; Monday - Saturday, 8:30 am - 5 pm.

Sam Goody

145 Greenwich Avenue, 862.9630

www.samGoody.com

A chain store with a wide selection of videos and DVDs for sale, a pleasant staff and great hours. Good music web site.
Hours: Monday - Saturday, 9 am - 9 pm; Sunday, 11 am - 6 pm.

Saturnia

39 Lewis Street, 625.0390

www.shopsaturnia.com

A favorite clothes store of the younger set. A good place to find a cute dress, leather pants or the perfect sweater.
Hours: Monday - Saturday, 9:30 am - 6 pm; Sunday, noon - 4 pm.

Scandia Food and Gifts

30 High Street (off US1), Norwalk, CT, 203.838.2087

www.ScandiaFood.com

The area source for Scandinavian food and gifts.
Hours: weekdays, 9 am - 5 pm; Saturday, 10 am - 5 pm.
Directions: I-95 N to exit 16, L on East, L on US-1, L on High.

Schultz's Cider Mill

103 Old Route 22, Armonk, NY, 914.273.8720

Their fantastic cider is made fresh (no preservatives) every Friday from mid-September to mid-May. They also have a nice selection of fresh fruits and vegetables. Delicious donuts are made fresh every Saturday and Sunday until 4 pm. If you want the best, its worth the trip. Especially if you are visiting Village Prime Meats.
Hours: Every day 8 am - 5:30 pm. Closed June.
Directions: I-95 S to I-287 W to I-684 N to exit 3S. Continue R to 22 S, R at 2nd light onto Rt 128 (Main Street). First Left onto old Route 22.

SHOPPING

Secret Garden
28 Sherwood Place, 869.6246
Tucked away behind the Greenwich Women's Exchange, this small store is indeed a secret place. They have unique garden ornaments and a selection of small antiques. Hours: Monday - Saturday, 10 am - 4 pm; during the summer, Saturday hours may vary.

Serenity Path
239 East Putnam Avenue, Cos Cob, 861.1551
This rather out of the way store sells a variety of wellness products such as aromatherapy oils, soaps and creams as well as homeopathic remedies and spiritual books.
Hours: weekdays, 10:30 am - 6:30 pm; Saturday, 11 am - 5 pm.

Shanti Bithi
3047 High Ridge Road, Stamford, CT 329.0768
www.webcom.com/shanti
Wonderful greenhouse of Bonsai trees as well as supplies and lessons to create your own bonsai. They also have a nice selection of Asian garden ornaments.
Hours: Monday - Saturday, 9 am - 5 pm.
Directions: Merritt Parkway N to exit 35, L on High Ridge. Store is about 5-miles on the right.

Shippan Center for Arts and Antiques
614 Shippan Avenue, Stamford, CT, 353.0222
www.ShippanCenter.com
The newest of a cluster of 5 antique centers in Stamford.
Hours: Monday - Saturday, 10:30 - 5:30; Sunday, noon - 5 pm.
Directions: I-95 N to exit N to exit 8, R on Canal

Shoes N More
251 Greenwich Avenue, 629.2323
A fun assortment of boys and girl's clothing, sizes 2T - 16. They have an excellent shoe selection including Astor, Elefanter, Nike and Merrill. They carry some western boots and accessories. Twice a year they have a very good shoe sale (summer & after Christmas).
Hours: weekdays, 10 am - 8pm; Saturday, 10 am - 7 pm;
Sunday, noon - 7 pm.

SHOPPING

Silk Purse

118 Main street, New Canaan, 203.972.0898
Nice quality consignment shop, for furniture, silver and jewelry.
Hours: Monday - Saturday, 10 am - 5 pm; Sunday, noon - 5 pm.
Directions: Merritt Parkway N to exit 37, L on Rte 124/South Street, R on Elm, L on Main

Simon Pearce

325 Greenwich Avenue, 861.0780
www.simonpearce.com
Beautiful handblown glass, pottery, lamps and furniture. Very reasonable prices for the quality.
Hours: Monday - Saturday, 10 am - 6 pm; Sunday, noon - 5 pm.

Smart Kids Company

17 East Elm Street, 869.0022
www.SmartKidsToys.com
The toys in Mary De Silva's shop may look like a lot of fun, but most have been selected to help in your child's growth and educational development through play. This local shop has a global clientele from the website.
Hours: Monday - Saturday, 9 am - 6 pm; Sunday, 11 am - 5 pm.

Smith & Hawken

30 East Avenue, New Canaan, CT 203.972.0820
www.SmithandHawken.com
An upscale store selling stylish garden furniture and some home furnishings.
Hours: Monday - Saturday, 10 am - 6 pm; Sunday, 11 am - 5 pm
Directions: Merritt Parkway N to exit 37, L on Rte 124/South Street, R on Elm, L on Main, R on East.

Sophia's Great Dames

1 Liberty Way, 869.5990
Wonderful shop for vintage clothing, antiques, collectibles, gifts and costume rentals. Fun to visit.
Hours: Monday - Saturday, 10 am - 5:30 pm; open later during holidays.

SHOPPING

Sound Beach Sportswear

239 Sound Beach Avenue, Old Greenwich, 637.5557

The sportswear is an interesting mix of casual dressiness. The owners are in tune with what Greenwich residents like to wear. They also carry adorable infant and children's wear. Expect a friendly reception in this family-owned business.

Hours: weekdays, 10 am - 6 pm; Saturday, 10 am - 5 pm

Sportif Ltd

41 Greenwich Avenue, 629.8874

A large selection of sporting goods and clothing including, skiing, snow boarding, tennis and inline skating.

Hours: Monday - Saturday, 9:30 am - 6 pm; Sunday, noon - 5 pm; Winter, Thursday & Friday - 7 pm.

Sportsman's Den

33 River Road, Cos Cob, 869.3234

Supplies and classes on angling and fly tying.

One visit and you will be hooked. They are an excellent source and the only good one in Greenwich. Captain Bill Harold is the best saltwater guide in the area.

Hours: weekdays, 9 am - 5 pm (Monday until 2 pm);
Saturday, 8 am - 5 pm; Sunday, 8 am - 2 pm.

TIP: HAVING A TAG SALE

No Town permit is required. The best days for sales are Saturday and Sunday 9:00 am to 4:00 pm. The best seasons are Fall and Spring. Avoid sales on or near a holiday. Advertise one week before and the weekend of the sale in *The Greenwich Time* (629-2204) in Friday Tag Sale section.

If you are planning a large sale, off-duty Greenwich Police can help you manage crowds. Call the traffic division (622-8016). Professional Tag Sale managers typically charge from 20% to 30% commission, depending on the services rendered.

SHOPPING

St. Moritz
383 Greenwich Avenue, 869.2818
Luscious, rich pastries and cakes. Be sure to try the Sarah Bernhardt cookies.
Hours: Monday - Saturday, 7 am - 6 pm; Sunday, 8 am - 1 pm.

Stamford Antique Area
Tucked away in converted manufacturing buildings are five collections of antique dealers with enough collectibles and antiques to suit just about anyone. With antiques from over 350 dealers, it's hard to imagine anyone not finding something they want. A great outing for the antique enthusiast.
Hours: Monday - Saturday, 10:30 am - 5:30 pm; Sunday, noon - 5 pm.
Directions: I-95 N to Exit 8, R on Canal (at second light), continue straight or L on Jefferson.

Antique and Artisan Center
69 Jefferson Street, 327.6022
Look in the Modernism Room and see their collection of 20th Century "antiques-in-the-making."

Hiden Galleries
481 Canal Street, 323.9090

Stamford Antiques Center
735 Canal Street, 888.329.3546
Open every day 10:30 am - 5:30 pm

Stamford Town Center
Stamford, CT, 324.0935
A large, attractive mall with plenty of brand-name shops. Macy's (964.1500), Saks Fifth Avenue (323.3100) and Filene's (357.7373) are the anchor stores.
Hours: weekdays, 10 am - 9 pm; Saturday, 10 am - 6 pm;
Sunday, noon - 6 pm.
Directions: I-95 N to exit 8, L on Atlantic, R on Tresser, L onto ramp.

Staples
1297 East Putnam Avenue, 698.9011
Yes, they have staples, too.
Hours: weekdays, 7 am - 10 pm; Saturday, 9 am - 9 pm;
Sunday, 10 am - 7 pm.

SHOPPING

Strauss Warehouse Outlet

140 Horton Avenue, Port Chester, NY, 914.939.3544, 7132
Gift wrapping, party favors, balloons, paper goods, just about any-
thing you might want for a party at great prices. They carry a huge
selection of Halloween costumes during October.
Hours: weekdays, 8 am - 7 pm; Saturday, 8 am - 5 pm;
Sunday, 10 am - 3 pm.
Directions: Post Road to Main Street in Port Chester, R on Wilkins,
L on Locust, R on Horton (Horton is a one-way).

Stew Leonard's

100 Westport Avenue, Norwalk, 203.847.7213
www.stewleonards.com
Famous throughout the metropolitan area - worth the trip. This huge
food store has been called the Disneyland of grocery stores by the New
York Times. Bring your children.
Hours: Every day, 7 am - 11 pm.
Directions: I-95 N to exit 16; L on East; R on Westport (6th light).

Steven B. Fox Fine Jewelry

8 Lewis Street, 629.3303
A full service family-owned jewelry store specializing in precious jew-
els, pearls, watches, estate jewelry and objects d'art. Repairs done on
the premises. They make estate purchases.
Hours: Monday - Saturday, 9:30 am - 5 pm; Sunday noon - 5 pm, from
Thanksgiving to Christmas.

Stickley - Audi Company

50 Tarrytown Road, White Plains, NY 914.948.6333
www.Stickley.com
Stickley mission furniture and fine English reproduction furniture.
There is a clearance center for Stickley in the same shopping center at
53 Tarrytown Road
Hours: Monday - Saturday 10 am - 5:30 pm (Monday & Thursday to 9
pm); Sunday, noon - 5 pm.
Directions: I-95 S to exit 21 (I-287 W); I-287 W to exit 8 (Westchester
Ave); Continue on Westchester Avenue which becomes Tarrytown Rd
(NY-119).

SHOPPING

Stop & Shop Home Shopping

Local Store located at 161 West Putnam Avenue, 625.0624
Place orders through www.StopAndShop.com or www.PeaPod.com
Call 800.573.2763 for information.
For orders over $75.00 the delivery fee is $4.95, for orders less than
$75.00 the delivery fee is $9.95.
The minimum order is $50.00.

Super Handy Hardware

1 Riversville Road, Glenville Center, 531.5599
A good old-fashioned hardware store with most everything you would
need for light and heavy-duty home projects.
Hours: Monday - Saturday, 8 am - 5 pm; Sunday, 9 am - 1 pm.

Sweet Art

374 ½ Greenwich Avenue (facing the parking lot behind Figaro's
Restaurant), 869.2683
Bob and Margaret Gorman (both pastry chefs) create original cakes
and pastries.
Hours: Limited hours, call for an appointment.

Sweet Lisa's Exquisite Cakes

3 Field Road, Cos Cob, 869.9545
www.sweetlisas.com
Wonderful cakes, party pastries and designer cookies by special order
only. They usually require seven days notice.
Hours: Tuesday - Saturday, 10 am - 6 pm.

TIP: THRIFT SHOPS
Donating your unwanted valuables to thrift shops is a
practical way to help our neighbors in need. Proceeds
from these shops, which are often run by volunteers,
go to helping others. So donate with a happy heart
and take a moment to explore the shops for a treasure—they can be found! To donate books see *Darien
Book Aid Plan* in the section on books.

SHOPPING

Sweet Spot
187 Sound Beach Avenue, 698.9277
Bin style and gourmet candy shop. 150 different varieties of bin candy.
Gourmet sweets such as fudge and turtles.
Hours: weekdays, 10 am - 6 pm; Saturday 9 am - 4 pm;
Sunday 10 am - 4 pm.

Tack Room
153 Post Rd East, Westport CT , 203.227.6272
www.WestMall.com
A good source for western attire, boots and saddles.
Hours: Monday - Saturday, 10 am - 6 pm (Thursday - 9 pm).
Directions: I-95 N to exit 17, L to US 1, R on US 1.

Tahiti Street
113 Greenwich Avenue, 622.1878
If you are planning a trip to the Caribbean or you just want to look
elegant on the beach, stop in here. You can purchase bathing separates
in different sizes.
Hours: Monday-Saturday, 10 am - 6 pm

Talbots
151 Greenwich Avenue, 869.7177, 6770
www.Talbots.com
Talbots has classic clothes for business women of all ages as well as a
good sportswear line. They have a extensive women's petite department.
Hours: Monday - Saturday, 9:30 am - 6 pm (Wednesday & Thursday to
7 pm); Sunday noon - 5 pm.

Talbots Kids
165 Greenwich Avenue, 869.6770
A mix of casual and dressier classic children's clothes. Sizes from newborn to 12 years old.
Hours: Monday - Saturday, 9:30 am - 6 pm; Wednesday & Thursday
until 7 pm; Sunday noon - 5 pm.

Tallows End
41 East Elm Street, 661.5903
The largest selection of candles in the area, all shapes, sizes and scents.
They also have a nice selection of gifts.
Hours: Monday - Saturday, 9 am - 5 pm (Friday - 5:30 pm).

SHOPPING

Tetonia

28 Arcadia Road, Old Greenwich, 698.1240
Unique clothing, jewelry and gifts in the heart of Old Greenwich.
Hours: Monday - Saturday, 10 am - 5 pm.

Threads and Treads

17 East Putnam Avenue, 661.0142
www.threadsandtreads.com
www.roadhogs.org
Entry forms for the latest races are available here. This is a good source
for biking, swimming and running attire. They sponsor the Road Hogs
which conducts classes for runners, cyclers and swimmers, of all ages
and abilities.
Hours: Monday - Saturday, 9:30 am - 5:30 pm

Tiffany & Co

140 Greenwich Avenue, 661.7847
www.Tiffany.com
This famous store has a nice collection of jewelry and giftware, as well
as very helpful sales people.
Hours: Monday - Saturday, 10 am - 6 pm; Sunday, noon - 5 pm.

Toys "R" Us

59 Connecticut Avenue, Norwalk, CT, 203.852.6988
A typically mega-toy store.
Hours: Monday - Saturday, 9:30 am - 9:30 pm; Sunday, 10 am - 6 pm.
Directions: Just off I-95, exit 14.

Trader Joe's

436 Boston Post Road (US 1), Darien, CT (203) 656.1414
www.TraderJoes.com
The Trader Joe fans will be glad to know there is a store not far from
Greenwich. A grocery store selling healthy food at good prices. Try one
of their soups or frozen dinners.
Hours: every day, 9 am - 9 pm.
Directions: I-95 N to exit 13, Left to US 1, L on US 1.

TSE Cashmere

289 Greenwich Avenue, 629.3302
Classic cashmere sweaters and suits. Shoppers who once trekked to
New York are happy to see it on the Avenue.
Hours: Monday - Saturday, 10 am - 6 pm; Sunday, noon - 5 pm.

SHOPPING

Tulips Greenwich
91 Lake Avenue (at the Lake Avenue Circle), 661.3154
www.TulipsOfGreenwich.com
European floral design shop known for its creative and innovative bouquets of Dutch and French flowers. Besides their absolutely gorgeous arrangements, they also sell very realistic silk orchids.
Hours: weekdays, 9 am - 5 pm; Saturday 10 am - 4 pm;
August weekday hours 9:30 am - 4 pm.

Tuscany
360 Greenwich Avenue, 661.0444
A giftware store with lots of Italian ceramics with colorful and whimsical designs.
Hours: Monday - Saturday, 10 am - 5:30 pm.

United House Wrecking
535 Hope Street, Stamford, CT, 348.5371
www.unitedhousewrecking.com
An unusual source for the unusual. Thirty-thousand square feet of inventory with everything from collectibles to antiques to architectural items, to junk. Don't miss it.
Hours: Monday - Saturday, 9:30 am - 5:30 pm; Sunday, noon - 5 pm.
Directions: I-95 N to exit 9, Make first 2 lefts onto Rt 1, at 2nd light R on Courtland (Rt 106) , L on Glenbrook, R on Hope

(The) Upper Crust & Bagel Company
197 Sound Beach Avenue, Old Greenwich, 698.0079
Good place to sit down and chat. Great bagels and sandwiches.
Hours: Weekdays, 6 am - 4 pm; weekends, 7 am - 4 pm.

Vallin Galleries
516 Danbury Road (Route 7), Wilton, CT, 203.762.7441
Located far from the source of these antiques, is a quaint saltbox filled with a collection of Asian art, some rare, all beautifully displayed.
Hours: Wednesday - Saturday, 10:30 am - 5 pm; Sunday, 1 pm - 5 pm.
Directions: Merritt Pkw. N to exit 39 (Norwalk) or I-95 N to exit 15, Rte 7 N.

SHOPPING

Van Driver
24 East Elm Street, 869.5358
High quality men's clothing. They have been in Greenwich for over 50 years.
Hours: Monday - Saturday, 9:30 - 5:30.

Var Max Liquor Pantry
16 Putnam Avenue, Port Chester, NY, 914.937.4930
They have a large selection of well-priced wine and are often less expensive. Nice descriptions on their wine specials.
Hours: Monday - Saturday, 9 am - 9 pm (Friday & Saturday until 10).

Versailles
315 Greenwich Avenue, 661.6634
Pastries. We love their operas and eclairs.
Hours: weekdays, 7:30 am - 9:30 pm (Friday until 10 pm);
Saturday, 8 am - 10 pm; Sunday, 8 am - 8 pm.

Victoria's Secret
200 Greenwich Avenue, 661.0158
www.VictoriasSecret.com
A popular chain shop with lingerie and fashionable P.J.s
Hours: weekdays, 9 am - 7 pm; Saturday, 9 am - 6 pm; Sunday, noon - 5 pm.

Village Clock Shop
1074 Post Road, Darien, CT, 203.655.2100
They sell exquisite clocks and repair clocks worthy of their service.
Hours: Tuesday - Saturday, 10 am - 5 pm.
Directions: I-95 to exit 11, L on US 1.

Village Ewe
244 Sound Beach Avenue, Old Greenwich, 637.3953
www.thevillageewe.com
Beware of stopping here unless you are ready to get hooked on needlepoint. Individual lessons for beginners can be arranged. Group classes are offered in the fall and spring. They are a full service needlepoint studio with over 1,500 handpainted canvases.
Hours: Monday - Saturday, 10 am - 6 pm; Tuesday, Wednesday and Thursday, open until 9 pm.

SHOPPING

Village Prime Meats

475 Main Street, Armonk NY, 914.273.5222

There is still an old-fashioned butcher shop in our area. It is worth the trip when you want something special. Where else can you get rabbit, game birds, Peking or Muscovy duck or just that special cut of meat you need? They also have a number of unique food products, such as white or black truffle oil and a large number of fresh pates. While you are in Armonk, stop in at Schultz's Cider Mill.

Hours: Monday - Saturday, 8 am - 6 pm (Saturday until 5:30).

Directions: I-95 S to I-287 W to I-684 N to exit 3S. Continue R to 22 South, R at 2nd light onto Rt 128 (Main Street). It is in a shopping center on your left just past the main part of town.

(The) Vitamin Shoppe

Shopping Center, 535 Post Road, Port Chester, NY, 914.939.5189

www.vitaminshoppe.com

A national chain with a good web site. They have a large selection of products.

Hours: Monday - Saturday, 9 am - 9 pm; Sunday, 11 am - 6 pm.

WH Smith Gift Shop - at Hyatt Regency

1800 East Putnam Avenue, Old Greenwich, 637.1234

When we need a gift with "Greenwich" on it, we dash to this shop.
Best Buy: their silk ties!

Hours: weekdays, 7 am - 11 pm; Saturday 8 am - 11 pm; Sunday 8 am - 9 pm.

Waldenbooks

173 Greenwich Avenue, 869.6342

Greenwich's largest book store, very conveniently located.

Hours: Monday - Saturday, 9 am - 6 pm (Thursday - 8 pm); Sunday, 11 am - 5 pm.

Waterworks

23 West Putnam Avenue, 869.7766

www.WaterWorks.com

High end bathroom and kitchen fixtures as well as a very nice selection of tiles. Excellent customer service.

Hours: weekdays, 10 am - 5 pm (Thursday until 7 pm); Saturday, 10 am - 4 pm.

SHOPPING

Wendy Gee!

29 Kings Street, Chappaqua, NY 914.238.1241
They sell attractive furniture for children and adults, as well as lots of
gift items.
Hours: Monday-Saturday, 9:30 am - 6:pm.
Directions: King Street N to NY-120.

Wendy's Closet

375 Greenwich Avenue, 622.7130
A nice mix of trendy casual and business outfits.
Hours: Monday - Saturday, 10 am - 6 pm; Sunday, 1 am - 5 pm.

Westbrook Factory Stores

Westbrook, CT, 860.399.8656
www.charter-oak.com/westbrook
Just barely smaller than Clinton Crossing and only a few miles away. If
you are in the area, you should stop by.
Hours: Monday - Saturday, 10 am - 9 pm; Sunday, 11 am - 8 pm.
Directions: I-95 N to exit 65, L on Flat Rock Place.

Westchester Mall

White Plains, NY, 914.683.8600
An even larger mall than the Town Center. Primarily upscale shopping.
Neiman Marcus (914.428.2000) and Nordstrom (914.946.1122) are
the anchor stores.
Hours: Monday - Saturday, 10 am - 9 pm; Sunday, 11 am - 6 pm.
Store hours may vary.
Directions: I-95 S to I-287 W, exit 8 (Westchester Avenue), L on
Bloomingdale or on Paulding.

Whimsies Doll House & Miniature Shop

18 Lewis Street, 629.8024
The ultimate dollhouse store.
Hours: Monday - Saturday, 10 am - 5 pm.

SHOPPING

Whole Foods

90 East Putnam Avenue, 661.0631
www.WholeFoods.com
Our favorite natural and organic food store. When you shop here you are bound to meet your friends buying their Sunday bagels, fresh fish, vitamins, deli foods, cheese , beautiful flowers, fruits and vegetables. It is great to have an expert available in each food area to happily give you advice about selections. In addition to its amazing assortment of natural foods, the store has many strong departments including, seafood, produce, nutrition, meat and cheese. We love their first-class deli; they even have a sushi chef. The vitamin and herbal portion of the store is very complete.
Hours: Everyday, 8 am - 9 pm.

Whole Foods Home Shopping

Whole Foods, 90 East Putnam Avenue, Greenwich
Place orders by phone 496.0176 or fax 496.0176 or email Deliverme@Wholefoods.com
www.Wholefoods.com
Groceries are delivered Tuesday, Thursday & Saturday. Orders must be in by 8 am the day of delivery. Delivery fee is $30. The minimum order is $75.

Wine World on Elm

39 East Elm Street, 869.6008,5067
Hard-to-get wines are their specialty. The service and help can't be beaten. If you are intimidated by choosing the right wine, this is your store. You will enjoy their recommendations.
Hours: Monday - Saturday, 9 am - 7 pm.

Woodbury Commons

Harriman, NY, 914.928.4000
A huge outlet location with over 220 stores, including Burberrys and Brooks Brothers. Definitely worth the 60-minute drive.
Hours: Monday - Saturday, 10 am - 9 pm; Sunday, 10 am - 8 pm.
Directions: Take I-95 to I-287 W across the Tappan Zee Bridge and follow I-87 N (New York State Thruway) to exit 16 Make a right at the exit. You can't miss it.

SHOPPING

Zyns News
354 Greenwich Avenue, 661.5168
This store boasts the largest selection of magazines and newspapers in Fairfield County. It certainly seems that way.
Hours: Monday - Saturday, 6 am - 9 pm; Sunday, 6 am - 6 pm.

TIPS: SCULPTURES IN GREENWICH
Greenwich has 30 outdoor sculptures. Some are tucked away in parks, some are in public buildings. Have fun on a sculpture hunt. Stop in the Greenwich Arts Council (second of 299 Greenwich Avenue) and ask for the map of sculpture locations.

SINGLES

According to the 2000 US Census, Greenwich has an adult population of 54,557 of which 16,533 are singles. If you are single, no matter what your age or life style, there are many ways to meet others. In addition to joining one of the numerous volunteer organizations, there are a variety of organized social events.

Capers Professionals

PO Box 2126, Westport, CT, 06880, 203.221.2209
A Greenwich-based, for-profit singles club, created by Jim Godbout. It conducts respected, upscale, dressy singles events all over lower Fairfield County for ages 30 to 50+. Even when held in towns such as Westport, a great many of the attendees are from Greenwich.

Cotton Club

Christ Church, 245 East Putnam Avenue, 869.6600
Contact Alina Anderson Co-President, 203.357.0034 or
Frank Johnson Co-President, 203.323.2475
A social club, with approximately 350 members, for singles of all faiths, ages 35 and up. Members participate in a variety of activities, from hiking and tennis to attending the theater and polo matches. Be sure to get their newsletter.

Fridays-in-the-Round

Bruce Museum, One Museum Drive, 869.0376 x 239
Leslie McDonald
From September to July, the Bruce Museum is a gathering place for local singles, 25 to 45+, to meet, and to enjoy entertainment and the museum. The gatherings are usually the second or third Friday of the month, from 6:30 pm - 9:30 pm.

SINGLES

Greenwich Reform Synagogue Singles
www.greenwich-reform-synagogue-singles.com
Comprised of men and women in their 30s, 40s and 50s. Meetings are at private clubs in Fairfield and Westchester County.

Singles Under Sail
Contact: Joseph Defranco, 203.847.3456
Social events for singles who love sailing. Meetings are held on the first and third Thursday during the summer at the Norwalk Motor Inn.

Ski Bears of Connecticut
11 Wall Street (entrance in rear), Norwalk CT, 203.454.6498
www.skibears.org
A ski and social club for singles and married adults. Membership is open to anyone over 21. Emphasis is on outdoor activities.

Sound Sailing Club
37 Fieldstone Drive, Hartsdale, NY, 212.479.7767
Contact Joan Marnara, Rear Commodore 718.792.6981
A non-profit organization for singles ages 30 to 60 who enjoy sailing. Monthly weekend get-acquainted parties in Fairfield and Westchester counties, as well as NYC.

Tri-County Talls of NY & CT
Box 736, Bedford Hills, NY, 914.422.5664
A nonprofit social club for tall singles. It sponsors social events for people over 21 years. Men must be at least 6' 2", women 5' 10".

Westport Singles
Unitarian Church, Westport, CT, (203.227.8173: Recording)
A nonprofit singles group, with about 800 members, sponsoring programs at various locations in Fairfield County. Ask for their newsletter.

TIP: COMMUNITY CALENDAR
If you want to know the coming town events, you will love the Community Answers "Planning Ahead Community Calendar". Call Community Answers, 622.7979 and ask to be on their list.

TEENS/YOUNG ADULTS

See also: Teen Speak under NEWS/NEWSPAPERS Educator Program

Ambassadors in Leotards
Contact: Felicity Foote, 869.9373
For twenty-four years, Felicity, director of the Greenwich Ballet Workshop, has taken a group of accomplished 14-to-18-year-old dancers to Europe to dance for charitable events. Auditions are required.

Arch Street
100 Arch Street, 629.5744
Founded in 1991, Arch Street (also known as the Greenwich Teen Center, Inc.) is a refurbished warehouse right on the harbor. Whether at the dance floor and bandstand or the upstairs snack shop with booths, Arch Street provides teens with the opportunity to be together in a healthy environment. Arch Street is more than just a place to hang out, the Center provides everything from college application advice and counseling help, to opportunities for teens to participate in community service projects or to learn leadership. Although there is an adult board, the teens run Arch Street through the teen board. This board has sixty members, from 9th to 12th grades, and has representatives from both private and public schools. Arch Street is open to Greenwich students from 7th through 12th grade.

Educator Program, Bruce Museum
Bruce Museum, 1 Museum Drive, 869.0376
High school students are trained to teach young children in the Museum's Neighborhood Collaborative program. Topics covered relate to the Museum's exhibits, such as Japanese folk art, surrealism and Native American beadwork techniques.

TIP: BIKE PATH
The East Coast Greenway Alliance has created a bicycle route between Greenwich and New Haven. A map of this route, championed by local resident Franklin Bloomer, is available by calling 401-789-4625 or check out www.Greenway.org

---

TEENS/YOUNG ADULTS

Greenwich Cotillion
869.1979

Greenwich still has a Cotillion every year at the beginning of summer for young ladies who wish to debut. The Cotillion, sponsored by the Junior League of Greenwich, is often described as "a fun party with dignity," but perhaps is more accurately described as a series of dignified fun parties. Attendance is by open invitation on a first-come, first-serve basis. Some years you need to get your check and application in the moment it is received; other years there is less demand and the event fills up more slowly. To be included on the mailing list, contact the Junior League at 869.1979.

Midnight Basketball
YMCA, 50 East Putnam Avenue, 869.1630

From 10 pm - midnight, on the second and last Friday of every month, the Y provides supervised basketball for young adults ages 14 to 18.

Safe Rides
869-8445

A service run by young people to keep other young people safe. Staffed Friday and Saturday nights from 10 pm - 2 am.

YWCA Teen Programs
869.6501 x 225

www.ywcagreenwich.com

In addition to the Y's many traditional programs for teens they also offer the following winter programs:

Computer Cool Club: A program for children 10-14, provides a fun introduction to computers, animation and web site design.

Assets: A program for girls in 6th through 12th grades which trains them in leadership and team-building skills.

TRAVEL

AIRPORTS

The Verizon yellow pages has a handy airport map to La Guardia and JFK (or check the airport's web page).

Avistar Airport Valet Parking

800.621.7275

www.avistarparking.com

Avistar operates out of Kennedy, La Guardia and Newark. If you fly out of one airport, but return to another, they will transfer your car and have it waiting for you. Their web site has good instructions to each of their airport locations.

Kennedy Airport (JFK)

Queens, NY, 718.244.444

www.panynj.gov/aviation/jfkframe.HTM

La Guardia Airport

Queens, NY, 718.533.3400

www.panynj.gov/aviation/lgaframe.HTM

Newark Airport

Newark, NJ, 973.961.6000

www.panynj.gov/aviation/ewrframe.HTM

Of the major New York City airports, Newark in New Jersey takes the longest to get to (80 minutes). Newark Airport is nicer and somewhat less congested than the other two. In addition, flights out of Newark are sometimes less expensive.

Skypark

Newark Airport 973.624.9000   800.PICK U UP

SkyPark is self parking with frequent shuttle service to the airport. SkyPark has the bonus of giving you a free stay after ten visits.

Directions: Follows signs from I-95 (the New Jersey Turnpike) to Newark Airport, exit at Hayes Street onto Route 1 S. Skypark is on the R.

TRAVEL

AIRPORTS

Westchester County Airport
White Plains, NY, 914.285.4860
www.co.westchester.ny.us/airport
This airport is located on upper King Street. It is newly renovated and has good parking facilities. Commercial flights are limited and somewhat more expensive than those from the major NYC airports, but nothing could be easier or more convenient. Airlines that fly out of Westchester are American Airlines, US Air, Carnival, United (Chicago), Northwest & Business Express. If you have time, try the Sky Top Restaurant.
Directions: Glenville Road to King Street; R on King; L at light to Rye Lake Rd.

TIP: GETTING A PASSPORT
Weekdays from 9 am - 4 pm, you can start the process of obtaining a new or renewed passport at the Greenwich Avenue Post Office. It normally takes twenty-five days to get your passport, although for a fee you can expedite the process.
For passport photographs see PHOTOGRAPHY

TRAVEL
AGENCIES

Liberty Travel

45 West Putnam Ave, 625.8170

Agents speak a number of languages. Because Liberty is a large operation with over 189 stores, they have big buying power for packages in the Caribbean and Florida. They are a good place to go to get a packaged tour for just about any purpose, intimate hotels, adventure trips, etc. If you don't quite know what you want, this could be a good bet. They are open every day, a real benefit if you are on a trip and need help immediately. They don't deliver tickets.

Hours: Monday - Thursday, 9 am - 7:30 pm; Friday, 9 am - 7 pm; Saturday, 10 am - 5 pm; Sunday, noon - 4 pm.

Unleashed Adventures of Greenwich

869.4522

www.unleashedadventures.com

Unleashed@aol.com

This Greenwich business, founded by Kathleen Snoddon and Diane Terry, is for women only. They provide one-week adventure trips to exotic places. They cater to the civilized who will enjoy and benefit from an uncivilized experience. Returnees give their experience rave reviews.

TIP: TRAVEL IMMUNIZATIONS

The Department of Infectious Diseases at Greenwich Hospital offers many types of immunizations required for foreign travel to less developed countries.

Call 863.3270 for an appointment. It is best to schedule one, at least, 6-weeks before your departure.

TRAVEL

BUS

Connecticut Transit (CTtransit)
203.327.7433
www.cttransit.com
CTtransit provides frequent bus service from Greenwich and Old Greenwich to Port Chester, Stamford and Norwalk.

Norwalk Transit
800.982.8420
www.NorwalkTransit.com
Norwalk Transit provides two commuter bus routes around town.

CLUBS

AAA / CT Motor Club
623 Newfield Avenue, Stamford, 765.4222
www.aaa.com
The Place to get your International Drivers's License or other help for a trip.
Hours: weekdays, 8:30 am - 5:30 pm, Saturday 8:30 am - Noon.
Directions: I-95 N to exit 8, follow exit ramp to State Street. @ 3rd light, L on Elm. It will become Grove, then Strawberry Hill, then Newfield. AAA is on right in Newfield Green Shopping Center.

Travel Club of Greenwich
For information call 661.4456 or 637.8383
Founded in 1903, it is the oldest travel club in the U.S.

TRAVEL

COMMUTING

See also: AUTOMOBILES

Travel Information

Local commuters can untangle their morning commutes by consulting the following commuter transportation web sites:

Metro-North Railroad: www.mta.nyc.ny.us/mnr/index.html
Offers the latest schedule information for all CT/NY/NJ MTA Metro North lines.

MetroPool: www.metropool.com
The site offers news and information on commuting in and around Fairfield and Westchester counties.

New York City traffic cams www.nyc.gov
Click on link to traffic cams for real time traffic cameras focused on trouble spots.

Tappan Zee bridge webcams
www.thruway.ny.us/webcams

Interstate 95 webcams
www.dot.state.ct.us
www.i95coalition.org

TRAVEL

TAXI/LIMOUSINE

CT Limousine Service

800.472.5466

If you are traveling alone, this may be your least expensive way to get to La Guardia or Kennedy. Pick up at the Stamford Marriot.

Eveready (Yellow) Cab Company

At Cos Cob RR Station, 869.1700

Greenwich Police

622.8006, 8015

A Greenwich off-duty policeman will drive you to any of the NY area airports and pick you up in your own car. This is often less expensive than a limousine service.

Greenwich Taxi

At Greenwich RR Station, 869.6000

An old stand-by for getting around town or to the train station - call ahead and make a reservation to be picked up. This is a good way to get to Westchester Airport, LaGuardia or Kennedy. Greenwich Taxi is open until 1:30 am.

Orix Limo-Car Service

203.322.7068

A very flexible auto service willing to pick you up at all hours. They will not only take you to the New York City theaters and airports, they will handle long distance trips to places such as Atlantic City.
Hours: 24 hours a day.

Rudy's Limousine Service

869.0014

A comfortable, reliable service. When several people travel together, this is a wise choice. Their drivers are very professional and pleasant.
Hours: 24 hours a day.

TRAVEL

TRAINS

Amtrak
800.USA.RAIL
www.amtrak.com
Operates from Stamford Station and connects to cities throughout the US and Canada.

Metro-North Commuter Railroad
800.638.7646 or 869.2663
www.mnr.org
Offers frequent service to Grand Central Station, New York City, Monday through Friday. Check weekend and holiday times.

Cos Cob Station
Sound Shore Drive, off Exit 4 of I-95

Greenwich Station
Railroad Ave, off Exit 3 of I-95

Old Greenwich Station
Sound Beach Ave, off Exit 5 of I-95

Riverside Station
Between exits 4 & 5 off I-95

INDEX

INDEX

INDEX

INDEX

INDEX

INDEX

INDEX

INDEX

INDEX

INDEX

INDEX

INDEX

INDEX

H

Häagen-Dazs 231
Habana 231
Hadassah, Greenwich Chapter 84, 204
HAIR SALONS 162
Hallmark 312
Hamilton Avenue Elementary School 274
Hamilton Avenue School 41
Handyman 173
Hank May's Goodyear 329
Harbor House Inn 179
Harbor View Antiques Center 330
Hardware 328, 363
Harmony 161
Harriman, NY 294
Harrington's of Vermont 330
Harris Restaurant Supply 330
Harvest Time Assembly of God 201
Hayday 231, 330
Hazardous Waste 171
Head Start 266
HEALTH 164
HEALTH - Equipment, Furniture & Products 288
HealthGain.Org 166
Helen Ainson 330
Helping Hands 43
Henri-Burton French Antiques 331
Hertz Rent-a-Car 39
Hickory & Tweed 331
Hiden Galleries 361
HIGHWAY MAP 25
Hiking trails 154
Hill House 279
Historical Society of the Town of Greenwich 84, 101, 102
HISTORY 23
Hoagland's of Greenwich 331
Hobby Center 331
HOCKEY, Field & Ice 132
Hockey, Roller 133

Holly Hill Resource Recovery Facility 171
Hollywood Pop Gallery 112
HOME 169
HOME - Accessories 288
HOME - Appliances 289
HOME - Furniture (indoor and outdoor) 289
HOME - Hardware, Lighting & Decorating 289
Home Depot 331
Home Depot Expo 332
Home Hair Styling Services 281
Home Shopping 363
Home Works 332
HomeGoods 332
Homestead Inn 179, 256
Honey Doo Services 173
Hoop Start USA, Summer Basketball Camp 117
Hopscotch 162
Horse Ridge Cellars 173
HORSEBACK RIDING 134
Horseneck Liquors 332
Horseneck Tavern 232
Hortulus 85, 158
HOSPITAL 18
Hospital Auxiliary 82, 168
Hospital for Special Surgery 166
Hospital, Greenwich 165
Hospital Thrift Shop 332
HOSPITALS 164
Hostaria Mazzei 232
Hot Spots 210
HOTELS 179
House of Fins 31, 333
Housewarmings 333
HOUSING 20, 279
Hubba_Hubba 232
Humane Society 30
Hunan Café 233
Hunan Gourmet 233
Hunter 145
Hyatt Regency 180

INDEX

INDEX

K

Kagetsu 234
Kaleidoscope - YWCA 42
Kamp Kairphree 74
KARATE 138
Kate Spade 335
Katonah Museum of Art 102
Katzenberg's Express 234
Katzenberg's Gourmet Deli 235
Kay-Bee Toy 335
KAYAKING 123
Kazu 235
Kelsey Farm 135
Kennedy Airport (JFK) 376
Kennedy Security Services 173
Kennel Club 31
Kenneth Lynch & Sons 336
Kerr's Village Pharmacy 336
Kids Corner Head Start at Armstrong
    Court. 266
Kids in Crisis 63
Kid's Night Out 44
Kid's Supply Co. 336
KidsEvents.com 66
Kiev USA 177, 336
Killington 147
Kinder Musik 50
Kindergarten 272
Kindness Counts 282
Kinkos 336
Kittatinny Canoes 123
Kiwanis Club 83
Klaff's 337
Kneaded Bread 235, 337
Knollwood Garden Club 85, 158
Kohl's 337
Kokusai Gakuen, Greenwich 267
Kykuit 57

L

La Guardia Airport 376
Labor Ready 173
LACROSSE 138
Lacrosse Camps 138
Lacrosse Clinic 73
Lacrosse, major league 53
Lake Compounce Theme Park 57
Lamaze classes 64
Land Trust 83, 193
Landfall Navigation 337
Landmark Diner 235
Landmark Document Services 337
Lane's Hair Stylists 162
Language Workshop for Children 49
LANGUAGES 49
Languages, Adult Education 261
Latin American Restaurants 207
Laura Ashley 338
Lauren Groveman's Kitchen 95
Le Club des Enfants 49
Le Leche League 64
Le Potager Catering 111
Leaf Collection 171
League of Women Voters 22, 85
Leather 177
Left of the Bank 338
L'Enfance Magique 338
Libby Cooke Catering 110
Liberty Travel 378
Liberty Village 338
LIBRARY 17
Licensed placement service 43
Light Touch 338
Lighting fixtures 337
Lillian August 338
Lillian August Home Outlet Store
    339
Lime Rock Park 140
LIMOUSINE 381
Lingerie 289

INDEX

INDEX

INDEX

INDEX

INDEX

INDEX

INDEX

INDEX

INDEX

INDEX

INDEX

INDEX

INDEX

INDEX

INDEX

Z

ABOUT THE AUTHORS

Carolyn and Jerry Anderson

At what age does one discover that the ordinary is extraordinary? For Jerry and Carolyn Anderson, it was when they returned to Greenwich. Jerry had been away at Harvard as an undergraduate, and then as a graduate at Columbia where he received his Masters in Business and Doctorate in Law. Carolyn had been at Boston University as an undergraduate and then at Columbia where she received her Masters. Jerry and Carolyn were introduced by a Greenwich friend, married, and in 1968 they bought their home on Clapboard Ridge Road in Greenwich. No other town was ever considered.

Jerry grew up in Deer Park and went to Brunswick. His youth was filled with sailing on the sound, playing tennis in the town tournaments and working on homework in the Greenwich Library. He learned to drive when Greenwich Avenue was a two-way street and dance lessons still required white gloves for boys as well as girls.

Carolyn is the President of Anderson Associates, a real estate firm specializing in Greenwich residential properties. She is a licensed appraiser and a professional member of the American Society of Interior Designers. Prior to opening Anderson Associates, she designed and renovated many restaurants and residences in Greenwich. In her spare time she writes cookbooks. Jerry and Carolyn rarely miss a new restaurant.

Their children, Clifford and Cheryl, were born in Greenwich Hospital. They thrived in the public school system, which launched them to successful academic careers at Harvard and Princeton. Cheryl and Clifford enjoyed the benefits of Greenwich's many resources: water babies at the Y, scouting, running in town races, camping on Great Captain's Island and visiting the wonderful exhibits at Bruce Museum.

However, this book is not just the work of Carolyn and Jerry. It is the product of all of the Anderson Associates. The Anderson Associates are a diverse group. They are all ages and lifestyles, with one interest in common—Greenwich. They live in, work in and love Greenwich. Most grew up and went to school in Greenwich. Each in their own way, has come to the realization that Greenwich is extraordinary.

ABOUT THE AUTHORS

Cheryl Anderson

Cheryl Anderson is the daughter of Jerry and Carolyn Anderson. She attended school in Greenwich from kindergarten through high school, then attended The American University and Harvard. She currently attends medical school in Portland, Oregon. She writes from her own experience growing up in Greenwich.

Amy Zeeve

Amy is Vice President of Anderson Associates and the inspiration for the first Anderson Guide. Amy is an active participant in the Greenwich community and continues to be a strong contributor to the Guide.

ABOUT OUR ILLUSTRATOR

Vanessa Chow

Vanessa, a Greenwich resident, created the maps and drawings. She graduated from Greenwich High School, where she was one of their top art students, won awards at the Old Greenwich Art Society. Vanessa graduated magna cum laude from Connecticut College. She has studied art at Parsons School of Design, Silvermine, New York University, The Art Students League, The Chinese Academy of Fine Arts and Oxford University. She is a graphic designer in New York City.

FEEDBACK FORM

We would appreciate your input.

IS THERE SOMETHING WE'VE MISSED?

_____

_____

_____

_____

HAVE YOU FOUND A MISTAKE?

_____

_____

_____

_____

HAVE YOU FOUND THIS BOOK USEFUL?
[ ] yes   [ ] no
Comments: _____

_____

_____

_____

Please mail this form to:
    Anderson Associates, Ltd.
    164 Mason Street
    Greenwich, CT 06830

ORDER FORM

Please send me ____ copies of The Anderson Guide to Enjoying Greenwich Connecticut 5th Edition

Total number of copies _____ @ 15.00
Price includes postage and sales tax.

Amount due $_____

I wish to pay by [   ] check or [   ] VISA or MasterCard

Name: _____

Address: _____

City: _____

State: _____ Zip: _____

Telephone: _____

Credit Card Number _____ _____ _____ _____

Expiration Date: ____/____

Name on Card: _____

Signature: _____

You can fax, mail, email or phone your order to
Avocet Press Inc
19 Paul Court
Pearl River, NY 10965-1539
Toll free phone: 877-4-AVOCET
Fax number: 845-735-6807
Email   books@avocetpress.com